Family

Relations:

CONCEPTS AND THEORIES

EDITED BY:

RAYMOND J. R. KING

UNIVERSITY OF OTAGO

(New Zealand)

THE GLENDESSARY PRESS – *BERKELEY, CALIFORNIA*

CONTENTS

FAMILY RELATIONS: Concepts and Theories

Introduction

Raymond J. R. King

It is taken as axiomatic today that no one theory is sufficient to provide the complex and deep understanding of the family that the sociologist seeks. Some theories make a greater contribution to such an understanding than do others, however. The primary objective of this collection of articles is to acquaint readers with those perspectives that to date have emerged as most promising. A secondary objective may also be seen: to alert the reader to possible obstructions to understanding that might inhere in inter-linkings of varied theories. Effective comparison and the merging of findings from diverse studies, that is, depend on accurate identification of assumptions and careful specification of the conceptual frameworks underlying each of the studies.

Concepts and Conceptual Frameworks

A conceptual framework is generally defined as a cluster of interrelated but not necessarily interdefined concepts that describe and classify phenomena — in this case, phenomena relevant to the study of the family. Logically constructed conceptual schemes both act as a means of arranging empirical data and guide research along theoretically significant paths.

But a close study of frameworks popular today discloses an overcrowding of concepts that are closely related in meaning (Hill, 1966, 12). Ironically, in the midst of this over-abundance is a semantic poverty of terms adequate to the complexities of whole family behavior or to changes over the life span of the family group. If, as Mogey (1966, 28) suggests, the goal of theory building is a maximum level of generalization with a minimum of concepts, then solutions to problems of conceptual redundancy and impotence must be found. The interdefinition of concepts suggests a partial solution. The number of redundant concepts is reduced by rigorous selection and then the remaining concepts are defined in terms of one another (Hill, 1966, 14). Its potential for theory building is suggested by the consequent gains claimed for this technique: reduction in the number of concepts, clarity in definition, and increased likelihood of generating propositions for family theory. Identical-appearing concepts based on differing assumptions may imply contrasting meanings, as is demonstrated in the contrast of frameworks organized in "structural" terms with those organized in "processual" terms. "Structural" concepts emphasize the stability of social forms, and their tendency is to preserve or maintain a given form or state. In contrast, "processual" concepts emphasize the dynamics of interactive processes of widely varying degrees and intensities of both association and dissociation. In structural terms the concept "process" may refer to movement directed towards stability but in processual terms it may refer to continuous change and elaboration.

The difference in theoretical viewpoints also has implications for the nature of the propositions formulated in research studies and their interrelationship as theories (Zetterberg, 1965, 69).[1] For the present discussion propositions or statements may be seen as either descriptive or interpretative.[2] Descriptive statements characteristically describe phenomena in terms of changes in only one variable: interpretative statements are those made about the interdependence of two or more variables (Hill, 1966, 16). Interpretative propositions, then, not only describe the occurrence of phenomena, they offer explanations for their occurrence. A theoretical viewpoint that emphasizes a structural stability invites the formulation of descriptive (categorizing) statements whereas a processual viewpoint encourages explanation and produces interpretative propositions. This suggests the wisdom of seeking a conceptual framework in which structure and process are closely integrated.[3]

Interrelationships between descriptive propositions lead to the formulation of descriptive theory while interpretative theory emerges from interrelated interpretative propositions (Zetterberg, 14).[4] Family theory encompasses both descriptive theory, generalizing about the mapping and charting of family phenomena, and interpretative theory, attempting explanations about why the phenomena occur. The family sociologist can point to an extensive literature of information-packed studies of the family containing descriptive statements about the ordered arrangement of data, but more effort is required to unearth empirical studies which offer generalizations relating interpretative propositions about aspects of family phenomena.

The present task demanded of the family theorist (and indeed of the social theorist) is explanation and verification rather than description and classification. The need, then, is for formulating interpretative propositions and for the empirical testing of the interrelationships among stated propositions. Central to this need is incisive evaluation of propositions about marriage and the family; in turn, prerequisite to this evaluation is a clear understanding of the principal frameworks utilized in family research and the similarities and differences in the theoretical viewpoints which differentiate them.

In the following sections the reader is introduced to frameworks more commonly encountered in family studies. The discussion, while making no pretense to be definitive, focuses on the similarities and contrasts in the theoretical viewpoints which differentiate the frameworks.

As in the work of Hill and Hansen (1960), five clearly identified frameworks are introduced: institutional, structure-functional, situational, symbolic interactional, and developmental.[5] In addition, the anthropological approach provides an example of an application of the functional framework and the discussion of the game theory approach (which is not yet widely used in family research) serves to introduce the development of systems theory in family sociology.

The Institutional Framework

While there is general agreement among most sociologists about the importance of institutions, practical difficulties arise when attempts are made to develop methods of institutional analysis. Institutional studies produce a variety of definitions, some of which are imprecise and inconsistent in the context of the conceptual framework utilized in the studies. But some consensus about the definition of institution has emerged and common usage has stabilized four areas of meaning: "cultural systems," in which institutions represent the overall arrangement of structures, practices and norms which surround social behavior; "cultural complexes," in which institutions represent normative principles that regulate behavior within "cultural systems"; "institutionalization," in which emphasis is on the processes by which partially controlled or uncontrolled behavior becomes more ordered; and "institutional functions," in which emphasis is on the roles of institutions in the social order (Sirjamaki, 1967, 39). These focuses are not mutually exclusive; any institution is all of these, and more.

The institutional framework currently offers its greatest rewards in historical and cross-cultural comparative studies: it tends to offer few resources for the study of individual family patterns, or of interpersonal relationships among members of specific families. In itself, the framework has made the significant contribution of an extensive assembly of empirical data relevant to the universal character of the family and has revealed its distinctive role in particular societies. Empirical data produced by studies within the institutional framework tend to be descriptive and to contribute to descriptive theory; interpretative propositions capable of empirical verification are but seldom generated by such studies (Merton, 1957, 9).[6] Nonetheless, inasmuch as descriptive studies and theory can stimulate the elaboration of interpretative theory, the institutional approach can contribute to family sociology (Willer, 1967, xii).[7]

The Structure-function Framework

Inherent in functional perspectives are basic assumptions that have suffered considerable criticism. Criticism focuses on the central assumption that structures, or the interrelationships between the units of any functional system, be it family or community, may be profitably viewed as static. Because the structure-function framework combines aspects of both biological and mechanical models it is understandable that it is hard pressed to generate concepts which cope with both change and adaptation. Biological structures (organismic systems) can be regarded as relatively fixed for any particular species at a specific stage of development. Even under conditions of stress, biological organisms do not demonstrate any great capacity for structural changes and under severe stress an organism may die. Mechanical systems are also incapable of creating new and more complicated structural interrelations. Moderate changes in units of mechanical systems or in their interrelations are assumed to be counterbalanced by adjustments tending to stabilize the dominant system structure. Furthermore, when an organismic system concept is associated with the mechanically derived notion of equilibrium there is an assumption implied that the predetermined structure of the system must be the *best* way the units may be interrelated. This point is elaborated further in the discussion of the anthropological approach.

Clearly there are difficulties in using concepts derived from biological and mechanical models to describe or interpret social phenomena. When structures are defined in terms of more or less static patterns of interaction between units, some assumption has to be made as to what structural form is most characteristic of a given social system.[8] Account must also be taken of the fact that social systems respond to environmental influences in various ways and that they are not incapable of modifying their own structures. On the contrary, it is by means of structural changes that social systems preserve viability as ongoing systems. Advocates of functional frameworks have attempted to cope with this process but with no great success. Change as represented in the concept of equilibrium occurs in only one direction — towards a state of stability in which strains and conflicts among component parts of a system are reduced to a minimum (Moore, 1955, 111). Whereas a central assumption of change and adaptation would lead to the development of a framework which interrelates "processual" concepts, emphasis on the preservation or maintenance of a necessary stability provides a foundation for the building of frameworks interrelating "structural" concepts. It seems that Parsons' conclusion of some years ago appears valid even today: "a general theory of the processes of change of social systems is not possible in the present state of knowledge" (Parsons, 1951, 481).

Another trenchant criticism leveled against functional theory is that it does not lead to statements about why systems are as they are. The principal line of inquiry stimulating empirical investigation in terms of this framework points to the identification of functional imperatives or prerequisites of a society or of part of a society. But to identify the functions (adaptive consequences) of a structure is not to indicate why it exists but rather to demonstrate how it operates. The causal relationship between units of a functional system cannot be determined by what its consequences (functions) are (Bredemeier, 1962, 43).[9] Emile Durkheim warns of this assumption:

> ...to show how a fact is useful is not to explain how it originated or why it is what it is. The uses which it serves presuppose the specific properties characterising it but do not create them. The need we have of things cannot give them existence, nor can it confer their specific nature upon them (1938, 90).

These two criticisms are illustrated in the following section which discusses the anthropologist's utilization of structure-function concepts.

The Anthropological Approach

Anthropologists have customarily adopted a functional framework as an appropriate blueprint for the study of patterns of social behavior in various social situations. There is no anthropological framework identifiable as such, although recent studies employ distinctive concepts and identify some underlying assumptions (Rodgers, 1964, 262).[10] Studies have been for the most part descriptive, focusing on the persistent patterns of social behavior exhibited by individuals and groups within clearly defined social contexts, and on analysis of the institutionalized norms in response to which the social behavior of individuals is patterned. The observed patterns of formal social behavior assumed to be characteristic of a particular society are conceptualized as more or less rigid structures.

Attempts have been made to identify underlying structural principles and to assess their implications for social relations. Structures come to be so as necessary arrangements of interdependent sub-system elements, in response to inferred functions. The implicit assumption is that the particular interrelationship among the elements of any social system is a necessary one for the continuance of that system in some sort of status quo.

This viewpoint may be to some degree appropriate in so called primitive societies, but it is difficult to uphold when focuses are on highly differentiated industrial societies. Almost identical structures may display more than one set of functions when viewed under various situational conditions. On the other hand, as cross-cultural studies have demonstrated, solutions to universal functional prerequisites such as the care and socializing of the young may be provided by a variety of structural forms. To assume that this particular structure or that specific function is not only a possible but also a necessary condition is to ignore variations within prescribed patterns. A more complete analysis would include both the consequences of the given structural pattern and the conditions under which the consequences become necessary for the maintenance of the structure. In this respect, it is clearly insufficient to restrict attention to the influence of established patterns of behavior: attention must be given to the symbolic definitions that comprise the individual's motivations.

The tradition has been for anthropologists working within the functional framework to neglect opportunities for both interrelating the findings of relevant research and generating theories and for testing specific emergent propositions. Much of the emergent theory is therefore descriptive rather than interpretative. As social anthropologists direct their attention more to the study of sectors of complex societies, a need for emphasis on adequate empirical verification of well-grounded propositions becomes recognized as imperative.

The Situational Framework

Some similarities may be seen between the situational framework and the institutional. From each emerges a generalized view; on the one hand a cross-sectional analysis of the family situation, on the other a picture of the family as an institution. Both tend to be inattentive to individual families. The institutional approach allocates a central position to institutionalized patterns of behavior and the situational to norms, meanings and roles as conveyed in the form of situational stimuli to which the organism reacts − for example, the child responds not only to family stimuli but also to the roles and norms related to his position in the family.

Again, attempts are made in each approach to classify modal products or situations and to map changes over time, although compared with the situational approach, the institutional demonstrates a greater attention to processual concepts. The situational framework acknowledges that the elements (cultural elements, physical elements and persons) within an organized situation continually change positions and relationships to one another as they undergo mutually induced modifications. But the focus is not upon process: rather, concepts are utilized to analyze the situation as it exists momentarily, as if frozen in time. Moreover, in the situational framework, family situations are not those perceived by individual members and expressed in their own "definitions of the situation." Rather, situations are described as they are perceived "objectively," as through an observer's lens: the situation is studied in its own right, apart from the ways in which individual members perceive and respond to it.

Accounts of the overt behavior of family members therefore stress both the purposive-adaptive aspect of the members' responses to stimuli provided by the situation, and the situation as a set of stimuli influencing the behavior of family members. Furthermore, with the family as central, focus may shift to adjustments in the total family to stimuli external to the family (e.g., the neighborhood). Community assessments of the family's socioeconomic status or health, for example, have repercussions on the family (Stryker, 1964, 165).

The Interactional Framework

This approach looks at interactive processes which through continuous change display some order, permitting predictions about the course of family change. Within the family, members act and respond to the actions of others and also to the meanings which those actions convey to actor and observer. In interpreting the symbolic communications of others, the individual gains experience and competence in effective interpersonal relations, and in the process of interaction members develop common definitions about how they should act towards others in particular family situations. Thus prediction is made possible.

Close affinities are reported between the interactional and the situational frameworks but the ways in which the frameworks differ may be more crucial. The central position assigned to family members as motivated actors in the interactional framework contrasts with the situational focus on reactions of the family to situational stimuli. The product of the situational approach has been a more generalized picture of family interactions – the interactional more specifically individuated.

Interactional analysis stresses the individual's definitions of the situation rather than the "objective" situation. For example, the framework does not treat only those stimuli external to the individual (or the family) but acknowledges that men are actors as well as reactors and even generate their own stimuli. In the same way that they respond to the physical world as expressed in symbols that have special meaning to them, so they can produce their own symbols and respond to their own symbolic productions. In this sense the individual's behavior is goal-directed. That is, the actor perceives and evaluates the situation and himself in particular ways; he selects from available choices one course of action, thereby ruling out the achievement of other goals.

A view of man that accentuates his capacity to select and interpret sectors of his environment and respond idiosyncratically evokes a methodological emphasis on subjective elements of the individual's everyday experience. Much early research demonstrates such an emphasis in the utilization of personal documents, but at the present time more objective techniques such as interview schedules and questionnaires are considered more appropriate.

The basic focuses, then, are upon the interactions of family members rather than on the family as a unit in interaction, and upon the changes in the family unit which are the products of this interaction. In contrast to the functional framework, the emphasis is on change rather than stability: not all interactions produce systems, and the concept of equilibrium characteristic of the structure-function framework is considered inappropriate when interactive processes are in continuous flux.

Attention to the complex processes of interaction does not necessarily preclude the formulation of propositions about institutional or cultural patterns. Although usually held residual, social and cultural patterns may be viewed profitably in terms of the framework. For example, it is probable that the occupants of parallel positions among different families consistently will hold situational definitions in common. Once identified, shared definitions of the situation permit the formulation of generalizations about institutionalized patterns of family interaction. Thus the framework is not necessarily committed to either a rational or a deterministic view. Individuals act in terms of their perceptions of self and others, and cultural and social experiences to some extent do determine the actors' evaluations and definitions. But there is not complete determination by the social system as the functionalists would tend to suggest: the individual is actor and modifier as well as social reactor.

The Developmental Framework

The developmental approach, rather recently refined as a conceptual framework (Rodgers, 1964, 262-270), derives concepts and assumptions from many of the frames of reference already discussed. It has affinity with the situational approach in its view of the family as a unit of interacting personalities; with the interactional framework in its focus on analyses and processes of family interaction; and with the structure-function framework in its view of the family as a social system with boundary setting and maintaining functions.

But it has a particular, almost unique, emphasis unrepresented in the other frameworks discussed here. For example, it provides a means for the study of changes in family member roles as they are influenced by the social interaction of the individual within and outside the family. Yet at the same time it copes with the structural implications of positions and roles derived both from the society in which the family is embedded and from the size, age and sex composition of the particular family. In short, it utilizes concepts which refer to processes of family member interaction, the social setting of the family and the structure of the family system itself. The framework is consequently equally fruitful for macroscopic analysis producing some affinities with the institutional modal family viewed crossculturally and historically, as well as for microscopic analysis (Rodgers, 1966, 217).

Not the least of the unique concerns of the developmental framework is the attention it gives to the manner in which changes occur in role expectations (developmental tasks) of members in positions, as the family unit moves over time through the sequence of stages that make up the family life cycle. The quality of the interaction in the family system differs at various stages (or categories) in the family's career as individual family members reach critical points in their life cycles at different times. Although in a state of continuous change, the family career may yet be represented profitably as a sequence of stages in a complex interactive process, defined in terms of the dominant developmental tasks being faced by individual family members and by the family as a whole (Rodgers, 1966, 217).

In the same way that individual family members strive for and hopefully achieve their own personal goals often by unsynchronized routes, so the family as a whole is required to accept certain responsibilities and successfully manage socially imposed developmental tasks. The successful accomplishment of these tasks in the past (as in the case of individual tasks) has implications for patterns of future family and individual growth (Hill and Rodgers, 1964, 187).

Many of the criticisms of this approach center about the lack of empirical studies in support of assumptions and concepts utilized in the framework. The empirical validity of the concept of family and individual developmental tasks has been questioned as has the reference to failure and success in task performances, in the accepted definition of these concepts (Magrabi, 1965, 454). Yet recent studies have demonstrated a vital interest expressed in attempts at "long overdue" systematic testing of the developmental conceptual approach and there have been fruitful contributions in cross-cultural comparisons (Morioka, 1967, 595).

The Systems Approach and Game Theory

Several of the frameworks already discussed utilize the concept of "open system" but they differ in their definitions and in the centrality of emphasis they attach to the concept.[11] The potential of the concept for family sociology is hinted at in Allport's (1960, 301) criteria of open systems: intake and output of matter and energy; the achievement and maintenance of steady (homeostatic) states; generally an increase in order over time; and extensive transactional commerce with the environment.

The structure-function framework allocates central importance to a concept of system which includes aspects of Allport's criteria. For example, the individual family member is viewed as a reacting part of a social system and his behavior as contributing, in part at least, to the maintenance of the family system. Activity that produces consequences dysfunctional to the maintenance of the system stimulates a readjustment of elements within the system. The functional framework is committed to the inevitability of system re-equilibrium: it pays little attention to system elaboration or reorganization. Finally, the framework, although allocating considerable emphasis to system transaction with other systems (between dyads as sub-systems and the family system or between society as the total social system and the family sub-system), at the same time regards the family as a closed, boundary maintaining corporation (Hansen and Hill, 1964, 787-792).

Interactional analysis focuses on the individual's situational definitions, on self-elicited action and on those processes of interaction from which both individual personality and society are ultimately derived. The framework recognizes the contribution of equilibrium but denies an essential commitment to re-equilibration. Little attention has been given to the possibility of the family becoming more than it at present is, although such considerations are implied in the basic postulates of the framework. Finally the interactional framework accepts an integumented yet transactive view of personality and the family unit but less often treats this aspect in research.

Allowance for the enhancement of personality and the potential of a view of the family that stresses processes producing increasingly complicated interpersonal relationships within the family as members realize and practice new strengths is inadequate in most family frameworks. The systems approach could sensitize researchers to these possibilities.

Systems theorists identify two basic processes characteristic of the transaction of a complex open system with its environment. Morphostatic processes tend to maintain the system in its given state by counteracting the effects of external forces working towards change. Morphogenic processes, by contrast, tend toward the elaboration or reorganization of the system in response to influences in the environment (Buckley, 1967, 58). The concept of system clearly has potential to synthesize interactional and structural models into a coherent conceptual scheme, but current system theories demonstrate a close adherence to morphostasis rather than to morphogenesis.

The essence of the contribution of game theory to a systems approach is its emphasis on morphogenesis. The theory of games owes its original statement to von Neumann (1944) but others have contributed to its rapid growth, devising new and ingenious applications in business strategies and in the strategies of war games. Games of strategy differ from games of chance and games of skill in that the wisest course of action for each player in games of strategy must take into account the mutual expectations of the other players. The choices of decisions among players are therefore interdependent, and forecasting is based on mutual expectations. Traditionally, game theory has focused on the strategy of pure "conflict"[12] as represented in the zero-sum game,[13] and has applied methods and concepts found useful in this study to the nonzero-sum model.

Zero-sum games demonstrate characteristics appropriate to closed systems (Williams, 1954, 14).[14] Assets are merely passed back and forth between players usually limited in number and representing distinct sets of interests rather than persons. The alternative actions available to each player are completely itemized, and the objective is to maximize payoff at the expense of the opposing player. In this process all players are fully aware of and abide by the rules of the game declared at its commencement — they play within this structure. Finally, the consequences of the various strategies are measured in a pay-off matrix which catalogues the various values accruing to the players as they play alternative strategies (Burger, 1963, 2).[15]

But games of strategy need not partake of the order of closed systems. The pure "conflict" (competitive) zero-sum game is not the only kind of strategic game. Schelling (1960) has enlarged the category of nonzero-sum games to incorporate pure coordination and mixed motive (or bargaining) games, which involve, as the name implies, a mixture of mutual dependence and competition. In nonzero-sum games which allow the incorporation of new factors and which mix competition with mutual dependence, strategies must subsume different concepts and methods. For example, the mixed-motive game involves a dynamic process of mutual accommodation in which each of the players suffers damage if the attempts at accommodation of the other are poor. The incentive is not to score over the other player but to achieve a mutually satisfying relationship. The success of the outcome depends on how accurately the first player perceives the value system of the other player. Both symbolic and explicit communication provide necessary information for players about the values of payoffs which may change over time. But some information is inherently unknowable for some of the participants, and there are difficulties in declaring intentions to others who do not have identical or parallel interests. In addition, players may also be compelled to contend with patterns of developing reciprocal interaction, which rapidly increase in complexity.

Critics of game theory in family analysis have based their assessments variously on the questionable assumption of the rationality of the players, the theory's doubtful substantive utility and the serious omission of communication, apart from the moves themselves, in many models (Kimmel, 1966, 460; Homans, 1964, 960). Recent conceptualizations of game theory have to a considerable extent answered the more serious criticisms (see, for example, Scheff, 1967, and Hansen, 1969, as well as the excerpts from

Laing, *et al.,* and Bernard in this volume), but even adherents to the theory of games would acknowledge the need for more empirical studies especially in its application to interaction among family members.

*   *   *   *

The following readings were selected to provide examples of these major conceptual frameworks and at the same time to illustrate some of the identified problems in theory building. Selections were guided also by the need to supply links between readings to ensure some degree of integration. Thus the paper by Hill and Hansen, which has stimulated much of the subsequent study of conceptual frameworks since it appeared in 1960, introduces the collection, leading directly to the discussion of Sirjamaki and Berardo. Slater's paper, followed by Berger's comment, logically precedes Hansen's analysis which leads to those of Stryker and Rodgers. The paper by Bernard presents a beginning in systems theory development (at the time of the Hill-Hansen article there was virtually no systems research in the field of family study), providing a context for the Laing-Phillipson-Lee application of mixed-motive analysis in which communication is emphasized in the study of consensus and coordination.

A bibliography illustrative of the varied frameworks is found on pages 210-218, and short introductory paragraphs introduce each paper.

ENDNOTES

[1]Propositions are statements about the interrelationships among concepts. When research propositions are interrelated, they contribute to the formulation of theory.

[2]This classification is Hill's (1966). Six alternative classificatory types of propositions have been identified by Zetterberg (1965).

[3]Current developments in systems theory appear to be redressing this unfortunate divorce between the two approaches. See Buckley (1967).

[4]But when interpretative propositions rather than descriptive statements are interrelated, they generate varying degrees of theoretical significance. "Partial" (or middle-range) theories suggest explanations of specific aspects of social phenomena, while "grand" theory emerges from the integration of partial theories producing more inclusive, more universal, total explanations (Zetterberg, 1965, 14-21).

[5]As Stryker (1964) argues, the similarities between interactional and situational approaches appear greater than the differences.

[6]Merton (1957, 9) comments, "A large part of what is now called sociological theory consists of general orientations toward data, suggesting types of variables which need somehow to be taken into account, rather than clear, verifiable statements of relationships between specified variables."

[7]Willer discusses the doubtful contribution of cumulated survey and comparative data to the development of theory.

[8]"Functions are those observed consequences which make for the adaptation or adjustment of a given system; and dysfunctions, those observed consequences which lessen the adaptation or adjustment of the system" (Merton 1957, 9).

[9]For a simple but thorough discussion of functional analysis see Bredemeier and Stephenson (1962, 28-59).

[10]Rodgers differentiates between using a conceptual framework for viewing phenomena and taking a conceptual "approach." A conceptual "approach" is characterized by the use of a set of concepts which are rather loosely tied together and which are not in any definite sense interrelated or interdefined. "While in a conceptual approach there is some attempt to consider a problem at a level of abstraction above the purely descriptive, the approach does not achieve the tight interrelatedness of a framework."

[11]The concept of closed system is of little value when applied to family systems. Open systems more realistically depict the transaction between the family system and other systems.

[12]"Conflict" refers to competing contradictory impulses and implies the presence of emotional tension. "Pure conflict" is defined in respect to out-

comes, but is really a contradiction in terms — either there is or there is not a conflict situation. To avoid this suggestion of an emotive connotation and to widen the unnecessarily limited scope of the term, a more appropriate concept would be "competition." Competition is not restricted to conflict (but conflict is a type of competition — perhaps "pure competition") and has no emotive connotation.

[13] When winnings are allocated positive scores and losses negative scores, the payoff in zeor-sum games is zero. Otherwise the game is a nonzero-sum game.

[14] Reference here is particularly to finite, zero-sum, two-person games although to some extent the conditions apply to nonzero-sum games (Williams, 1954, 14).

[15] "A strategy of a player in a given game is a complete play of behavior which specifies the player's behavior, that is, his decisions, for all possible circumstances that may arise during the course of play" (Burger, 1963, 2).

WORKS CITED

Allport, Gordon W., "The Open System in Personality Theory," *Journal of Abnormal and Social Psychology*, 3 (1960), pp. 301-312.

Bredemeier, Harry C. and Richard M. Stephenson, *The Analysis of Social Systems*, New York: Holt, Rinehart and Winston, 1962.

Buckley, Walter, *Sociology and Modern Systems Theory*, New Jersey: Prentice-Hall, inc., 1967.

Burger, Ewald, *Introduction to the Theory of Games*, New Jersey: Prentice-Hall, Inc., 1963.

Durkheim, Emile, *The Rules of Sociological Method*, George Catlin, ed., Chicago: University of Chicago Press, 1938.

Hansen, Donald A., "Toward a Theory of Coordination in Counseling and Psychotherapy: Consensus, Influence and Communication," in Donald A. Hansen, ed., *Explorations in Sociology and Counseling*, Boston: Houghton Mifflin, 1969, pp. 124-148.

Hansen, Donald A. and Reuben Hill, "Families Under Stress," in Harold T. Christensen, eds., *Handbook of Marriage and the Family*, Chicago: Rand McNally, 1964, pp. 782-819.

Hill, Reuben, "Contemporary Developments in Family Theory," *Journal of Marriage and the Family*, 28 (1966), pp. 10-26.

Hill, Reuben and Donald A. Hansen, "The Identification of Conceptual Frameworks Utilized in Family Study," *Marriage and Family Living*, 22 (1960), pp. 299-311.

Hill, Reuben and Roy H. Rodgers, "The Developmental Approach," in Harold T. Christensen, ed., *Handbook of Marriage and the Family*, Chicago: Rand McNally, 1964, pp. 171-211.

Homans, George C., "Contemporary Theory in Sociology," in R. E. L. Faris, ed., *Handbook of Modern Sociology*, Chicago: Rand McNally, 1964, pp. 951-977.

Kimmel, Paul R. and J. W. Havens, "Game Theory Versus Mutual Identification: Two Criteria for Assessing Marital Relationships," *Journal of Marriage and the Family*, 28 (1966), pp. 460-465.

Magrabi, Frances M. and W. H. Marshall, "Family Developmental Tasks: A Research Model," *Journal of Marriage and the Family*, 29 (1957), pp. 595-606.

Merton, Robert K., *Social Theory and Social Structure,* New York: The Free Press of Glencoe, Inc., 1957.

Mogey, John, "Contemporary Developments in Family Theory, A Discussion," *Journal of Marriage and the Family,* 28 (1966), pp. 26-28.

Moore, Barrington, "Sociological Theory and Contemporary Politics," *American Journal of Sociology,* 61 (1955), pp. 107-115.

Morioka, Kiyomi, "Life Cycle Patterns in Japan, China, and the United States," *Journal of Marriage and the Family,* 29 (1967), pp. 595-606.

von Neumann, John and Oskar Morgenstern, *Theory of Games and Economic Behavior,* New Jersey: Princeton University Press, 1955.

Parsons, Talcott, *The Social System,* Glencoe, Ill., The Free Press, 1951.

Rodgers, Roy H., "Towards a Theory of Family Development," *Journal of Marriage and the Family,* 26 (1964), pp. 262-270.

Rodgers, Roy H., "The Occupational Role of the Child: A Research Frontier in the Developmental Conceptual Framework," *Social Forces,* 45 (1966), pp. 217-224.

Scheff, Thomas, "A Theory of Social Coordination Applied to Mixed Motive Games," *Sociometry,* 30 (1967), pp. 215-234.

Schelling, Thomas C., *The Strategy of Conflict,* Cambridge: Harvard University Press, 1960.

Sirjamaki, John, "Education as a Social Institution," in Donald A. Hansen and Joel E. Gerstl, eds., *On Education—Sociological Perspectives,* New York: John Wiley and Sons, 1967, 36-38.

Stryker, Sheldon, "The Interactional and Situational Approaches," in Harold T. Christensen, ed., *Handbook of Marriage and the Family,* Chicago: Rand McNally, 1964, pp. 125-170.

Willer, David, *Scientific Sociology: Theory and Method,* New Jersey: Prentice-Hall, inc., 1967.

Williams, John D., *The Compleat Strategyst,* New York: McGraw-Hill, 1954.

Zetterberg, Hans L., *On Theory and Verification in Sociology,* New Jersey: Bedminster Press, 1965.

The Identification of Conceptual Frameworks Utilized in Family Study

Reuben Hill and Donald A. Hansen

Although a need for theory building was generally recognized prior to 1960, attempts to systematically sort and classify the numerous studies on the family were few. Yet the identification of characteristic frameworks utilized in empirical studies of the family and the assumptions which underlie the frameworks are necessary steps towards the formulation of family theory. Now almost a decade old, the paper by Reuben Hill and Donald A. Hansen still provides the fundamentals of such an inventory. In specifying the more common frameworks utilized in family studies during the preceding decades, it broke new ground and provided a classificatory system which promoted further clarification and needed theory construction.

Marriage and the family as an arena of investigation has won the attention of hundreds of scholars in recent years. Research articles in the United States alone now number more than two hundred a year, and the research findings produced annually add up to a magnitude sufficient to baffle the research librarian. Yet the development of family theory based upon these findings is modest

Reprinted, with permission of the authors and publisher, from *Marriage and Family Living*, 22 (1960), pp. 299-311.

indeed. Even in the critiques of the field formulated to appraise progress in family research there has been only token attention to issues of theory.

Why? We have been so busy researching, piling finding on finding, that the essential task of inventorying has been badly neglected. We have lagged in developing a technology for coping with the range and quantity of research findings which would enable us to sift reliable from unreliable generalizations and note the extent to which findings from different conceptual approaches can be integrated into accretive theory. What is needed is a large-scale inventory which engages in codification of the mass of family research completed to date, providing us with an orderly, compact, and systematic arrangement of (1) substantive findings, (2) research procedures employed, and (3) theoretical propositions derived from these findings.

Such an inventory, conceived almost a decade ago, is now in progress at the Minnesota Family Study Center. Its major objectives include:

1. The identification of the empirical foci which have been investigated by marriage and family researchers.
2. The classification and summarization of the research findings among these foci.
3. The identification of the competing frames of reference which have been used as approaches by marriage and family researchers and the isolation of the major conceptual apparatus of each of the frameworks that is identified.
4. The organization, where possible, of research findings into a set of interrelated hypotheses and research propositions.[1]

In pursuit of these objectives, research articles have been systematically abstracted, utilizing an outline which requires the abstractor to note the research methods employed and to classify the findings by the conceptual framework employed. Objective three (identification of conceptual frameworks) is crucial to the entire inventory, *even to the seemingly mechanical classification and summarization of research findings.* To an even greater extent, objective four (accretion of propositions) cannot intelligently proceed divorced from identification of conceptual frameworks.

Conceptual frameworks, then, are the keys to fruitful codification; the step that raises the inventory beyond simple accumulation toward real significance. In previous articles seven frameworks have been identified, as have the disciplines which produced them and the major researchers who used them. Five of these have survived further scrutiny and are listed in Table I.[2]

Table I. Approaches to the Study of the Family Competing for Adherents in America

conceptual framework	developed in discipline of	exemplified by
1. The interactional approach	Sociology and Social Psychology	R. C. Angell, E. W. Burgess, R. Cavan, L. S. Cottrell, T. D. Eliot, R. Hill, M. Komarovsky, E. Koos, E. T. Krueger, H. Mowrer, S. Stryker, W. Waller, P. Wallin
2. The structure-function approach	Sociology and Social Anthropology	K. Davis, W. Goode, C. McGuire, T. Parsons, L. Simmons, L. Warner, and others
3. The situational approach	Sociology	W. I. Thomas, L. J. Carr, J. H. S. Bossard, R. Blood, and E. Boulding
4. The institutional approach	Sociology and Historical Sociology	J. Sirjamaki, A. Truxas
5. The developmental approach	Sociology, borrowing from Rural Sociology, Child Psychology, and Human Development	Approximations seen in research of R. Faris, P. Glick, M. Sussman, L. Stott, and writings of E. M. Duvall, R. Foster, R. Hill, and L. D. Rockwood

If conceptual frameworks are the source of hope for our inventory, they are also a source of danger; the frameworks are elusive to grasp, and even diligent students have been hard pressed to understand them.

Such confusion requires attention. The remainder of this article attempts to specify some dimensions of current conceptual frameworks. Specifically, we seek perspective which will:

1. Be valuable in classifying and accreting propositions in the inventory, thus working toward the development of middle-range theories about marriage and the family;
2. Sensitize research workers to available approaches to the study of marriage and the family; and

3. Aid students and other readers in understanding, evaluating, and placing in perspective, researches employing approaches which are basically different.

What is a Conceptual Framework

Though we can't trace every influence on each concept used in a study, we can take one step back and attempt to identify the conceptual framework within which the research was done.

This will by no means clarify exactly the meaning and underlying assumptions inherent in every concept within the framework. But it will often save us from the error of comparing propositions whose concepts are widely different in spite of common terms.

We attempt, then, to identify the conceptual environments in which concepts operate and the basic assumptions necessary if those environments are to be considered at all true or useful.

But the term "conceptual framework" is a confusing one. Some sociologists use it to refer to no more than a cluster of concepts brought together for some purpose, without concern for peculiar interrelationships or for assumptions. At the other extreme, the term is used to refer to full-fledged theory, including a set of interrelated concepts, a set of underlying and unifying assumptions, and a set of postulates.

In this article and in operations of the inventory, "conceptual framework" refers to clusters of interrelated but not necessarily interdefined concepts generally applicable to the arena of marriage and the family.[3] In identifying the frameworks we ignore most of the possible levels of abstraction which the concepts might attain and concern ourselves only with a simple dichotomy: only those concepts which are abstract and general (substance-free) are included. Substance-bound (specific) concepts are omitted. Thus we do not include concepts of such specificity as "son" or "parent" but do include "position." Though not so well divorced from specific objects or events as, for example, "unit," "position" is applicable to any substance area conceivable in marriage and family. Similarly "role" is a general concept, "father-role" a specific; "status" general, "divorced" specific; "significant other" general, "neighborhood hero" specific. It must be stressed we use this dichotomy only to simplify presentation; we do not claim there is any kind of gap between conceptual frameworks and the real world.

The task of winnowing and clustering concepts has been by no means an easy one. Too, the requirement that we set up an operationally useful scheme militates against perfection. Thus the interrelations identified are somewhat arbitrary and imperfect; the identified dimensions and assumptions less than pure.

But it is a start; there have been fruits.

Five Conceptual Approaches to Family Study

Conceptual frameworks are elusive and abstract; indeed, some students have found them to be almost ephemeral. How, then, do we identify them; how do we distinguish one from another?

Our procedure has been one of identifying the scope and focus of various writers who deal with marriage and the family and listing their most frequently used concepts. After reading hundreds of studies it has been possible to abstract out of the mass of concepts utilized those which refer primarily to structure, to processes, to solidarity, to development over time, and to spatial arrangements. The five approaches we describe in this paper cope with these dimensions quite differently.

Our mode of exposition is straightforward: a simple taxonomic arrangement of those relatively substance-free concepts which seem most crucial and necessary to the particular approaches. This arrangement permits easy comparison and distinction from one framework to another.

In the analyses that follow we include the following dimensions:

1. Organization (structural) concepts: Units studied and their interrelationships.

   a. *Units of study:* Type and number of units permitted by the conceptual development. Any one framework will have one or more units which may be used; each will have a basic unit (the unit to which autonomous reality is ascribed).

   b. *Unit configuration:* Positions and interrelations of units in the study, arranged hierarchically and "horizontally."

   c. *Unit interdependency:* Cohesion concepts which bind together the units of the structure (e.g., functions, services, normative demands).

2. Bridges: Conditions linking structure to overt, observable behavior and mechanisms which interpret the structure into behavior.

   a. *Conditions:* Those structural and environmental states important to the operational or dynamic qualities of the structure.

b. *Mechanisms:* Those inferred, usually sub-unit behaviors necessary to, present in, or preceding overt behavior or change.

It is readily recognized that this arrangement hardly takes advantage of all the clues available for identification of the various frameworks. Therefore, in our analyses we add these identifying characteristics of conceptual frameworks:

1. Overt behavior which can be sought or analyzed by the framework:

   a. *Transactional behavior:* Behavior of the family or sub-units with social or cultural elements outside the family.

   b. *Interactional behavior:* Behavior of sub-family units within the family or of a sub-family unit with the family as a whole.

   c. *Actional behavior:* Behavior of the single unit with itself or another object as referent.

2. Social space

   a. *Arena of study:* That particular aspect of the social and cultural whole to which the framework specifically addresses itself and with which it can adequately cope in analysis.

   b; *Environment:* The milieu within which the arena of central focus is studied.

   c. *Peripheral areas:* Those areas which enter study only as independent variables or which are considered only incidentally in analysis.

   d. *Residual areas:* Those areas explicitly neglected by the framework.

3. Social Time: The span of processual time which can be coped with by the framework. This can vary from specific acts or interacts to processes and change over broad sweeps of chronological time.

4. General characteristics of family studies with the framework: Those recurrent and generally present characteristics (in past studies) which are assumed specifically in family study, whether the assumption is necessitated (e.g., by the peculiar conceptual development) or arbitrary.

5. Basic assumptions: Those suppositions most basic to the particular framework — broad and general, but sufficiently specific to allow comparison.

The following discussion does not pretend comprehensiveness in even these selected dimensions of conceptual frameworks. Particularly, the basic assumptions and general characteristics are highly tentative and incomplete. We leave more intensive analysis to those more qualified and will welcome their elaborations and revisions when they are offered.

The Interactional Approach. The interactional approach, first developed in sociology and social psychology, has been the most frequently used in the past twenty years in American family sociology. The approach was a direct outgrowth of the work of George Herbert Mead and the University of Chicago group of symbolic interactionists. Notable among these, Ernest W. Burgess first suggested the feasibility of viewing the family as an interacting unity in 1928. Subsequent studies have gradually refined the interactional framework, the most basic dimensions of which are presented in Table II.

An interactional conception of the family takes these lines: The family is a unity of interacting persons, each occupying a position(s) within the family to which a number of roles are assigned, i.e., the individual perceives norms or role expectations held individually or collectively by other family members for his attributes and behavior. In a given situation, an individual defines these role expectations primarily in view of their source (reference group) and of his own self-conception. Then he role-plays. Most immediately the family is studied through analysis of overt interacts (interaction of role-playing family members) cast in this structure.

Characteristically, past studies have considered the family a comparatively closed unity which has little relation to outside agencies. Thus the hundreds of studies it has stimulated have focused on the internal aspects of the family but neglected consideration of the family as an entity in relation to the community or collateral associations.

Substantively, in addition to role analysis, the framework has focused on such problems as status and inter-status relations, which become the basis for authority patterns and initiative taking; processes of communication, conflict, problem solving, decision making, and stress reaction; and other aspects of family interaction and interactive processes from dating to divorce. Necessarily, propositions flowing from the use of this framework have been limited to statements about individual families or specified groups of families; institutional or cultural patterns of family life have been quite foreign to this framework.

Table II. Properties of the Interactional Framework

Social Time: Copes with time as stages and phases of process; can focus on short episodes of interacts, but in actual studies time is often frozen; processes treaded statically.

Social Space:
1. Area: Focuses on the family of interacting persons.
2. Environment: Strongly symbolic. Physical elements of little concern, except as mediated symbolically.
3. Peripheral: Agencies outside the family used as independent variables.
4. Residual: Social and cultural family patterns, institutions, personality system (with exception of self).

Structure (Illustrative Basic Concepts)

Units of study	Configurations	Cohesion
Act	Position (status)	Role (as norm or expectation
Interact	Role Sector	Expectations
Person	Intrapersonal role complex	Attribute expectations
Dyad	Concurrent roles	Behavior expectations
Triad	Sequential roles	Norms
	Role continuity	
	Interpersonal role complex	
	Complementary roles	
	Supplementary roles	
	Antagonistic roles	

Bridges (Illustrative Basic Concepts)

Conditions	Mechanisms
Reference groups	Definition of the situation (social
Generalized others	definition)
Significant others	Thought
Self (social self)	Memory
Personality	Fantasy
Motivation	Inhibition
Values	Role-taking
Needs	Reflexive role-taking
Emotions	Empathy
	Identification
	Role conflict tension
	Role-playing
	Playing at a role

Overt Behavior:
1. Transactional: Of only peripheral interest. Rarely treated, and then as discrete transactive event.
2. Interactional: Highly developed, primarily treated in terms of events and specific interacts.
3. Actional: Rarely treated, though conceptual development would allow treatment.

Reuben Hill and Donald A. Hansen

The Structure-Function Approach. The structure-function approach, which views the family as a social system, has its roots in anthropology and sociology and is rapidly winning adherents in the United States and Europe. Elaborated in the United States in more recent years by Talcott Parsons, Kingsley Davis, Robert Merton, George Homans, Marion Levy, and others, it has been applied to the family profitably at several levels from broad macroanalysis to intensive microanalysis. In family study, it is convenient to consider microfunctionalism as concerned with the specific behavior of *individual families;* macrofunctionalism as concerned with *the family* as an abstraction useful in institutional analysis. This distinction will be noticed in Table III.

Table III. Properties of the Structure-Function Framework

Social Time: Copes well with recurrent social act, interact, and transact. Is somewhat vague for specific acts, interacts, and transacts, although some work has been done in this area (Bales and Strodbeck). Deals poorly with social change and process.

Social Space:
1. Area: Copes with (1) the interaction of the individual family member with other individuals and subsystems in the family and with the full family system; (2) the interplay of subsystems with other subsystems and with the full family system; and (3) the transactions of the family with outside agencies and other systems in society, and with society (*the* social system) itself.
2. Environment: In family study, the social system is environmental; cultural elements are mediated through it.
3. Peripheral: Cultural system, personality system.
4. Residual: No residual areas apparent in theory.

Structure (Illustrative)

Units of Study	Configuration	Cohesion
Status-role bundle (basic to microfunctionalism)	Social structure	Function
	Group structure	Dysfunction
Individual (in position)	Sub-structures	Latent function
Groups (dyads, triads, etc.)	External system	Latent dysfunction
Family (as social system— basic to macrofunctionalism)	Internal system	Functional prerequisites, needs, requirements
	Pattern variable	
	Role	Functional equivalents
	Role patterns	Functional alternatives
	Role set	Functional substitutes
	Status	Functional autonomy
	Status set	Social norms
	Structure differentiation	Expectations
	Role differentiation	Interpersonal relations
		Interpenetration
		Reciprocal habits

Bridges (Illustrative)

Conditions	*Mechanisms*
Solidarity	Boundary maintenance
Sanction types	Integration
Personality	System input
Subjective dispositions	System output
Motives	Definition of the situation
Need-disposition	
Purposes	
Values	
Sentiment	
Reference groups	
Equilibrium	
Disequilibrium	

Overt Behavior:
1. Transactional: Strong theoretical development. Permits analysis of transaction of family members with other agencies and of family in social system. Macroanalysis of process is treated statically. Does not cope with change.
2. Interactional: Strong development, especially in analysis of structural arrangements.
3. Actional: Some development, but generally neglected.

The functionalist might conceive of the family as one of many components of the complete social system (society) and as best studied for the functions it performs in society. Internally, the family itself is composed of individuals who are best studied through their status-role bundles and who are significant for their functions in the maintenance of the family system and, ultimately, of the social system. Individuals contribute to the boundary maintenance of the system either by acting in response to demands of their structure or by acting under the constraint of the structure.

The family structure includes the expectations of other members and is oriented toward boundary maintenance of the system. (Thus, status roles are best perceived as inseparable.) Subjective dispositions, reference groups, and definitions of the situation, as well as the more structural mechanism of boundary maintenance, mediate this structure into overt behavior or "function as consequences" of structure and mechansim.[4] Behavior, then, is studied in the context of its contribution to this maintenance of the structure. Thus the researcher's goal can be either the understanding of the system by studying its components, or the understanding of the component by studying its relation to the system.

The term "function" is unfortunately an ambiguous one and will be found in almost any study done in any framework. Functionalists usually use the term to refer to (1) the part played by a particular unit in the maintenance of the system, or (2) to the interrelationship of the parts which compose the system, or (3) (most often) to both. It does not, Merton points out, refer to a mathematical relation, to subjective dispositions (aims, motives, purposes), or to a number of other more common definitions.

The scope of the functional approach to the family is broad. Homans indicates the framework posits both an internal system for regulating relations within the family and an external system for dealing with the transactions between the family and non-family agencies and events. The framework thus encompasses the interplay between (1) the family and collateral systems like the school, the occupational world, and the market place, and (2) the transactions between the family and the smaller subgroups of the husband-wife dyad, the sibling cliques, and the individual personality systems of family members.

Characteristically, studies employing this approach view the family as open to outside influences and transactions, and at the same time as a system which tends to maintain its boundaries. The individual family member is viewed more as a reactive bundle of statuses and roles than as an active, action-initiating person; similarly, the family is viewed more as a passively adapting element of the system than as an agent of change. In short, this framework to date has tended to emphasize the statics of structure and neglect change and dynamics. Whether this will remain the case is to be seen.

The approach is extremely versatile and, as is seen in the chart, not only stimulates development of concepts but also readily adapts concepts from other areas. It is important, then, to take careful note of definitions when behavioral concepts such as "role," "definition of the situation," "reference groups," and institutional-type concepts such as "family types," "stratification," "institution" appear in a study. Such key concepts really offer no key if divorced from precise definitions (which unfortunately are rarely offered) or from the cluster of other concepts employed in the report.

The Situational Approach. The situational approach has had provocative but limited use in America. Developed from basic theoretical work by W. I. Thomas and Lowell Carr, it has been applied and refined as an approach for family research by Bossard and his students at the University of Pennsylvania.

The psychological habitat-ecological approach of psychology developed independently by Barker and Wright of Kansas is closely similar to the situational approach of sociology. Differences in terms impose limitations on interchange between these approaches, but these differences seem to be mostly in labeling rather than in meanings: lack of intercourse appears due more to indifference than incompatibility. A more important distinction between the two is in their focus: situational analysis studies the situation itself, or the individual's overt behavior in response to the situation. Complementarily, psychological habitat analysis centers attention on the individual's psychological milieu, emphasizing the uniqueness of each individual's habitat and perception of appropriate behavior.[5]

With some interrelating, we might hope the psychological approach would offer the situational increased precision in the concept category, "bridges." At this time, however, only illustrative concepts directly applied in the sociological situational approach are included in Table IV.

Situationists would agree with interactionists that the family is a unity of interacting persons who experience relatively continuing relationships. But rather than emphasizing interaction, situationists turn to the study of the family as a social situation for behavior. "Social situation" is defined as: ". . . (a) a number of stimuli, external to the organism, but acting upon it; (b) organized and operating as a unit; and, (c) with a special relatedness to each other as stimuli of the specific organisms involved."[6]

The family, then, is seen as a unit of stimuli acting toward a focal point (e.g., child). But the framework allows not only for analyses of the behavior of that focal point in the family situation; Bossard strongly urges study of the situation itself (as he has done in his study of family rituals). In either case it is assumed that: "All behavior is purposive in relation to the situation which calls it forth. It is a solution to the problem or 'crisis' which the situation presents, an answer to or definition of the situation, made by the individual on the basis of other situations and previous experience."[7] This does not, of course, imply that all behavior is rational; it is only purposive in that it is an attempt to resolve a problem posed by the situation.

Characteristically, the family is considered relatively open to

Table IV. Properties of the Situational Framework

Social Time: To capture the situation, time is frozen like still photographs. With observation techniques, short span of interaction is recordable. For longer periods (using interview techniques), time is inexplicit, vague, no specified time units developed.

Social Space:
1. Area: The immediate situation (milieu) of an individual or group.
2. Environment: The entire situational *field* (of which an individual's immediate situation is only a part) including persons, cultural elements, and physical elements.
3. Peripheral: Any nonfamilial part of the situational field may be treated peripherally.
4. Residual: Institutional interaction, personality systems.

Structure (Illustrative)

Units of Study	Configuration	Cohesion
Family situation (basic)	Structural forms	Interactive processes
Life situation	Family patterns	Functions
Family interaction	Family system	Purposes
Family institution	Family relationships	Culture content
(cultural design)	Structural relationships	Environmental norms
Group	Location	
Structural element	Position	
(polar point)	Role	
	Status (hierarchy)	

Bridges (Illustrative)

Conditions	Mechanisms
Family adaptability	Gestalt awareness
Adjustment potential	Definition of the situation
Needs, drives	Role assumptions
Motivation, expectation	Situational adjustment
Values	Social dynamics
Background patterns	Behavior cycle
Primary groups	Opposing cycles
Casual groups	Cycle intersection (collision)
Purpose organizations	
Events	
Occurrences	
Social changes	
Problem situations	
Personality (as social reflection)	

Overt Behavior:
1. Transactional: Some development possible. Focal point of situation may be outside family, permitting analyses of family unit in relation to outside agent or event.
2. Interactional: Strong development. Focal point of situation usually considered within family, permitting analyses of family interaction, family adjustment to the individual, or situational (family) adjustment of the individual.
3. Actional: Little development (developed, however, in psychological-habitat analyses).

outside influence. Though it may be a unit of stimuli for the family member, it is not the only source of stimuli. Nonetheless, the work done in this area to date has centered within the family: focal points range from individual child development in a family situation, through family table-talk, to family rituals and space utilization policies.

The Institutional Approach. Institutional study, one of the first developed sociological approaches to marriage and the family, from its beginnings was strongly allied with historical analysis.

Early institutional study, however, viewed institutions as an aspect of a society as an organismic whole, a system supported and maintained by its component parts. Such an approach is more closely compatible with the structure-function framework (which, it will be remembered, can and does regard the social institution as a functioning part of the social system) than it is with the institutional framework to be described below. The few remaining advocates of the early, organismic-type approach, represented by C. C. Zimmerman, are thus residual to the institutional framework of our inventory in spite of their persistent emphasis on institutional study.

Institutions may also be studied as cultural patterns (modes of life available or permitted within a culture) and as social patterns of recurrent overt behavior or structure. Modern institutionalists (who may be termed "institutional nominalists") may emphasize either of these, though both are necessarily studied as aspects of the same thing.

Because of the continued connection with historical analyses, a highly developed conceptual framework is not employed, and often studies take an almost pure descriptive stance. Penetrating analyses are possible, however, with the concepts developed, as illustrated in Table V.

Contrary to the advocates of the organismic approach, institutional nominalists emphasize the family as a social unit in which individual and cultural values are of central concern. Sirjamaki's definition of institution is illuminating:

> The term "institution" is used in a nominalist sense to mean a group of persons organized according to cultural principles to carry on activities which fulfill certain of their basic individual and social needs as human beings ... the functions of an institution are defined as the satisfaction of these wants ...."[8]

Table V. Properties of the Institutional Framework

Social Time: Deals best with social change and family development over long spans of time. Can cope with broad sweeps of time, such as epochs, eras, centuries, and with evolutionary movements. Does not deal with individual acts, interacts, or transacts.

Social Space:
1. Area: Deals best with transaction of the family institution with other social or cultural structures. Individual families with living members rendered residual.
2. Environment: The social cultural milieu.
3. Peripheral: Cultural components, often those producing change.
4. Residual: The individual personality system, individual families as functioning groups.

Structure (Illustrative)

Units of Study	Configuration	Interdependence
Institution (basic)	Institution structure	Institutional
Institutional elements	Social structure	Value system
Cultural traits	Status (generalized)	Norms
Institutional traits	Role (generalized)	Charter
	Institution types	Cultural configuration
	Institution forms	Societal regulations (e.g.,
	Institution patterns	law, ethics)
	Institutional practices	Institutional roles
	Cultural forms	Social functions (service
	Cultural practices	to persons)
	Cultural patterns	
	Social class	
	Power structure	

Bridges (Illustrative)

Conditions	Mechanisms
Biological conditions	Institutional adjustment
Biological limitations	Social process
Environmental conditions	Life process
Environmental limitations	Evolution
Social conditions	Development
Social limitations	Culture transmission
Culture lag	Stratification
Social problems	Differentiation
Conflict	Acculturation
Social change	Assimilation
	Stabilization

Overt Behavior:
1. Transactional: Well able to cope with transactional behavior of family with other cultural elements, and of family positions (generalized) with other cultural elements. (Specific events and elements are residual.)
2. Interactional: Copes only in highly generalized fashion with interaction as a process (as in changing family status and roles).
3. Actional: Cannot cope with action or with covert or idiosyncratic behavior.

Conceptual Frameworks   33

This emphasizes institutional members as active elements in a society; but continuity is assured, for the individual's values and learned needs are transmitted from generation to generation within the individual family systems which make up the institution and from the more general cultural milieu in which the family exists. The cultural milieu is expressed in the family as a complex of cultural values (culture complex) or, again in Sirjamaki's terms, in cultural configurations:

> Configurations are the moral principles, or working rules, which rise at the level of the culture to rationalize the activities of an institution and to motivate or instruct its members. They derive their name from the fact that they organize or configurate behavior into specific overt patterns of activity.[9]

With this nominalist definition, it is almost necessary to assert that there is not just one but many family institutions within any one society; nonetheless basic shared values and behaviors will allow abstraction of a basic family institution, which for convenience may be called *the* family.

Characteristically, even today the institutional approach is closely allied with historical, cross-cultural, and descriptive works. Of the frameworks herein described it remains the most closely rooted in substantive analysis. The family institution is often, though not necessarily, described as the most important of institutions, in spite of a loss of functions in contemporary society.

It is difficult to tell whether the number of works in this framework is increasing; it is obvious that few have been accomplished. It does seem clear, however, that there is a *need* for an institutional approach which does not involve commitment to the organismic analogy; whether the need is for this particular approach or another (for example, the more generally popular and better developed "actional" approach applied by Riesman, Weber, Mills, and Martindale to other sociological areas) remains to be seen. It is also apparent and understandable that organismic institutional analyses are increasingly rare outside the functional framework.

The Developmental Approach. The developmental approach is not at this moment a precisely unique framework but is really an attempt to transcend the boundaries of several approaches through incorporation of their compatible sections into one unified scheme. From rural sociologists it borrowed the concept of stages of the family life cycle. From child psychologists and human development specialists came the concepts of developmental needs and tasks. From the sociologists engaged in work in the professions it incorporated the concept of the family as a convergence of inter-contingent careers. From the structure-function and interactional approaches were borrowed the concepts of age and sex roles, plurality patterns, functional prerequisites, and the many concepts associated with the family as a system of interacting actors.

It has been shown, however, that as the framework is presently developing, an individual set of basic assumptions is emerging, but

Table VI. Properties of the Developmental Approach

Social Time: Copes well with action and interaction, as well as with change and process over time. The time span is the life cycle of the nuclear family, the basic time units are stages demarcated by spurts of growth and development.

Social Space:
1. Area: Emphasizes changing internal structure and development of family. May cope with family systems and collateral systems and with the personality system of members.
2. Environment: Cultural imperatives and demands.
3. Peripheral: Agencies outside the family; members' outside activities, physical elements.
4. Residual: Not determinable. Potentially can cope with full array of social and cultural elements with which the family has contact, including the social system (in structure-function terms).

Structure:
1. Units of study: Family group (basic); interacting individuals, individual.
2. Configuration: Basically life cycle and stages, family tempos and rhythms.
3. Cohesion: Basically developmental tasks (interrelating stages with one another) and roles and functions (interrelating individuals within stages).

Bridges:
1. Conditions: Basically teachable moment (physical maturation, cultural pre-requisites, communication) and psychological elements such as perception, identity formation, and motivation.
2. Mechanisms: Little development apparent. Can probably borrow heavily from interactional and microfunctional approaches.

Overt Behavior:
1. Transactional: Treatment of transactional behavior only now beginning; only limited development shown.
2. Interactional: Strong development likely. Can cope with individual interacts as well as process within a stage; stages and development allow treatment of long-range changes and process over time.
3. Actional: Little added development to date but leans on psychology of child development for identification of stages of individual growth and development.

that these are as yet closely similar to those of the interactional school. Table VI indicates other characteristics of the developing framework. The array of basic concepts is not as extensive as in the preceding frameworks, for the framework has not yet reached full term. It is too soon to say whether the developmental approach will turn out to be a variant or an extension of interactional analysis rather than a unique approach in its own right.

As does the interactional approach, family development views the family as an arena of interacting personalities, intricately organized internally into paired positions (e.g., husband-father, son-brother). Norms prescribing the appropriate role behavior for each of these positions specify how reciprocal relations are to be maintained as well as how role behaviors may change with changing ages of the occupants of these positions. This intimate small group has a predictable natural history designated by stages, beginning with the simple husband-wife pair and becoming more and more complex with each additional position that is activated, then becoming less complex as members are launched into jobs and marriage and the group contracts to the husband-wife pair once again. As the age and member composition of the family change, so does the quality and type of interaction.

In the interaction arena, each personality strives to obtain the satisfaction of his basic desires. As a result, at some stages of development parents and children are good company, at other stages their diverse developmental strivings are strikingly incompatible.

Using these concepts, a number of well-defined stages of the family life cycle can be identified, each with its own peculiar sources of conflict and solidarity. Each of these stages can be seen along three dimensions of increasing complexity: (1) the changing developmental tasks and role expectations of the children; (2) the changing developmental tasks and role expectations of the parents in their capacities as providers, homemakers, spouses, and persons, and (3) the family developmental tasks of the family as a family, which flow from the cultural imperatives at various stages of growth and from the personal developmental requirements of children and parents.

The approach furnishes an opportunity for the accretion of generalizations about the internal development of families from their formation in the engagement and wedding to their dissolution in divorce or death. In spite of increasing interest in the approach, however, the framework implies use of the longitudinal method of research, which, because of its expense and slow yield, has seen limited use in family research to date.

Basic Assumptions of the Five Frameworks

Perhaps the most significant elements in differentiating one framework from another are the underlying assumptions which each makes about the nature of man, the family, and society. Unfortunately, the last persons to identify their assumptions are usually the advocates of a particular approach to a given problem area. Moreover, it is difficult to disentangle basic underlying assumptions from the unifying assumptions which tie together the concepts within a framework. The importance of the latter should be recognized, for they also introduce differences into the propositions in completed studies. But such unifying assumptions can be dropped or modified[10] within the conceptual framework without reducing greatly the differences between the frameworks general orientations to man, family and society.

In this concluding section we limit our task to specifying the differentiating basic assumptions, recognizing that hard work by those most deeply immersed in this type of analysis has yielded to date only a few suppositions thought basic.

Interactional
1. Social conduct is most immediately a function of the social milieu.
2. A human is an independent actor as well as a reactor to his situation.
3. The basic autonomous unit is the acting individual in a social setting. (Emergence is not an issue.)

Structure-Function
1. Social conduct is best analyzed for its contribution to the maintenance of the social system, or for its nature under the structures of the system.
2. A social human is basically a reacting part of the social system; self-elicited (independent) action is rare and asocial.
3. The basic autonomous unit is the social system, which is composed of interdependent subsystems (e.g., institutions, family systems, etc.).
4. It is possible to profitably study any sub-units of the basic system.
5. The social system tends to homeostasis.

Situational

1. Social conduct is a function of the situation (social, cultural, physical milieu).
2. Behavior is purposive (i.e., problem solving, though not completely rational) in relation to the situation which elicits it.
3. The basic autonomous unit is the individual in a situation.
4. Situations and human groupings, as unities of organization, have emergent realities (i.e., have a reality beyond that of its component parts).

Institutional

1. Social components (e.g., conduct and change) are best analyzed for their service to the institution member (generalized, nonspecific member of social institution); institutions are generally responses to human needs and values (cultural norms).
2. Institutions are active as well as reactive to other social, material, and cultural components; institution members are active as well as reactive.
3. The basic autonomous unit is the institution.
4. There is emergence in social groupings; this emergence goes at least to the level of institutions. Culture and society are most often held to be only configurations of elements.

Developmental

1. Human conduct is best seen as a function of the preceding as well as the current social milieu and individual conditions.
2. Human conduct cannot be adequately understood apart from human development.
3. The human is an actor as well as a reactor.
4. Individual and group development is best seen as dependent upon stimulation by a social milieu as well as on inherent (developed) capacities.
5. The individual in a social setting is the basic autonomous unit. (Issue of emergence is skirted.)

Summary and Implications for Further Work

As a necessary step in building an inventory of research propositions on marriage and the family, this article has attempted to identify competing approaches to family study. It has been posited (1) that irrevocable differences in propositions are introduced by descriptive concepts which themselves refer not to the real world, but to other concepts, (2) that such concepts flow from basic assumptions about the real world and from the other concepts with which they are related.

At this point, we cannot attempt to trace the history of every concept used in family research. But we can seek to discover the general conceptual framework in which the research was done. Identification of the framework employed will forestall unthinking accretion of propositions across framework lines; such accretion of propositions with even identical-appearing concepts can be quite misleading, luring us from insight to error.

We have attempted to distinguish five frameworks from one another in basic concepts, definitions of the family, and underlying assumptions. These have been presented in a way that hopefully will be of use in the development of new family and marriage research as well as in the mining of past research for the meaningful accretion of research propositions.

This article represents one step along a path on which many strides must still be taken. The following steps might now be taken to sharpen the cutting edge of the instrument we have assembled:

1. Further work on distinguishing and examining the assumptions of the five identified frameworks and of other frameworks developed in collateral fields which may not yet have been identified as relevent for marriage and family study.
2. Further work on conceptual interrelations within the frameworks. We need an ordering of concepts by generality, abstraction, and observability.
3. Identification and examination of gaps between the concepts within each framework, re-evaluation of frameworks as gaps are recognized, and bridging or filling those gaps where it is possible.

Whatever the accomplishment of this article in itself, its significance must be seen in light of the objective of codifying family research in an inventory of research propositions. Though still incomplete, framework clarification opens the door to development of numerous potentials in the inventory and promises tools of value to marriage and family students, researchers, and theory builders.

FOOTNOTES

This is the third in a series of articles reporting progress on the Inventory of Research in Marriage and Family Behavior now located at the University of Minnesota. See also Reuben Hill, Alvin M. Katz, and Richard L. Simpson, "An Inventory of Research in Marriage and Family Behavior: A Statement of Objectives and Progress," *Marriage and Family Living,* 19 (February, 1957), pp. 89-92; and Alvin M. Katz and Reuben Hill, "Residential Propinquity and Marital Selection: A Review of Theory, Method and Fact," *Marriage and Family Living,* 20 (February, 1958), pp. 27-35.

In preparation of this article we wish to acknowledge especially the help of Professor Don Martindale of the University of Minnesota and Dr. Sheldon Stryker of Indiana University, whose criticisms, suggestions, and insights greatly strengthened the manuscript.

[1] A research proposition is defined as an empirically validated generalization which often takes one of these forms: (1) a descriptive statement of observed conditions (e.g., the course of family adjustment to crisis follows a roller coaster pattern of disorganization — recovery attempts — readjustment); (2) an antecedent-consequent statement (e.g., if the family has had previous success in meeting crises then there is greater probability that a subsequent crisis will be successfully met); or (3) a statement of co-variance (e.g., crisis proneness increases as a family's socio-economic position declines).

[2] The person acquainted with the inventory will notice a number of minor changes and complete omission of two frameworks previously included. The "household economics-home management approach" was dropped because of its apparent failure to generate a full-fledged conceptual framework. Relying on a "balance sheet" presentation, the approach does not seem to have risen from the level of description, and, except when allied with a separate theoretical framework, it involves no important assumptions about the real world. This does not mean that propositions derived in this area will be neglected in the inventory; they will be treated adequately without concern about a framework, as would any descriptive propositions. The "learning theory-maturational approach" was dropped more arbitrarily: to keep the inventory within working boundaries, it is necessary to consider only approaches which can deal with the family as a whole and/or with the full array of its internal relationships. The promise that learning theory showed a decade ago of developing such a framework has not been realized, and today it still focuses exclusively on the individual. The "psychological-habitat" aspect of the situational approach was dropped for the same reason. Provocative writing about personality in a family context abounds in the literature, utilizing concepts from these approaches and from the rich store of psychoanalytic terms, but to date they have been unable to cope with the family conceptually.

[3]Clustering of concepts is, ideally, dictated by the interrelations of the concepts themselves. In our discussion we have not been able to go beyond a taxonomic presentation of the framework; to offer more would be to presume insights apparently not yet gained by the most advanced students of each of the frameworks. Propositions are, ideally, not a part of the framework; indeed, the term "generally applicable" indicates the framework should be relatively substance free (i.e., abstract and general, as opposed to substance bound) and applicable to any substance area not rendered residual by the framework itself.

[4]Robert K. Merton, *Social Theory and Social Structure,* Glencoe, Illinois: Free Press, 1957, pp. 20-25.

[5]As was noted, the psychological-habitat is not included in the frameworks, not because it fails to yield information pertinent to family study, but because it does not cope with the family as an entity or with its possible subgroupings.

[6]James H. S. Bossard and Eleanor Stoker Boll, *Family Situations,* Philadelphia: University of Pennsylvania Press, 1943, p. 37.

[7]James H. S. Bossard, *Parent and Child,* Philadelphia: University of Pennsylvania Press, 1956, p. 23.

[8]John Sirjamaki, *The American Family in the Twentieth Century,* Cambridge: The Harvard University Press, 1953, p. 8.

[9]*Ibid.,* p. 8.

[10]An example of this may be seen in Merton's now generally accepted criticism of the functionalists' postulate of functional indispensability. See Merton, *op. cit.,* pp. 32-36.

Culture Configurations

in the American Family

John Sirjamaki

This selection by John Sirjamaki introduces the Institutional framework with a discussion of the significance of value configurations for an understanding of the behavior patterns characteristic of American families. Observations of family behavior have suggested eight more important configurations which motivate and integrate the behavior of family members. Pitfalls inherent in generalizations about American cultural patterns are stressed.

Most sociological studies of the family deal with it either as a social system or as a social institution. An important supplement to these approaches is the cultural analysis of the family in terms of its dominant configurations. When these can be specified for the family, it is possible to interpret the basic moral ideas which give the family its distinctive and identifying characteristics.

Culture configurations are the moral principles which comprise the social philosophy of a society. They are patterns of covert behavior; as such, they are the culturally approved rules or sentiments which motivate overt behavior and which integrate it into consistent patterns; and they can be deduced only from behavior. Such configurations exist on the level of the culture and arise in the context of everyday living. Members of a society comprehend the meaning of such precepts in the process of socialization, even

Reprinted, with permission of the author and the publisher, from *American Journal of Sociology*, 53 (1948), pp. 464-470.

when they are expressed tenuously or obscurely; and, indeed, configurations are difficult to state abstractly inasmuch as they generally operate below the level of awareness. Taken together, the configurations delineate the ethos of a culture.[1]

Configurations are thus the basic units of the value system of a society. They differ from the absolute ethics of religious or philosophical systems in that they are mundane, practical, this-worldly; having developed within the culture, they express the dominant values which are thought to be necessary for the continued functioning of the society. Ordinarily configurational values are stigmatized by philosophers as base and inferior; Fromm has called them "socially immanent ethics" as contrasted to universal ethics.[2] For the social scientist, however, it is necessary to understand the configurations of a culture, since they motivate behavior much more continuously than do absolute ethical systems. The configurations will tend to support the total culture and to achieve an interrelatedness among themselves. As Sumner indicated, there is a strain for consistency in the mores.[3]

The concept of the configurations of the culture, and a knowledge of the manner in which these are expressed within an institution, illuminates the study of the family. Configurations reach into the most intimate areas of individual and family behavior; they furnish the meanings and determine right and wrong behavior in courting, in husband-wife and parent-child relationships, in heterosexual social activity, and in ideas about sex. Thus they supply the moral sentiments by which family members are influenced and make explicable the vagaries of their behavior.

At least four qualifications may be raised concerning the validity of applying culture configurations to the study of the American family. First, since such configurations are inferred by the investigator from the overt behavior of people, he must have available a considerable amount of observational data which, however, is currently lacking. Second, the use of such configurations should await an analysis of the total culture, and this has been attempted thus far in the most tentative manner.[4] The analysis of parts of the culture, however, will assist in the determination of the total culture ethos. Third, generalizations about American culture must be stated in the most broad terms and can attempt only to strike an average, since regional and ethnic subcultures obviously differ from the main pattern. To whom, it may be asked, do configurations apply? The answer is that configurations are generally valid, or will tend to become so, for the entire American society, in the sense that they represent the moral standards by which all behavior is evaluated, and which exert a social pressure to secure some degree of conformance. Families of ethnic minorities thus quite apparently have patterns dissimilar to those of native-born families, but in time the American culture configurations come to influence the actions of at least the immigrant children and to bring their behavior into conformity with the general requirements of society. Finally, configurations are not easily amenable to quantification; they may seem to be accurately stated, but they are difficult to measure. There is no real answer to this objection other than to predicate the statement of configurations upon as careful objective analysis as is possible. A value system patently exists in every culture, and its appriasal should be sought by the social scientist.

The following configurations, among others, appear in the American family:

1. *Marriage is a dominating life-goal, for men as well as for women.* — It is felt that married life is the normal, desired condition for all adults, that it brings the greatest personal happiness and fulfilment, and that it permits the proper exercise of sex for the procreation of children and for individual satisfaction. The single adult life by contrast, according to this attitude, is empty and barren. That there is a considerable societal concern that women marry is generally recognized, but the greater courting and sexual initiative assumed by men has obscured the comparable pressure on them to marry, and adult men who postpone marriage into their thirties become objects of distress and conspiracy among friends and relatives. Most Americans marry in their twenties, and, for a considerable share of them, marriage at that age means a happy union of individual volition and social pressure.

Long ago Professor E. A. Ross pointed out that Americans are the most marrying nation in Western Christendom. United States census figures have shown that since 1890 they have married in steadily increasing proportions and at earlier ages.[5] About 92 per cent of adults will have been married at some time in their lives by the age of sixty-five,[6] and this is a sufficiently high number to suggest that nearly all persons marry who are physically and mentally capable of contracting marriage.

2. *The giving and taking in marriage should be based on personal affection and choice.* — Marriage is thought to be preeminently the

linking of the lives of two young people drawn to each other by personal attraction. Arranged marriages, or those based on fraud or calculation, receive considerable disapprobation.

Dating is thought by many sociologists to precede serious courting and to be an educational process leading to it. Waller first analyzed it in terms of its distinctive cultural patterns.[7] In dating, the young woman undoubtedly receives the greatest cultural estimation of her personal qualities: merely to be a young, nubile female of attractive phenotype means that she is the object of considerable masculine attention and chivalry.[8] But, despite this high evaluation of young women, most men grow up in American society with the assumption, culturally derived, that the decision to marry rests with them; they expect in the fulness of time to lead some dear girl to the altar. Women, on the other hand, regardless of their personal qualities, can never be completely sure that they will receive a marriage proposal which they can consider seriously, or, more to the point, be asked to marry by the man upon whom they have fastened their desire.[9] The culture does not permit them to undertake active courting by themselves; to be a man-chaser is to suffer an ostracism which is enforced by the women themselves. Women are obviously not completely helpless in these sentimental matters, but they must use guile and finess to bring the male to their side.

Since the biological fact of bisexuality predisposes women for the having and rearing of children, and therefore for the maintenance of a home, they are compelled to drive as good a bargain in the marriage market as they can. This they can manage only by a careful exploitation of the rules which specify correct maidenly deportment. Men, on the other hand, have greater volition in their marriage choices and are much more disposed as a result to manage their marital ventures in the bathos of culturally approved romance.

3. *The criterion of successful marriage is the personal happiness of husband and wife.* — Mutual compatibility is made the basis of marriage, and marital bliss becomes dependent upon the emotional sentiments, fluctuating and volatile as they may be, with which a couple regard their relationship. Ultimately their fullest felicity is believed to be achieved by having children, whose arrival and subsequent nurture are viewed as bringing satisfaction to basic biological and social needs. Childless couples are sometimes regarded as possessed of a selfishness which blights their union.

Happiness in marriage is thus predicated upon a personal equation, the individual satisfaction and the opportunity for development of the couple.

The cultural accent upon happiness in marriage is of relatively recent origin. Marriages are ordinarily contracted and their success gauged by their contribution in the struggles of life. These may be the partnership co-operation of man and wife, the production of children, the social recognition of adult status, or the stability of marital status. Many such marriages may be buttressed by institutional supports, the most important of which is generally the exchange of property. The spouses may be selected for each other by the parents or other adults, after a careful scrutiny of their relative merits and upon some property agreement, in the belief that normal young people, once married, can fashion for themselves a successful marital life.[10]

A corollary of the American patterns of courtship and marriage which is not always recognized is the logical necessity of a relatively easy system of divorce. From a cultural viewpoint, if marriages are made on the basis of personal and inevitably shifting emotions, without the added support of other institutional devices, then they should be equally easy to dissolve. Persons marry to find happiness and, finding it not, turn to divorce as a way out. The present high divorce rate, therefore, is in this sense made explicable and partially condoned by the cultural rules of marriage.

4. *The best years of life are those of youth, and its qualities are the most desirable.* – A high evaluation is placed upon youth and early middle age in American society, while the old are sometimes treated with indifference and even callousness. Youth is regarded as a period of innocence, energy, and enthusiasm; it is inventive and pragmatic when faced with new experiences and is glad of change – qualities fondly believed to be typical of Americans in general.

Among the young, the unmarried girl, aged perhaps twenty, attractive of face and limb, is the center of attraction in thought and deed. In other societies young men, or old men, or mothers are variously regarded as ideal symbols;[11] in the United States it is the young, pretty girl. She therefore receives at this age the greatest gratification of her ego drives which will probably ever come to her. With men the ideal age is somewhere in the thirties; they need time in which to win occupational and social placement and need not depend so much upon chronological age for their acceptance.

From this high esteem on youth there derive important social consequences. Wherever the young are involved, whether it be in the conduct of schools, or juvenile delinquency, or maltreatment of children, or provision for their play opportunities, there is likely to be at least a quick emotional response to their needs.

Such sentiments as these do not, of course, arise in a social vacuum. They exist, rather, and become understandable in terms of American social history. Youth has received a high evaluation, precisely because its resourcefulness and resilience were valued qualities in the exploitation and development of the American continent. There have been, in addition, as compared to the age groups in European societies, relatively high proportions in the younger age categories in the American population; Americans have in this sense been a young people and correspondingly eager to admire the virtues of youth. The aged, on the other hand, have emerged as a significant social group only recently, and they are not yet favorably regarded.

Related to this cultural theme of youth is the existence of a considerable rift, not to say antagonism, between the generations. The conflict between the old and the young is common enough in human groups; what is significant is its intensity in American society. This is due, in large part, to the rapidity of social change in the United States and to the differing rates with which the generations have adjusted to those changes. Keller speaks somewhat nostalgically of the aged in primitive society as revered "repositories of wisdom";[12] in American society they are unlikely to be regarded as possessors of a truth that has any relationship to their age.[13]

5. *Children should be reared in a child's world and shielded from too early participation in adult woes and tribulations.* — This configuration is obviously closely related to the high cultural esteem of youth. It is modified by social class: the sentiment is held most strongly by the upper levels of society, much less so by the lower, but even among the poor the social conditions of the American community prevent a too considerable precocity among the children.[14]

The cultural ideal is that children shall mature slowly in terms of their nature and age-sex grades in a prolonged child's world, which is characterized by a segregated class of children's activities.[15] In this juvenile social world they are allowed to grow, develop their abilities, indulge in play, and occasionally to perform such small and often artificial tasks as may be assigned them. Generally they are protected from the responsibilities of adults, and laws and custom prevent their too early gainful employment. In many American homes, particularly in the cities, there is actually not much useful work that children can perform even if they wish. Especially in middle-class families is the configuration most completely observed. The child is accepted as an individual, and his relationships with parents are often warm and affectionate.

Folsom has contrasted this pattern with that which prevails in certain western European families, in which the child is incorporated into the family of adults and in which he lives in their world rather than in a segregated youth society.[16] Moreover, unlike the American middle-class child who may become somewhat exhibitionist in his behavior because of the attention shown him, the European youth is often hastened along in the process of maturation and trained to deference and respect toward parents and elders in general.

Such training as the American child receives may start him off with a psychologically secure character structure,[17] but in other respects it prepares him inadequately for later life. Sometimes he has not broken the emotional ties with his parents or developed definite heterosexual interests; hence his fondness for "Mom."[18] During World War II the British thought the American soldier adolescent.[19] James Graham Leyburn has pointed out that the American family is itself often at fault because of its inadequate integration with the larger community.[20] It may be unable, as a result, to prepare and to place its members into job, school, clique and class, association, and other social relationships in the society. Thus it delays the processes of maturation.

6. *The exercise of sex should be contained within wedlock.* – Prior to marriage premarital intercourse is strongly condemned, and sex knowledge is kept hidden from children lest it be damaging to their moral character. After marriage, adultery is similarly proscribed. Sex may thus be legitimately expressed only within marriage, and the speaking of marriage vows makes highly moral sexual behavior which before then had been grossly immoral. The couple, previously prohibited from intercourse, may now embark upon an active, and socially approved, sex life. Sex, to speak figuratively, explodes upon marriage.

About sex there is considerable tension, preoccupation, frustration, shame, and deceit in American society. Judeo-Christian influences, and more immediately Puritanism, have given a sinful cast to sex and have condoned its expression in marriage only because of the grossly physical method of human reproduction. The tradition has particularly valued virginity, more especially in women, before marriage. But the strong interdictions upon sex have tended to heighten rather than to lessen the fascination with sex which exists among Americans. The furtiveness with which it is often approached and the numerous colloquialisms which refer to it indicate the uneasiness with which it is treated. Kinsey's exploration of the sex histories of American males has documented their actual performances.[21] These data indicate that the sex configuration is held with varying intensity at the several levels of society, apparently least so in the lower class. Even here, however, the materials re-emphasize the manner in which restrictive cultural attitudes condition and limit sexual outlets.

7. *Family roles of husband and wife should be based on a sexual division of labor, but with the male status being superior.* — According to this configuration, the husband is head of his family, its main economic support, and its representative in the larger community. Women, consigned to domesticity, are mothers and homemakers. These roles, biologically and culturally conditioned, provide for the structuring of all types of heterosexual relationships, in which the presumption of dominance generally rests with the males. Men are trained to develop the qualities necessary to fulfil their roles in economic, social, sexual, and other activities and to view themselves with self-respect when they have secured a competence in their performances. Women, too, are trained to their respective feminine roles, and these generally involve some degree of catering to men, somewhat as a complement to the expectation of greater male initiative. Terman's analysis of the desired pattern of sex typing in husband and in wife indicated how the cultural conception of the manly man and the womanly woman fall into the cultural mold.[22]

Women's behavior is governed by a double standard of morality which expects greater masculine enterprise not only in the sexual spheres but in many other areas of life. Women live, in male estimation, under a blanket of oppressive mores which restrains their ordinary, everyday movements. Where men have a relative freedom of action, women must cater to a public opinion of what is womanly behavior. In social life women are under greater disapproval than men when they smoke or indulge in narcotics. On the job they may encounter much male prejudice which affects their pay and possibilities of promotion. They are more protected by social legislation which governs their hours and conditions of employment.[23]

These cultural attitudes persist despite the social and economic events of modern times which have released women from the control of husbands and fathers. Before the law women have achieved a near-equality with men; they may seek gainful employment and retain their earnings; they have equal rights with men to education; they have all the freedoms necessary to live their own lives as they wish. Democratic sentiments further foster the desire that women develop as persons to enjoy the manifold blessings of American life and to have many of the privileges given men.

Women are thus caught in a process of social change, in which the cultural configuration restrains them to traditional roles, while new ones are proffered by economic and social forces. There is much confusion among them as a result. The young college girl, for example, may have difficulty in knowing to which force to respond: should she be content with the domestic role and look to the main chance of marriage, or should she seek outlets which include both marriage and other roles?[24] Apparently some urban upper-level women find the puzzle extremely hard to resolve and respond to it neurotically.[25]

Men, too, it must be pointed out, suffer in the realignment of roles, since they as much as women are conditioned to the status quo and may find it hard to accommodate themselves to change.

8. *Individual, not familial, values are to be sought in family living.* – The family is obviously affected by the considerable cultural affirmation of individualism, and the lack of a tradition of familism in American culture has further aided in the development of a configuration in which the family exists for the benefit of its members. The emphasis has been upon the individualization of all members of the family, the children as well as the parents, the wife as much as the husband. Obviously, the husband's prerogatives, nurtured in the bosom of the patriarchal family have had to be parceled out to the other members.

There are many important social consequences from the stress on individualism in the family. On the one hand, its promise is for the richer, fuller development of personality. On the other hand, it weakens the unity of the family. The stresses of American life, including industrialization, urbanization, internal migration, and social class, press hard against the frail shell of the family, attenuated as it is by the thinning of larger kin groups and often limited to its own resources in times of crisis. Further, since the family is not primarily important in placing its members into positions in the larger community, its members feel the strain of loyalties divided between the family and the outside affiliations.

If some of the configurations of the American family have been correctly stated, they indicate a social philosophy in which the values of individualism are paramount, or, more specifically, those which support the development of individual personality in the context of family and community relationships. A primary stress is placed on the family as a social group rather than on the functions which it performs for society. The family exists for its members rather than the members for the family. In this respect the family is in relatively close adjustment to the total culture, in which the democratic realization of the potentialities of all its members is an ideal.

But the family is pre-eminently an association based on antagonistic co-operation, and in times of hardship the antagonisms may predominate. The straining of family members for individualistic goals may blunt their sense of obligation to each other and to the larger society. When achievement of the desired values for which they grope seems far off and difficult, individualism may decay into gross egotism and selfishness. The family based on the chimera of personal values seems then faced with a dolorous future.

The American family, however, is not without resources. Contributing to its strength is the immense popularity of marriage, and through marriage the possibility of parenthood, both of them regarded as major life-goals. Staying power is also given the family by the affection and compatibility which draws two people into marriage, the warmth of relationships between parents and children, and the individualization of all members of the family. The structure of the family is such as to permit the desired nurturing of stable and democratic personalities.

In view of the ethos of the culture the direction of evolutionary change in the family, and of desirable efforts at rational adjustments, is in the continued emphasis upon the social relationships within the family and upon the family as a social system through which fundamental life-purposes can be achieved.

FOOTNOTES

[1] I have adhered to Clyde Kluckhohn's definition of configuration in his chapter, "Patterning as Exemplified in Navaho Culture," in Leslie Spier, A. Irving Hallowell, and Stanley S. Newman (eds.), *Language, Culture, and Personality* (Menasha, Wis.: Sapir Memorial Publication Fund, 1941), pp. 109-30, and exemplified in part in Clyde Kluckhohn and Dorothea Leighton, *The Navaho* (Cambridge: Harvard University Press, 1946), pp. 216-38. My indebtedness is considerable to Ruth Benedict, "Configurations of Culture in North America," *American Anthropologist*, XXXIV (1932), 1-27, and *Patterns of Culture* (Boston: Houghton Mifflin Co., 1934). For the study of value systems configuration has appeared to be a more useful concept than most, in that it refers to positive rules which organize behavior into patterns, while the mores are generally stated as unitary negative injunctions (see William Graham Sumner, *Folkways* [Boston: Ginn & Co., 1906], p. 30; and William Graham Sumner and Albert Galloway Keller, *The Science of Society* [New Haven: Yale University Press, 1927], I, 33-35). Bronislaw Malinowski has used the concept of "charter" in his definition of a social institution as a means of studying values (*A Scientific Theory of Culture and Other Essays* [Chapel Hill: University of North Carolina Press, 1944], pp. 52-53). Alfred McClung Lee has analyzed social values from an interesting and useful approach in "Levels of Culture as Levels of Social Generalization," *American Sociological Review*, X (1945), 485-95, and in "Social Determinants of Public Opinions," *International Journal of Opinion and Attitude Research*, I (1947), 12-29.

[2] Erich Fromm, *Man for Himself* (New York: Rinehart & Co., Inc., 1947), p. 241.

[3] *Op. cit.*, pp. 5-6.

[4] John Sirjamaki, "A Footnote to the Anthropological Approach to the Study of American Culture," *Social Forces*, XXV (1947), 253-63; Clyde Kluckhohn, "The American Culture: Definition and Prophecy. Part II. The Way of Life," *Kenyon Review*, III (1941), 160-79; Clyde Kluckhohn and Florence R. Kluckhohn, "American Culture: Generalized Orientations and Class Patterns," in Lyman Bryson, Louis Findelstein, and R. M. MacIver (eds.), *Conflicts of Power in Modern Culture* (New York: Harper & Bros., 1947), pp. 29-109; Robert S. Lynd, *Knowledge for What?* (Princeton: Princeton University Press, 1939), pp. 63-99; Robert S. Lynd and Helen Merrell Lynd, *Middletown: A Study in American Culture* (New York: Harcourt,

Brace & Co., 1929), and *Middletown in Transition* (New York: Harcourt, Brace & Co., 1937); and Oscar Waldemar Junek, "What Is the Total Pattern of Our Western Civilization? Some Preliminary Observations," *American Anthropologist*, XLVIII (1946), 397-406.

[5] *Sixteenth Census of the United States, 1940, Population*, IV, Part I, 16.

[6] *Fifteenth Census of the United States, 1930, Population*, Vol. II, chapter on marital condition.

[7] Willard Waller, "The Rating and Dating Complex," *American Sociological Review*, II (1937), 727-34.

[8] Weston LaBarre, "Social Cynosure and Social Structure," *Journal of Personality*, XIV (1946), 171.

[9] Ernest R. Groves, *Marriage* (New York: Henry Holt & Co., Inc., 1933), pp. 89-90.

[10] Ralph Linton, *The Study of Man* (New York: D. Appleton-Century Co., Inc., 1936), p. 175.

[11] LaBarre, *op. cit.*, p. 179.

[12] Sumner and Keller, *op. cit.*, p. 464.

[13] Margaret Park Redfield, "The American Family: Consensus and Freedom," *American Journal of Sociology*, LII (1946), 177.

[14] W. Lloyd Warner and Paul S. Lunt, *The Social Life of a Modern Community* (New Haven: Yale University Press, 1941), pp. 92-111; and Allison Davis, Burleigh B. Gardner, and Mary R. Gardner, *Deep South* (Chicago: University of Chicago Press, 1941), pp. 84-136.

[15] Joseph K. Folsom, *The Family and Democratic Society* (New York: John Wiley & Sons, Inc., 1943), p. 184.

[16] *Ibid.*, p. 105.

[17] Abram Kardiner, *The Psychological Frontiers of Society* (New York: Columbia University Press, 1945), p. 361.

[18] Edward A. Strecker, *Their Mothers' Sons* (Philadelphia: J. B. Lippincott Co., 1946), and Philip Wylie, *Generation of Vipers* (New York: Farrar & Rinehart, Inc., 1942).

[19] Mass-Observation, London, "Portrait of an American?" *International Journal of Opinion and Attitude Research*, I (1947), 96.

[20] In lecture at Yale University, May 2, 1947.

[21] Alfred C. Kinsey, Wardell B. Pomeroy, and Clyde E. Martin, *Sexual Behavior in the Human Male* (Philadelphia: W. B. Saunders Co., 1948).

[22] Lewis M. Terman, *Psychological Factors in Marital Happiness* (New York: McGraw-Hill Book Co., Inc., 1938), pp. 145-66.

[23] Constantine Panunzio, *Major Social Institutions* (New York: Macmillan Co., 1939), p. 430.

[24] Mirra Komarovsky, "Cultural Contradictions and Sex Roles," *American Journal of Sociology*, LII (1946), 184-89.

[25] Ferdinand Lundberg and Marynia F. Farnham, *Modern Woman: The Lost Sex* (New York: Harper & Bros., 1947).

The Anthropological Approach to the Study of the Family

Felix Berardo

Felix Berardo examines the varying perspectives — sometimes competing, other times shared — from which Sociologists and Social Anthropologists view the family. Concepts are defined, assumptions basic to the anthropological approach are identified, and the reader gains some appreciation of the contribution of the Hill and Hansen article to the stimulation of studies aimed at the clarification of frameworks.

There is a certain consensus that the field of social anthropology — often referred to as *comparative sociology* — is based upon sociological conceptions and anthropological data. That is to say, its theoretical orientation is properly with sociology rather than with anthropology, for the comparative sociologist is concerned with social explanation, rather than cultural, [and] . . . tries to derive generalizations about behavior of persons in groups, rather than about cultural continua; to seek both the sociological imperatives that operate irrespective of particular cultures and the sociologically derived variations between cultural forms." (Goldschmidt, 1953, p. 287.)

Reprinted, with permission of the author and publisher, from *Emerging Conceptual Frameworks in Family Analysis*, edited by F. Ivan Nye and Felix Berardo, New York: The Macmillan Co., 1966, pp. 16-37.

Theoretically, societies are viewed as functioning wholes, all the parts of which are closely interrelated. To evaluate any particular subunit or system such as the family, one must (1) indicate its place in the society as a whole, (2) show its relation to other subsystems, and (3) attempt to specify the particular functions that it performs in promoting the existence of society. The essence of this approach is captured in an early statement by one of its original proponents, Bronislaw Malinowski, who remarked how the functionalist point of view "aims at the explanation of anthropological facts at all levels of development by their function, by the part which they play within the integral system of culture, by the manner in which they are related to each other within the system, and by the manner in which this system is related to the physical surroundings." (1926, pp. 132-33.) A contemporary exponent of British social anthropology, Evans-Pritchard, has expressed a similar notion:

> A total social structure, that is to say the entire structure of a given society, is composed of a number of subsidiary structures or systems, and we may speak of its kinship system, its economic system, its religious system, and its political system. . . . The social activities within these systems or structures are organized round institutions such as marriage, the family, markets, chieftainships, and so forth; and when we speak of the functions of these institutions we mean the part they play in the maintenance of the structure. (1952, p. 20.)

It is this type of perspective which has served as the theoretical background for a number of recent studies in England on marriage, the family, and kinship, such as those conducted by Firth and his associates in 1956.

The approach has been characterized as holistic, and its major interest lies in what has been termed *macrosocial organization.* It involves what Hill has called *macrofunctionalism,* which concerns itself with the family — as opposed to individual families — as an abstraction useful in institutional analysis. As Hill and Hansen have observed (1960), the functionalist approach to the family is broad:

> the framework posits both an internal system for regulating relations within the family and an external system for dealing with the transactions between the family and non-family events. The framework thus encompasses the interplay between (1) the family and collateral systems like the school, the occupational world, and the market place, and (2) the transactions between the family and the smaller sub-groups of the husband-wife dyad, the sibling cliques, and the individual personality systems of family members.

In this framework, then, the family is perceived as an open system sensitive to external influences and transactions (the family treated as a dependent variable) as well as a system which tends to maintain its boundaries (the family treated as a closed system). Social anthropological investigations lean heavily toward the former viewpoint, that is, treating the family in relation to external factors. In this connection, "the individual family member is viewed more as a reactive bundle of statuses and roles than as an active, action initiating person." (*Ibid.*)

Foci of Study

Homans has stated that in studying primitive kinship one crosses the line that divides sociology from social anthropology. (1950, p. 192.) Social anthropologists have, for the most part, concentrated their efforts on investigations of primitive or communal societies which are typically small, with a relatively simple division of labor and a limited differentiation of roles.[1] In such societies, immediate families and larger kinship groups often nearly exhaust the group memberships and constitute the important units within the society as a whole. Anthropological investigations have often revealed that in this type of social structure behavior is regulated primarily by custom or tradition. The family – or some larger kinship group – is taken to be the most significant social unit to which individuals belong, and the majority of any one individual's roles and relationships are viewed as being heavily dependent upon such membership.[2]

Social anthropologists focus on the *formal aspects* of the systems of marriage and the family, such as composition, residence rules, kinship obligations, parental-authority patterns, marriage forms and regulations, separations, and so on, and attempt to trace the structural implications of these aspects for the community as a whole. Thus, Fortes, in discussing the study of marriage, states: "A complex and fundamental problem in the comparative sociology of marriage is that of the regulations, conditions and criteria governing the choice of a spouse and the procedure of espousal entailed thereby. For everything connected with marriage is directed to this outcome." (1962, p. 2.) In analyzing the manner in which marriages are terminated, for example, and the frequency with which this occurs, the social anthropologist concerns himself with distinguishing the pattern of divorce which characterizes a society and tracing the ways in which this is related to other features of the social system. He deals with such questions as: who initiates divorce, at what point in a person's life divorce is most likely to occur, the reallocation of rights and obligations which follow divorce, the available alternatives, and the spatial correlates of divorce. (Goody, in Fortes, 1962, pp. 14-54.)

The social anthropologist also engages in analyses of the nature of affinal roles and relationships and their connection with other institutions. In a recent investigation, for example, Harris attempts "to seek out the interconnection between the form of affinal relationships on the one hand and, on the other, the distribution of affinal ties − between the *how* and *who* of affinity," and "the interconnection between the dominant forms of affinal relationships as related to the age-status system on the one hand and other features of the social structure on the other." (In Fortes, 1962, pp. 55-87.)

More often than not, however, the social anthropologist will choose to focus primarily on the kinship system at large, attempting to gain some understanding of its underlying principles and the structural implications of these principles. (Olderogge, 1961.) Firth has commented on the theoretical importance of such analyses: "The study of kinship is a perennial theme for the social anthropologist. An understanding of the kinship system in any society is essential as clues to the working of some of the most fundamental relationships − sexual, marital, economic, in that society. It also may be of prime importance in the process of socialization, in developing patterns of reaction to authority and in providing important symbols for the moral evaluation of conduct." (1956, p. 11.) In a similar vein, Radcliffe-Brown's introductory statement to *African Systems of Kinship and Marriage* aptly conveys the importance of this aspect of social organization to social anthropological inquiries concerning family life:

> In these essays I have referred to "Kinship systems." The idea is that in a given society we can isolate conceptually, if not in reality, a certain set of actions and interactions amongst persons which are determined by the relationships of kinship and marriage, and that in a particular society these are interconnected in such a way that we can give a general analytical description of them as constituting a system. The theoretical significance of this idea of systems is that our first step in an attempt to understand a regular feature of a form of social life . . . is to discover its place in the system of which it is a part. (1950, p. 6.)

It should be noted that the quotation also contains certain assumptions regarding the framework under discussion, and these assumptions shall be examined more fully in the appropriate section below.

In sum, it may be said that the social anthropologist concerns himself with a variety of problems revolving around the institutionalized forms in which human groups are organized, how the group members conventionally seek their mates, the lines along which such mating is permitted, and the resulting family structures, as well as how these primary groupings proliferate into the broader units of social organization.

Comparative Analysis

A related and integral aspect of the anthropological approach to family study is the comparative method. In an early statement by Mead, the comparative analysis is viewed as an attempt to arrive at a general understanding of an institution of universal occurrence — such as the family — by a "critical comparative study of its various manifestations in differing cultures at different periods in history." (1932, p. 23.) According to Mead, this method may further serve as a "useful corrective of attempts to theorize upon the family's loss of functions; for the comparative student will realize that the family has had many and various functions, of varying degrees of social importance, as it has occurred in different types of culture." (*Ibid.*)

Social anthropologists engage in comparative analyses of related cultural forms, such as the comparison of forms of marriage and divorce, to provide clues to the function any specific form may serve in a given society. "The essence of the comparative method in social anthropology is that comparison is made between items of behavior in different major social units, with the object of establishing types and seeing variants from them." (Firth, 1951, p. 18.) Perhaps more to the point, the comparative method allows concise testing of specific hypotheses, illustrated by Murdock's study (1950) of family stability in non-European societies.

Comparison may be carried out either on the quantitative or qualitative levels of analysis. The former type of comparative method is illustrated by Murdock's well-known *Social Structure* (1949) which concentrates on family and kinship organization in relation to the regulation of sex and marriage. Here the emphasis is on cross cultural investigation of a large sample of societies in terms of a limited number of traits or variables by means of statistical analysis.[3]

A second type of comparative approach is illustrated in *African Systems of Kinship and Marriage*, edited by Radcliffe-Brown and Forde. In the introduction to this volume, the authors propose that:

> Analysis . . . is a procedure that can only be applied to something that is in itself a whole or synthesis. By it we separate out, in reality or in thought, the components of a complex whole and thereby discover the relation of these components to one another within the whole. To arrive at an understanding of kinship systems we must use comparison and analysis in combination by comparing many different systems with one another and by subjecting single systems to systematic analysis.
>
> A study of kinship systems all over the world by this method reveals that while there is a very wide range of variation in their superficial features there can be discovered a certain small number of general structural principles which are applied and combined in various ways. It is one of the first tasks of a theoretical study of kinship to discover these principles by a process of abstractive generalization based on analysis and comparison. (1950, p.2.)

The method proposed here has tended to take a highly qualitative form emphasizing analytical description of the systems under investigation, with considerably less emphasis on statistical procedures for mobilizing the data and arriving at generalizations. The general assumption underlying this method is perhaps most simply expressed by Timasheff: "Qualitatively, if two social situations could be found differing by the presence or absence of a particular trait or partial structure, the differential consequences of this dissimilarity for the survival and prosperity of the total system may be established." (1957, p. 229.)

Social anthropologists, of course, can and do utilize both quantitative and qualitative methods at the same time, and a variety of comparative techniques have been described and suggested in the literature. Discussions by Schapera (1953), Eggan (1954), and McEwen (1963), are particularly recommended in this connection. McEwen's remarks are especially revealing regarding attempts by social anthropologists to validate their findings.

Concepts

Anthropologists employ a plethora of significant concepts in their analysis of the family and society. Many of these concepts have proliferated into the general language of the behavioral sciences; for example, those relative to the forms of marriage, such as monogamy and polygamy, or to the rules of marriage, such as endogamy and exogamy. Others have been found to be quite amenable to interdisciplinary research on family life. And still others remain unique to the field itself. Consequently, only a limited selection of the major concepts utilized by contemporary social anthropologists are presented in the form of definitions or illustrations taken directly from the literature; others have been simply listed.[4]

An attempt has also been made to loosely group those concepts which would ordinarily be found occurring together in the analysis of a particular subsystem, such as the family. Finally, it must be noted that there is a good deal of terminological debate among anthropologists regarding nomenclature. The conceptualization of the family, for example, has often been subject to debate.[5] It is obvious, therefore, that some of the definitions and/or illustrations presented do not necessarily have complete consensus among family and kinship specialists. With the latter precaution in mind, we may proceed.

Concepts	*Definition and/or Illustrations*

Family
  Nuclear family
  Extended family (joint)
  Family of orientation
  Family of procreation
	The family, as distinguished from the more embracing kinship structure, consists of a group made up of "adults of both sexes at least two of whom maintain a socially approved sexual relationship, and one or more children, own or adopted, of the sexually cohabiting adults." (Murdock, 1949.)

	"The unit of structure from which a kinship is built up is the group which I call an 'elementary family,' consisting of a man and his wife and their child or children. . . . The existence of the elementary family creates three special kinds of social relationship, that between parent and child, that between children of the same parents (siblings), and that between husband and wife as parents of the same child or children. . . ." (Radcliffe-Brown, 1941.)
	"But certain important groupings depend upon bilateral and also affinal kinship, and

are frequently associated with common residence. The best known and most widespread grouping founded on kinship is the extended family, sometimes called the joint family because of their common claims to land and certain kinds of property. The extended family is a group founded on kinship and locality, and resulting from the rules of patrilocal or matrilocal marriage. It is a socially recognized group of individual families living together in close association, which are bound together by the fact that either: (A) The men in each of the individual families are genealogically related in the male line (the patrilineal or patrilocal extended family); or (B) The women in each of the individual families are genealogically related in the female line (the matrilineal or matrilocal extended family)." (Piddington, 1950.)

Conjugal family system
Consanguineal family system

A system in which the conjugal ties are given preponderant importance is called a *conjugal* family system; one in which ties to blood kin are emphasized is called *consanguine:* "In societies organized upon the conjugal basis we can picture the authentic functional family as consisting of a nucleus of spouses and their off-spring surrounded by a fringe of relatives. In those organized on the consanguine basis we can picture the authentic family as a nucleus of blood relatives surrounded by a fringe of spouses." (Linton, 1936.)

Marriage and parenthood
  Exogamy
  Endogamy
  Levirate
  Sororate
  Hypergamy
  Hypogamy
  Monogamy
  Polygamy
  Polygyny
  Polyandry

Marriage consists of the rules and regulations which govern the relationships between spouses. Such rules define how the relationship shall be established or terminated, the expectations and obligations it entails, and the persons who are eligible to enter such a relationship. "Marriage cannot be defined as the licensing of sexual intercourse but rather the licensing of parenthood." (Malinowski, 1930.)

"If we regard marriage as a relationship not just between individuals, but also, at least potentially, between groups, then an important distinction is that between endogamy and exogamy. The terms . . . simply mean that one must 'marry in' or 'marry out'; that is, inside or outside of a social group to which one belongs. Since the terms are relative, it is necessary when using them to define the group within which, or outside of which, one must marry." (Beattie, 1964.)

"Under the levirate, when a man dies his widow becomes the wife of one of his brothers. In some communities a man must marry his deceased brother's wife, in others he may waive the right. . . . The term sororate is a somewhat ambiguous one, being used in three different senses by various writers to refer to: (a) the rule whereby a man who marries a woman has a preemptive right to marry also her younger sisters as they reach maturity; (b) the rule whereby if a man wishes to marry more than one wife, the subsidiary wives must be sisters of his first wife; (c) the rule whereby if a man marries and his first wife dies, then his wife's kinfolk are under an obligation to provide him with another wife, particularly if the first wife had died childless." (Piddington, 1950.)

Kinship systems
Descent systems
    Patrilineal (unilateral)
    Matrilineal (unilateral)
    Bilateral
    Ambilineal

From the point of view of the individual, kinship refers to "any relationship . . . to another through his father and mother. All kinship ties thus derive from the family, that universal and fundamental group which everywhere and in some way or another incorporates the institution of marriage." (Evans-Pritchard, 1951.)

"A kinship system is therefore a network of social relations which constitute part of that total network of social relations which is the social structure. The rights and duties of relatives to one another are part of the system and so are the terms used in addressing or referring to relatives." (Radcliffe-Brown, 1950.)

"A rule of descent affiliates an individual at birth with a particular group of relatives with whom he is especially intimate and from whom he can expect certain kinds of services that he cannot demand of non-relatives, or even of other kinsmen. The fundamental rules of descent are only three in number: patrilineal descent, which affiliates a person with a group of kinsmen who are related to him through males only; matrilineal descent, which assigns him to a group consisting exclusively of relatives through females; and bilateral descent, which associates him with a group of very close relatives irrespective of their particular genealogical connection to him." (Murdock, 1949.)

Consanguineal groups
  Lineage
  Sib
  Phratry
  Moiety
  Clan
  Kindred

"When the members of a consanguineal kin group acknowledge a traditional bond of common descent in the paternal or maternal line, but are unable always to trace the actual genealogical connections between individuals, the group is called a sib. . . . Occasionally two or more sibs recognize a purely conventional unilinear bond of kinship, more tenuous than that which unites a sib but nevertheless sufficient to distinguish the constellation of sibs from others of its kind. A consanguineal kin group of this higher order is called a phratry. When a society has only two sibs or phratries so that every person is necessarily a member of one or the other, the dichotomy results in so many distinctive features in social structure that a special term, moiety, is applied to them." (*Ibid.*)

Residence rules
  Matrilocal
  Patrilocal
  Bilocal (ambilocal)
  Neolocal
  Avunculocal

Joint families are often established by means of common residence. "If custom requires the groom to leave his parental home and live with his bride, either in the house of her parents or in a dwelling nearby, the rule of residence is called matrilocal. If, on the other hand, the bride regularly removes to or near the parental home of the groom, residence is said to be patrilocal. It should be emphasized that this rule implies, not merely that wife goes to live with her husband, but that they establish a domicile in or near the home of his parents. Some societies permit a married couple to live with or near the parents of either spouse. . . . The rule of residence in such cases is termed bilocal. When a newly wedded couple . . . establishes a domicile independent of the location of the parental home of either partner, and perhaps even at considerable distance from both, residence may be called neolocal. . . . A fifth alternative, which we shall term avunculocal residence, prevails in a few societies which prescribe that a married couple shall reside with or near a maternal uncle of the groom rather than with the parents of either spouse or in a separate home of their own." (*Ibid.*)

Social status
Social roles
Social norms
Social patterns

"The place in a particular system which a certain individual occupies at a particular time will be referred to as his status with respect to that system, and 'role' will be used to designate the sum total of the culture patterns associated with a particular status. It thus includes the attitudes, values, and behavior ascribed by the society to any and all persons occupying this status. It can even be extended to include the legitimate expectations of such persons in other statuses within the same system. Every status is linked with a particular role . . . a role is the dynamic aspect of a status; what the individual has to do in order to validate his occupation of a status." (Linton, 1945.)

Social processes
Social action

Social process is "the operation of the social life, the manner in which the actions and very existence of each living being affect those of other individuals with which it has relations." (Firth, 1951.) Again, social process "is the immense multitude of actions and interactions of human beings, acting as individuals or in combinations or in groups." (Radcliffe-Brown, 1952.)

And more recently, "process consists of the manner in which every social organization operates to maintain itself and/or to undergo change due to external pressure or internal impetus." (Hsu, 1959.)

Social relations
Social usages
Sentiments
Social control
   Folkways
   Mores
   Sanctions

"We can regard these observations as facts of custom — as standardized ways of doing, knowing, thinking and feeling — universally obligatory and valued in a given group of people at a given time. But we can also regard them as facts of social structure. We then seek to relate them to one another by a scheme of conceptual operations different from that of the previous frame of reference. We see custom as symbolizing or expressing social relations — that is, the ties and cleavages by which persons and groups are bound to one another in the activities of social life." (Fortes, 1953.)

"By a social sanction I meant broadly, any institution a consequence of which is to incline persons occupying certain roles to conform to the norms and expectations associated with these roles . . . any social system must provide some institutionalized means of constraining individuals to at least some degree of conformity to accepted norms." (Beattie, 1956.)

Socialization
   Age-sex categories
   Age grades
   Age sets
   Age classes

Socialization may be generally defined as "The way in which a society integrates its members and the process by which individuals learn to adapt to their society." (*Dictionary of Anthropology*, 1956.)

One aspect of social structure is the classification of a society's members on the basis of age and sex. Thus, "membership in asso-

ciations and statuses within the family organization bear a very close relation to age-sex
categories . . . before an individual can assume
the status of father in a new conjugal family
unit he must belong to the adult male category in the age-sex system." (Linton, 1942.)

|Institution
Integration
Equilibrium

An institution has been defined as a fairly
permanent cluster of social usages. It is a
reasonably enduring complex pattern of behavior by which social control is exerted
and through which basic social desires or
needs can be met. (*Dictionary of Anthropology,* 1956.)

"A system implies a state of equilibrium in
which elements are in mutual dependence.
If change is introduced at one point, change
follows at another. If the first change is not
too great — that is, if it is not so great that
destruction of the system ensues — then subsequent changes do not alter the situation
out of recognition. Far from it, since the
elements are woven into a common whole,
the effect of the change is soon dissipated.
. . . The system reverts to its former state. It
may be said to have thus an equilibrium which
it regains after each disturbance." (Arensberg
and Kimball, 1948.)

Social structure
Social function
Social organization
Social system
Social stratification
Social field

"In studying a field of social relations, whether we are using the notions of society, of
culture, of community, we distinguish their
structure, their function, and their organization. These are separate but related aspects . . . by the structural aspect of social
relations we mean the principles on which
their form depends; by the functional aspect
we mean the way in which they serve given
ends; by the organizational aspect we mean
the directional activity which maintains their
forms and serves their ends." (Firth, 1951.)

"By social organization (or social structure)
is meant the division of society into social

groups, based upon conventionally standardized social relations between the individuals concerned. . . . In modern democratic countries most social groups are of the voluntary type, and here we find the most striking contrast with primitive cultures in which the individual's place in the social structure is determined, in general, by such factors as kinship, locality and hereditary social class which cannot be changed except by certain special social mechanisms. (Piddington, 1950.)

Functional prerequisites
Social imperatives

Functional prerequisites and *social imperatives* refer "broadly to the things that must get done in any society if it is to continue as a group concern, i.e. the generalized conditions necessary for the maintenance of the system concerned." (Aberle, 1950.)

A related term is *social imperatives,* by which is meant "those insistent interpersonal problems that every culture must face. For man is committed to living in society, and group life requires certain organizational features through which each individual compromises his personal interests with the demands of others. Social imperatives are then those general organizational features that are requisite to the continuation of social life irrespective of cultural form." (Goldschmidt, 1953.)

Culture
Society
Community
    Neighborhood
    Village
    Band

The terms *culture, society,* and *community* refer to the most general terms used in the description and analysis of group life; each is commonly used to express the idea of totality.

"If society is taken to be an organized set of individuals with a given way of life, culture is that way of life. If society is taken to be an aggregate of social relations, then culture is the content of those relations . . .

the term community emphasizes the space-time component, the aspect of living together . . . a body of people sharing in common activities and bound by multiple relations in such a way that the aims of any individual can be achieved by participation in action with others." (Firth, 1951.)

"a society or a social institution, is not a thing at all. It is a concept, an abstraction from people's observed behavior; and it exists only in the minds of the people who are concerned with it. Whether as members of the society or as investigators of it. . . . It is simply a number of people who are related to one another and to their environment in innumerable ways. When we use the term 'society' in a strict sense we are not referring simply to this human collectivity . . . rather we are referring to the complex of institutionalized interpersonal relationships which bind them together, or to some aspect or aspects of them." (Beattie, 1964.)

Basic Assumptions

Hill and Hansen have suggested that "perhaps the most significant elements in differentiating one framework from another are the underlying assumptions which each makes about the nature of man, the family, and society." (1960, pp. 309-11.) In this connection they present a list of five basic assumptions which are felt to be peculiar to the structure-functional approach of sociology and social anthropology, namely:

1. Social conduct is best analyzed for its contribution to the maintenance of the social system or for its nature under the structures of the system.
2. A social human is basically a reacting part of the social system; self-elicited (independent) action is rare and asocial.
3. The basic autonomous unit is the social system, which is composed of interdependent subsystems, (for example, institutions, family systems, and so on).
4. It is possible to profitably study any subunits of the basic system.

5. The social system tends to homeostasis.

Unfortunately, Hill and Hansen do not provide the specific source or give illustrations of the above assumptions; nor do they attempt to elaborate upon them to any extent.

The three basic "postulates" underlying functional analysis as it is expressed by anthropologists were explicitly stated and critically evaluated in a much earlier publication (1949) by Merton: "These postulates hold first, that standardized social activities or cultural items are functional for the entire social or cultural system; second, that all such social and cultural items fulfill sociological functions; and third, that these items are consequently indispensable." (Revised edition, 1957, pp. 19-84.) While many contemporary social anthropologists have either rejected or modified these postulates,[6] one still finds examples of them in the literature. Thus, Evans-Pritchard writes: "A social system has a functional unity. It is not an aggregate but an organism or integrated whole." (1952, p. 54.) Similarly, Fortes has suggested "that a culture is a unity in so far as it is tied to a bounded social structure." (1953, p. 23.)

A fourth assumption holds that a knowledge of the kinship system is necessary for the comprehension of social behavior. In the words of one social anthropologist, "an understanding of the kinship system in any society is essential as a clue to the working of some of the most fundamental relationships — sexual, marital, economic, in that society." (Firth, 1956, p. 11.) The idea here is that kinship systems exhibit regularities and systematic forms which are socially significant and that the nuclear or elementary family is not an isolated unit. In short, the notion of kinship is posited as basic to the study of society.

A fifth assumption is that the history of any society or sub-system of society, such as the family, is unnecessary for understanding its present nature. Thus we are told that "societies are systems, and these systems are natural systems which can be reduced to variables, with the corollary that the history of them is irrelevant." And again, "an institution is not to be understood, far less explained, in terms of its origins, whether these origins are conceived of as beginnings, causes, or merely in a logical sense, its simplest forms." (Evans-Pritchard, 1952, pp. 38-49.) The idea here is that a knowledge of the origin of an institution such as the family cannot tell us how it functions in a society. "To know how it has come to be what it is, and to know how it works, are two different things." (*Ibid.*) Contemporary social anthropologists assume that the study of institutions in their present form must precede any inquiry into their origin and development, if proper conception of their function is to be gained.

A sixth assumption, noted by Hill and Hansen, and documented here, is that a human being is basically a reacting part of the social system. It is said that "most people are shaped to the form of their culture because of the common malleability of their original endowment. They are plastic to the molding force of the society into which they are born . . . the great mass of individuals take quite readily to the form that is presented to them." (Benedict, 1934, p. 221.) Similarly, Radcliffe-Brown in his presentation of the functionalist perspective notes how such a point of view implies "that we have to investigate as thoroughly as possible all aspects of social life, considering them in relation to one another, and that an essential part of the task is the investigation of the individual and of the way in which he is molded by or adjusted to the social life." (1935, p. 400.)

A seventh and final assumption holds that a knowledge of cultural or societal forms of institutions is necessary for the comprehension of human behavior. It is suggested, for example, that "the chief requirement for a discussion of culture is that it should be based on a wide selection of possible cultural forms. . . . If we are interested in human behavior, we need first of all to understand the institutions that are provided in any society." (Benedict, 1934, p. 29.) A similar notion is apparent in the list of basic assumptions by Hill and Hansen presented earlier in this section, especially number three.

Product

It is somewhat difficult to assess the theoretical and research contributions of functional social anthropologists to the field of marriage and the family. Social anthropology has been primarily a qualitative discipline, and its studies of the family have been highly descriptive, for the most part, with little emphasis on theory formulation and hypothesis testing.

Nonetheless, the close relationship between social anthropologists and sociology — and their identification with it has resulted in some fruitful contributions. Homans' comment on this relationship in *The Human Group* is of interest.

If we agree that there is only one sociology, a sociology of human organization, we can hardly admit any division between sociology and social anthropology. A social anthropologist is a sociologist of primitive peoples, a sociologist, an anthropologist of civilizations. The anthropologists are indebted to some of the ideas of the earlier sociologists, and the other side of the exchange has been even more rewarding. In many of the social sciences, ideas worked out by anthropologists have been adopted and found fecund, and anthropologists, self-trained in the bush, have gone on to make excellent studies of civilized communities using the techniques of gathering material and analyzing it that they learned among the primitives. This book, for one, leans heavily on their findings and ideas. (1950, pp. 192-93.)

With regard to the "studies of civilized societies," Homans has in mind such works as the *Yankee City* series by W. L. Warner and his associates; *Family and Community in Ireland* by C. M. Arensberg and S. T. Kimball; *Deep South,* by A. Davis, B. Gardner, and M. Gardner; as well as the well-known *Middletown* by the Lynds.

As has been previously noted, social anthropologists apply sociological conceptions to anthropological data. But the reverse is also true. An examination of past as well as current sociological textbooks — in particular the sections dealing with marriage and the family — reveals a heavy reliance upon anthropological conceptions, ethnographic data, and results of comparative analyses. This is especially true in discussions of marriage forms and regulations, functions of the family, premarital practices, duration and dissolution of marital ties, and so on.[7]

Social anthropological emphasis on kinship systems and their functions in the structuring or patterning of familial relations has led to fruitful hypotheses concerning the extended family in Western civilization. The widely read study of Arensberg and Kimball of the Irish family, for example, and Sussman's sociological research on extended family relations in American communities (1962) got their impetus from social-anthropological demonstrations of the utility of kinship analyses for theory as well as for research.

Social anthropology along with anthropology in general has made an impact on the field of psychology and, in particular, on psychoanalytic theory. . . . "Recognition of the extent to which the activities of the members of a society are culturally patterned and of the extraordinary range of variation in modal patterns as one moves from society to society led to a veritable revolution in psychological thinking that is still working itself out today."

(Smith, in Gillin, 1954, p. 59.) The classic example here is Malinowski's test of the Freudian hypothesis concerning the universality of the Oedipus complex. Malinowski revealed how the manifestation of this phenomenon is dependent upon family structure; his finding that the role of the uncle in Trobiand society is central has led to a modification of Freud's original statement. In other ways psychological researchers draw upon the comparative data and analyses of social anthropologists for cross-cultural validation of specific hypotheses. This is particularly true of those researchers engaged in so-called culture and personality studies.

In the areas of culture contact and change, social anthropologists have investigated the impact of Westernization on various societies.[8] This has led in turn to an interest in the concomitant variation in family organization and disorganization. . . . The manner in which the family in different societies adapts to changing situations has been noted and observed. Such observations have contributed to the general field of social disorganization and have suggested hypotheses in that area. That the methods and approaches developed in social anthropology have made substantial contributions to studies of the family in complex societies is well documented by Eisenstadt (1961).

Values

An attempt was made to uncover any outstanding value judgments or value objectives, either implicit or explicit, within the structure-functional framework of contemporary social anthropologists, especially as this framework relates to the study of the family. The results were, for the most part, negative. The heavy emphasis on kinship does at times project an underlying outlook which views extended relationships other than those organized around the marriage bond as best suited to the welfare of society, the family, and the individual.

The Framework

The structure-functional framework of social anthropology may be briefly summarized, as it deals with the family, in the following manner. Society is viewed as a functioning whole composed of various subsystems or institutions, all of which are closely interrelated. The family and kinship systems must be perceived in terms of their relations or interactions with the other subsystems

– economic, political, religious – which make up the total society. When the social anthropologist speaks of the functions of the family he is, in general, referring to the part it plays in perpetuating itself and in maintaining the total social system or structure, that is, society.

The family here is viewed as a social system, and its evaluation must be in terms of its place in the society as a whole and the special functions it performs in the existence of society. This is best accomplished by focusing on the formal aspects of the family and/or kinship systems – composition, residence and inheritance rules, kinship rights and obligations, parental authority patterns, marriage forms and regulations, separations – and tracing the structural implications of these aspects for social relations. The goal is to deduce the underlying structural principles and derive generalizations about behavior of persons in groups which eventually may be useful in comparative analyses.

In focusing on the formal aspects of family and kinship systems, the social anthropologist pays particular attention to the normative patterns evident in the social relations occurring within these systems. Eisenstadt has commented on this aspect of the framework:

> This type of analysis is achieved through the great emphasis on social behavior as related to various norms which are said to be operative in the social structure. Most of the social-anthropological descriptions of social behavior are studies of the ways in which major norms found in these societies are upheld by individuals, of the interrelationships between these different norms, and of the ways in which these norms influence and regulate the relations between different groups in society. . . . Thus, various norms and the patterns of behavior which uphold them are seen mostly as institutional directives upholding the interrelations among the society and the continuity of the society as a whole. In this way, most anthropological studies combine in one basic model the analysis of social behavior, institutional norms, groups and societies. They explain patterns of social behavior through the analysis of group structure, institutions and "total" societies. (1961, pp. 201-02.)

Eisenstadt cites a considerable amount of substantive research conducted by social anthropologists as illustrations of the application of this to both simple and complex societies.

FOOTNOTES

[1] The characteristics of such a community in its "ideal" state have been summarized by Chinoy: "In the communal society social roles are inclusive rather than segmental, social relationships are personal and intimate, and there are comparatively few sub-groups other than family and kinship units. In this typically small, isolated, non-literate and homogeneous society, with a strong sense of group solidarity, tradition permeates all aspects of life and the range of alternative patterns of behavior open to individuals is inevitably restricted." (1961), p. 89.

[2] See Chinoy's comments on how numerous anthropological investigations have revealed the difficulty of distinguishing economic, political, and religious institutions and roles from those of marriage and the family in such societies. (1961), p. 106.

[3] For more recent and statistically sophisticated analyses along these lines see Homans and Schneider (1955), Schneider and Gough (1961), and Gouldner and Peterson (1962). The latter study, for example, is an exploratory analysis of data from seventy-one primitive societies and has the following objectives: "(1) It seeks to identify fundamental dimensions or subsystems common to such societies, and (2) To examine some of their relations to each other, thus to see them systematically, and (3) To assess the relative importance of these dimensions. (4) It aims to pursue the above objectives with a systematic body of empirical data derived from the Human Relations Area Files and with statistical methods, rather than calling upon random anecdotal materials or impressionistic insight." p. 1.

[4] The concepts cited should be viewed as representative rather than exhaustive. For a recent publication in which some of the major terms peculiar to social anthropology are presented and discussed, see Mair (1963). A list of concepts and definitions specifically related to the study of kinship is provided by Zelditch, in Faris (1964), pp. 716-17.

[5] An overview of this question including pertinent references regarding the definitions and functions of the family may be found in Zelditch, in Faris (1964), pp. 680-82. His remarks concerning the disparity between the sociologists' use of the term *extended family* and the anthropological definition of this concept are also of interest.

[6] See, for example, Beattie (1964), especially Chaps. 3 and 4.

[7]Recognition of this close alliance between sociology and social anthropology has prompted Faris to remark: "Social anthropology . . . is mainly sociology, and there is little distinction between the two fields other than that resulting from the accidental and scientifically irrelevant differences in the routes by which the two fields came to their present interests. There is, of course, some practical division of labor in the fact that anthropologists undertake most of the descriptive studies of preliterate societies, although for more than a quarter of a century they have also conducted sociological research on communities in modern civilizations. Also, until recently anthropologists mainly employed their personal skills in recording and interpreting a society as a whole, while sociologists placed somewhat more confidence in the use of technical research methods and their application to problems of considerably smaller scope. At the present time, however, even this distinction is diminishing, and if present trends continue it may soon become pointless to attempt to distinguish between sociology and social anthropology." (1964), p. 31.

[8]A recent discussion of the social anthropologists' study of social change and its impact on family life may be found in Beattie (1964), Chap. 14.

WORKS CITED

Aberle, David F., *et al.* "The Functional Prerequisites of a Society," *Ethics*, 60 (Jan., 1950), pp. 100-111.

Arensberg, C., and Kimball, S. I. *The Family and Community in Ireland.* Cambridge, Mass.: Harvard University Press, 1948.

Beattie, John H. M. *Other Cultures: Aims, Methods and Achievements in Social Anthropology.* London: Cohen & West, Limited, Publishers, 1964.

Beattie, John H. M. "Social Anthropology," in Alan Pryce-Jones, ed. *The New Outline of Modern Knowledge.* New York: Simon and Schuster, Inc., 1956, pp. 252-278.

Benedict, Ruth. *Patterns of Culture.* New York: The New American Library of World Literature, Inc., 1934.

Eggan, Fred. "Social Anthropology and the Method of Controlled Comparison," *American Anthropologist*, 56 (Oct. 1954), pp. 743-763.

Eisenstadt, S. N. "Anthropological Studies of Complex Societies," *Current Anthropology*, 2 (June 1961), pp. 201-222.

Evans-Pritchard, E. E. *Kinship and Marriage Among the Nuer.* London: Oxford University Press, 1951.

Evans-Pritchard, E. E. *Social Anthropology.* New York: Free Press of Glencoe, Inc., 1952.

Firth, Raymond. *Elements of Social Organization.* London: C. A. Watts & Co., Ltd., 1951.

Firth, Raymond, ed. *Two Studies of Kinship in London.* London: The Athlone Press, 1956.

Fortes, Meyer, ed. *Marriage in Tribal Societies.* London: Cambridge University Press, 1962.

Fortes, Meyer. "The Structure of Unilineal Descent Groups," *American Anthropologist,* 55 (Jan.-March 1953), pp. 17-41.

Goldschmidt, Walter. "Values and the Field of Comparative Sociology," *American Sociological Review,* 18 (June 1953), pp. 287-293.

Goody, Jack, ed. *The Developmental Cycle in Domestic Groups.* Cambridge Papers in Social Anthropology No. 1. London: Cambridge University Press, 1962.

Hill, Reuben, and Hansen, Donald A. "The Identification of Conceptual Frameworks Utilized in Family Study," *Marriage and Family Living,* 22 (Nov. 1960), pp. 299-311.

Homans, George C. *The Human Group.* New York: Harcourt, Brace & World, Inc., 1950.

Hsu, Francis L. K. "Structure, Function, Content, and Process," *American Anthropologist,* 61 (Oct. 1959), pp. 790-805.

Linton, Ralph. "Age and Sex Categories," *American Sociological Review,* 17 (Oct. 1942), pp. 589-603.

Linton, Ralph. "The Scope and Aims of Anthropology," in R. Linton, ed. *The Science of Man in the World Crisis.* New York: Columbia University Press, 1945, pp. 3-8.

Linton, Ralph. *The Study of Man.* New York: Appleton-Century-Crofts, 1936.

Malinowski, Bronislaw. "Anthropology," *Encyclopaedia Britannica,* First Supplementary Volume. Chicago: Encyclopaedia Britannica, Inc., 1926, pp. 132-133.

Malinowski, Bronislaw. "Culture," *Encyclopedia of the Social Sciences*, 14, New York: The Macmillan Company, 1930.

McEwen, William J. "Forms and Problems of Validation in Social Anthropology," *Current Anthropology*, 4 (April 1963), pp. 155-183.

Mead, Margaret. "Contrasts and Comparisons From Primitive Society," *The Annals*, 160 (March 1932), pp. 23-28.

Merton, Robert K. "Manifest and Latent Functions," in his *Social Theory and Social Structure*. New York: Free Press of Glencoe, Inc., 1957, pp. 19-82.

Murdock, George P. *Social Structure*. New York: The Macmillan Company, 1949.

Murdock, George P. "Family Stability in Non-European Cultures," *The Annals*, 272 (Nov. 1950), pp. 195-201.

Olderogge, D. A. "Several Problems in the Study of Kinship Systems," *Current Anthropology*, 2 (April 1961), pp. 103-107.

Piddington, Ralph. *An Introduction to Social Anthropology*, 2 vols. Edinburgh: Oliver and Boyd, Ltd., 1950 and 1957.

Radcliffe-Brown, A. R. "The Study of Kinship Systems," *Journal of the Royal Anthropological Institute*, 71 (1941), pp. 1-18.

Radcliffe-Brown, A. R. *Structure and Function in Primitive Society*. New York: Free Press of Glencoe, Inc., 1952.

Radcliffe-Brown, A. R., and Forde, Daryll, eds. *African Systems of Kinship and Marriage*. New York: Oxford University Press, Inc., 1950.

Schapera, I. "Some Comments on Comparative Method in Social Anthropology," *American Anthropologist*, 55, (Aug. 1953), pp. 353-366.

Smith, M. B. "Anthropology and Psychology," in John Gillin, ed. *For a Science of Social Man*. New York: The Macmillan Company, 1954, pp. 32-66.

Sussman, Marvin B. "Unheralded Structures in Current Conceptualizations of Family Functioning," *Marriage and Family Living*, 24 (Aug. 1962), pp. 231-240.

Timasheff, Nicholas S. *Sociological Theory: Its Nature and Growth*, rev. ed. New York: Random House, Inc., 1957.

Wenick, Charles. *Dictionary of Anthropology*. New York: Philosophical Library, 1956.

Parental Role Differentiation

Philip Slater

Confusions can and do occur when identical concepts utilized in various conceptual frameworks carry diverse meanings. In this reading, Philip Slater takes issue with the theory of parental role differentiation advanced by Talcott Parsons and Robert F. Bales. In his "Comment" on Slater's article, Bernard Bergen traces the source of the points at issue to the very different meanings which the writers (Parsons-Bales and Slater) attach to the concept of "role."

Some of the most confused segments of psychoanalytic theory are those which attempt to deal differentially with intra-familial relationships. The difficulties seem due largely to a failure to isolate the effects of formal, structural properties, based solely on variables such as the age and sex of family members. This defect has recently been remedied to a considerable extent by the work of Parsons, who attempts to integrate a formal analysis of this kind with classical psychoanalytic theory.[2] One of the more valuable products of this effort is a considerable clarification of the difficult concept of identification.[3]

At several points, however, the conceptual scheme advanced by Parsons encounters both theoretical and empirical difficulties. These involve the problem of role differentiation in the nuclear family. They may be stated as three hypotheses:

Reprinted, with permission of the author and publisher, from *American Journal of Sociology*, 62 (November, 1961), pp. 296-311.

1. Role differentiation along an "instrumental-expressive axis" is a universal characteristic of the nuclear family.

2. Role differentiation between parents facilitates the child's identification with the same-sex parent.

3. Role differentiation between parents is essential to normal personality development in the child.

The position taken in this article is that parental differentiation along the "instrumental-expressive axis" is an optional feature of nuclear family structure and that under some conditions, notably those obtaining in large segments of our own society, it may actually impede identification with the same-sex parent and affect adversely the personality development of the child.

The Universality of Differentiation

In the concluding chapter of *Family, Socialization and Interaction Process,* Parsons and Bales refer to "the universal presence of two axes of differentiation, namely, an hierarchical axis of relative power and an instrumental-expressive axis."[4] The first difficulty we encounter in attempting to evaluate this statement is the lack of an adequate criterion for determining when differentiation is present and when it is not. If role differentiation is to be conceived as a quantitative variable — and it is difficult to see how it could be viewed otherwise — then the chance of finding a negative case is one divided by the square of the number of points on the scale used. If, of course, all that is meant by the statement universality is that no two people exhibit a given type of behavior to exactly the same extent, then it cannot be questioned.

More than this is meant, however. Basic to the entire discussion of familial role differentiation is the notion that, in a family characterized by sharp differentiation of roles, it should be grossly apparent that the majority of the instrumental functions are being performed by one parent — the father — and the majority of the expressive functions by the mother.[5]

But now a second difficulty arises, for this formulation ignores the problem of parental salience. In many cultures one parent, usually the mother, is both more expressive (nurturant) and more instrumental (demanding). Thus in Pukapuka, "the child is mainly cared for by its mother. The father has no specific duties to perform. He is sympathetic and lavish in his affection for his child, caring for it, however, only when it is necessary or convenient.

... Authority over the infant is largely focused in the mother. Love, dependence, and affection on the other hand tend to diffuse themselves among many members of or visitors to the household."[6] This description, a negative instance not included in Zelditch's cross-cultural survey,[7] could be applied to a large number of societies, including (save for the final sentence) our own middle class. Considering each parent alone, one may see a marked emphasis on instrumental or expressive behavior, but this should not lead us to ignore the fact that one parent plays a distinctly secondary role in the performance of both functions.

This problem is not considered by either Parsons or Zelditch, perhaps because of the apparent assumption that instrumental and expressive behavior are negatively related, so that if one is stressed the other must be minimized. This idea is implicit in the use of the term "axis" with regard to the relationship between the two roles. But there is no way in which such an assumption of a negative relationship can be justified. In small-group studies, to which analogical appeals are often made in the Parsons and Bales volume, there is actually a positive correlation between the two roles.[8]

The argument for a negative relationship receives its ultimate expression in the following quotation from Zelditch: "Why after all, are *two* parents necessary? For one thing, to be a stable focus of integration, the integrative-expressive 'leader' can't be off on adaptive-instrumental errands all the time."[9]

We must be forgiven our pedantry for stressing, along with Briffault,[10] that the only time in a child's existence when two parents are "necessary" is when it is conceived. Passing over this issue, however, we note that the main weight of Zelditch's argument rests on the notion that role differentiation occurs because two discriminable types of behavior cannot be performed at the same time. One cannot, for example, work and play at once,[11] although the universality of work songs suggests that even this statement must be qualified. But it is not at all clear why differentiation should be limited to the instrumental-expressive "axis." If a special person is required to lead the laughing and playing, as Zelditch suggests, then it follows that still another person will be required to lead the weeping and mourning, since clearly a person cannot laugh and mourn at the same time. On the instrumental side, this role fragmentation becomes even more complicated. According to Zelditch's view, the farm family must at all times send two persons to the well, one to lower the bucket and one to raise it up, since the bucket cannot be raised and lowered at the same time.

We must not, however, overlook the grain of truth in Zelditch's statement. It would undoubtedly be possible to find persons so incompetent as to be capable only of lowering or only of raising a bucket. Similarly, many persons are too rigid or limited in their interpersonal repertory to shift easily from the performance of instrumental to the performance of expressive functions, and vice versa.[12] This was originally suggested as the basis of role differentiation in experimental groups,[13] and there is no reason to assume a different foundation in the family. From this viewpoint, role differentiation could be characterized as a mechanism which takes nothing for granted with regard to the personalities of the incumbents.

It would be a rare society, however, which left such matters to chance, and we would expect societies characterized by sharp differentiation of parental roles to encourage role rigidity in individuals. In our own society the reverse is true, as the use of the work "role" and our fascination with Goffmanesque modes of analysis might suggest. The ability rapidly to alternate instrumental and expressive role performances is highly valued, and we have developed concepts such as "interpersonal flexibility" and "role-playing ability" to express this value. We must therefore be cautious in our inferences about personality, since societal pressures may have caused the ability to shift roles to have atrophied in the first instance and to have hypertrophied in the second, perhaps at the expense of other capacities.

Unidimensional Differentiation

The "human-limitations" theory of role differentiation assumes bidimensionality, that is, it is based on the assumption that instrumental and expressive roles are roughly independent of each other. The theory could not be maintained, however, if in some way it could be demonstrated that instrumental and expressive behavior were in fact incompatible, that is, opposite poles of a single dimension, as Parsons and Zelditch seem at times to imply. While we expect an adequate individual to be capable of varying his behavior over time — to be able, in Zelditch's terms, both to call for a coffee break and eventually to terminate it without having to call in a back-to-work specialist — we do not ask of him that he behave in a truly self-contradictory manner. If a parent, for example, is alternately indulgent and depriving *in identical situations* we call him inconsistent rather than flexible. Knowing the situation, we expect to be able to predict his response with some accuracy on the basis of his previous behavior. If one parent is consistently depriving, it will be necessary, if we desire for the child a wide range of behavior on the depriving-indulgent axis, to have the other parent behave in an indulgent manner.

But if instrumental and expressive behavior were incompatible and differentiation were "built into" the family to avoid personal inconsistency, the incompatibility would simply have been externalized, so that in place of a whimsical individual we would now have quarreling parents, one saying "be lenient," the other saying "be strict."

It is usually argued, of course, that differentiation does not involve a conflict of aims but simply an agreement to specialize in different directions, with complementarity binding rather than separating the participants. But this distinction breaks down whenever there is the slightest contradiction between the two directions of specialization. Vogel and Bell, for example, present cases in which unidimensional parental differentiation is utilized to institutionalize internal conflicts.[14]

Consider, for example, Parsons' statement that "the mother-figure is always the *more permissive* and supportive, the father the *more denying* and demanding."[15] In a family strongly differentiated along these lines, if the child wishes something which he fears might be denied him, he will probably to to the mother for it. If the mother grants the child what the father would have denied, does the father nonetheless support her in the performance of her differentiated function, since they are, after all, in a "coalition"? The notion of collaborative differentiation in socialization assumes, if the differentiation is unidimensional, that there is no relationship between personality and role behavior. Yet if the father is "denying," the chances are rather great that it is not simply because he feels it is something that *he* should do, but because he thinks it is something that should *in general* be done to the child, in which case he will not support the mother's indulgence at all, but will instead probably accuse her of subverting his authority or "spoiling" the child.[16] The maintenance of a "coalition" under conditions of sharp unidimensional differentiation assumes that the differentiated parents *will never interact with the child at the same time,* since it would obviously be impossible to do so and still support each other. The idea of collaborative differentiation is therefore relevant primarily to the large and formal upper-class households of an earlier era, when mother, father, and child were rarely together at one time under circumstances which were disciplinarily problematic. It was easy under those conditions to "agree" that the child going from parent to parent and room to room should encounter different responses to the same behavior, and that when all were together the mother should place herself in a totally subordinate position. But in the less formal, more intimate middle-class household of today, any such arrangement would be an occasion for mirth. Major differences between parents in beliefs about what is "good" for the child can no longer be masked by drawing a kind of 38th parallel between the front and back of the house.

Often, as in the beautiful example given by Vogel and Bell,[17] unidimensional differentiation may serve to keep a conflict at a covert level, with the parents expressing their disagreement only through their orders and remarks to the child and never directly to each other. In such a case it might be correct to speak of "collaboration," since the parents are co-operating to avoid an open clash. But as Vogel and Bell point out, while such a technique may serve to keep the family "intact," it effectively prevents any ultimate airing and resolution of the conflict, and "keeps the peace" only at the cost of impairing the emotional health of the child.[18]

In short, while bidimensional differentiation (i.e., role differentiation in which the required performances are not incompatible) is obviously functional for all parties concerned under certain conditions specified below, unidimensional differentiation (i.e., in which the required performances are incompatible) seems to be primarily a mechanism for the ritual expression of intrapsychic and interpersonal conflicts in and between the marital partners and is usually dysfunctional for the child and for the society as a whole.

Differentiation and Identification[19]

Parsons' position on the relationship between differentiation and identification is clearly stated: "If the boy is to 'identify' with his father in the sense of sex-role categorization there must be a discrimination in role terms between the two parents."[20] For the sake of simplicity let us follow Parsons' example and concentrate on the identification of the male child with the father.

Since Parsons has defined the differentiated role of the father as being "more denying and demanding," we would expect identification to be a function of the father's strictness. That being "denying" is inherently paternal is problematic, in view of findings such as that of Payne and Mussen, 87 per cent of whose adolescent male subjects saw their fathers as more rewarding than their mothers,[21] but let us disregard this issue for the moment. That identification is a function of parental frustration is also a hoary psychoanalytic concept.[22] Empirically, however, the reverse seems to be the case. Chronic punitiveness seems actually to impede identification, while an underlying nurturant attitude toward the child seems to facilitate it.[23]

There is some evidence, moreover, which is in more direct contradiction to Parsons' statement. Beier and Ratzeburg found that males identified preferentially with whichever parent was least extreme in the performance of his or her sex role, while the author found that the more denying and strict the father and the more supportive and lenient the mother, the more the son identified preferentially with the latter.[24] These findings suggest that in our society at least, unidimensional parental role differentiation, and perhaps also an extreme degree of bidimensional differentiation, may actually inhibit the son's identification with the father, and Parsons' statement should therefore be qualified to that extent.

The reason for this is implicit in Parsons' discussion of the process of identification in the family. Parsons argues that the child forms several identifications, the first being with the mother.[25] Once this maternal identification is formed, the male child must at some point extend his identification to the father. If, however, the parents are highly differentiated with respect to their socialization behavior, and particularly if the father is primarily a source of frustration for the child, the transition will be a difficult one. There will be no inducement for the child to adopt this entirely new frame of reference. Parsons states that "before he has internalized the father as an object the child cannot be fully sensitive to his attitudes as sanctions. He can, however, be motivated to do things *which please both mother and father* and be rewarded by mother's love and nurturance. By some such process he comes to cathect the father — *because mother loves father and backs him up* — and from this generalized parental object then a qualitatively different object can be differentiated out."[26] This process will only take place, however, if the parents are not differentiated to such an extent that (*a*) it is impossible to please both at the same time, and (*b*) it is impossible, either emotionally or conceptually, to form a "generalized parental object." For it should be emphasized that a major aspect of identification is "taking the role of the other" in G. H. Mead's sense, that is, adopting the viewpoint of the other with respect to oneself. The importance of paternal identification is that it makes possible the development of a "generalized other" from the perceived viewpoints of the two parents. If the parents' attitudes toward the child are reasonably similar, such generalization is possible, but if they clash, the child is thrown back on a particularistic orientation toward them. He may be able momentarily to empathize with first one and then the other, but he cannot easily form a generalized self-concept from these conflicting perceptions.

Differentiation and Personality Development

Since Parsons argues that the human personality is a structure composed of internalized systems of social objects,[27] and that this structure develops through an internal differentiation which reflects a differentiation among the social objects,[28] it is clear that parental differentiation is not seen, on the whole, as pathogenic.

Empirical studies, however, show a consistently negative relationship between degrees of parental role differentiation and the emotional adjustment of the child. Lazowick found greater "semantic similarity" between the parents of his less anxious subjects than between those of his more anxious subjects.[29] Manis found that his adjusted subjects saw their parents as more alike than did the maladjusted subjects.[30] A study by the author showed significant positive correlations between degree of perceived parental role differentiation and most of the pathological scales in the Minnesota Multiphasic Personality Inventory.[31] Wechsler found that subjects who perceived a high degree of role differentiation between father and mother also experienced conflict in their self-perceptions.[32] At the very least, one would be forced to conclude from these data that for the child parental role differentiation is not always an unmixed blessing.

One cannot, of course, generalize these findings beyond the specific context of the American middle class. In a society characterized by extended families, for example, the effects of sharp differentiation between the parents may be diluted by the presence of substitute figures. Our own society is remarkable in the extent to which it concentrates the socialization process in the nuclear family. Furthermore, in a social system predicated upon parental role differentiation, the healthy offspring of undifferentiated parents might feel himself constricted while the less healthy child of differentiated parents might find himself fulfilled.

The studies cited above deal primarily with college students, a segment of the population in which parental differentiation is traditionally less marked,[33] so that the children of differentiated parents have developed in a family environment which was in some sense "deviant." The apparent adverse "effects" of differentiation may be entirely due to this deviant position of the family, or to its antecedents and correlates. But they are even more likely to be a simple function of the child himself being illsuited to the society in which he later finds himself, a possibility suggested by a finding of the author's. In small experimental laboratory groups, subjects showing the greatest tendency toward role specialization, whether in a task or social-emotional direction, also tended to report that one parent (more often but not necessarily the father) was denying and demanding and the other permissive and rewarding.[34]

When we consider the high degree of specialization in occupations in our society, however, we might well wonder why the development of specialized children should be anything but functional for both individual and society. Is there, nevertheless, some sphere in which role differentiation is discordant with American society?

Differentiation and Isolation

While it is impossible to do justice to a question of this magnitude within the scope of this paper, a promising hypothesis is suggested by Bott's study of the relationship between the degree of differentiation and segregation of conjugal roles and the kind of social matrix in which the marital couple finds itself. Bott distinguishes between "loose-knit networks" in which friends, neighbors, and relatives of the couple tend not to know each other, and "close-knit networks," in which the people known by a couple tend more often to interact also with one another.[35]   She finds:

> Couples in close-knit networks expected husbands and wives to have a rigid division of labor. There was little stress on the importance of shared interests and joint recreation. It was expected that wives would have many relationships with their relatives, and husbands with their friends. Both parents could get help from people outside the family, which made the rigid division of labor between husband and wife possible. Successful sexual relations were not considered essential to a happy marriage.
>
> In contrast, families in a loose-knit networks had a less rigid division of labor, stressed the importance of shared interests and joint recreation, and placed a good deal of emphasis on the importance of successful sexual relations. They were more self-conscious about how to bring up their children than couples in close-knit networks. They were aware that the people they knew had a great variety of opinions on this subject and they were worried about which course they themselves should follow.[36]

Note that Bott associates this lack of differentiation with conjugal solidarity. She goes on further to suggest that the relationship is a causal one — that couples who cannot rely upon a stable and supportive external social context must develop a more intimate relationship with each other than a rigid division of labor permits. This is achieved through an increase in joint, shared activities.[37]

Bott also associates loose-knit networks with social and geographical mobility.[38]   This suggests the hypothesis that couples will tend to decrease role differentiation whenever the welfare of the family is predicated upon a high degree of non-commitment to (or lack of dependence upon) external social relationships.[39] This degree of commitment, furthermore, may vary not only from couple to couple, but also within the same couple over time. De-differentiation typically occurs with a family whenever it is removed from its usual social context, such as during a vacation or a change in residence.[40]

Such a situation obtains in large segments of the American middle class and is particularly marked in families in which the husband works for an organization whose offices are widely distributed, so that advancement requires frequent changes of residence; or when such advancement necessitates the formation of new relationships at each status level.[41] But it seems clear that if a couple living in this kind of context does show a rigid division of labor it is much more likely to be associated with conflict and strain within the family than would be the case if both husband and wife could turn for support, friendship, and tension release to stable lifelong relationships outside the nuclear family. Furthermore, if a pattern of behavior appropriate to close-knit networks is formed in the absence of such networks, it would seem reasonable to expect that some of the burden of filling this vacuum would be placed upon the child, thus generating the negative relationship found above between parental differentiation and the emotional adjustment of the child.[42]

But apart from any considerations of emotional health, is there any more universal effect of parental role differentiation upon the child – one which might be functional in some social contexts and dysfunctional in others? Does parental role differentiation help foster, for example, a personality trait or constellation which is maladaptive for children growing up in a fluid social environment but necessary for life in a stable one?

One possibility is suggested by a study of the Gusii by LeVine. Testing a prediction by Whiting that authoritarian sanctioning would develop with parental role differentiation, LeVine found that among the Gusii, who tend to violate cultural norms when authority figures are absent, the father is a non-nurturant and punitive disciplinarian, while the mother tends to specialize in the nurturing role, using the threat of paternal punishment as a principal means of control. "The child thus learns to fear the father's painful ministrations and to avoid them by being obedient and performing his tasks; but he does not internalize the father's evaluation of his behavior."[43]

It is not difficult to see why this is so. To the extent that the father is non-rewarding he will tend to appear as an alien ruler to the child. His demands will be acceded to when he is present, for the same reason that other forms of reality command obeisance, but when he is not present and cannot exert his authority, nothing is to be gained by obedience. To the extent that he is rewarding, however, much is to be gained by being a "good boy" even when the father is away. In other words, the internalization of parental values tends to occur to the degree that nurturance and discipline come from the same source. This point, which seems to be fairly well established today, is stressed by Eleanor Maccoby in an analysis of the effects upon children of the mothers working. She cites Solomon's work with dogs, noting that "punishment by a stranger, or a person who has been primarily cold and restrictive toward the animal in puppyhood, does not seem to last very well in its effects when the trainer's back is turned," and even goes so far as to recommend that "if nurturant caretaking is divided between two people ... then discipline should be similarly divided."[44]

But accustomed as we are to the serious consequences of a severe failure of internalization in our own society, it should perhaps be emphasized that in a society with a less fluid social structure a high degree of internalization is not only unnecessary to insure social control, but may in some instances be actually disruptive — if, for example, the society is heavily committed to a complex system of external controls with regulated violation, as in the case of chaperonage, or if such intensive internalization tends to erode other personality characteristics valued by the society, as Bronfenbrenner suggests.[45]

At the same time, an additional reason for the importance of internalization in our own society is suggested by this analysis. When large numbers of individuals spend their lives in shifting loose-knit networks, social control cannot be based on external sanctions to the extent that is possible with a stable and integrated social context; the need then is for a family structure that promotes the internalization of parental values.

The de-differentiation of parental roles also tends to palliate one of the major strains besetting the mobile nuclear family, that is, the potentially fragile relationship between child and father due to the latter's absence from the home during most of the child's waking hours. For as the burden of socialization has become increasingly concentrated in the nuclear family, the availability of the father to share this burden has remained unchanged and in many instances (e.g., the suburban commuter) actually decreased. Assuming that the importance of such sharing is non-problematic, it seems clear that in the mobile nuclear family a great deal of pressure exists to soften and familiarize the paternal role. The specialized disciplinarian of other times and places, in an immobile and "connected" nuclear family, was in a sense the immediate representative of a like-minded community of persons well known to the child; if the child did not fully internalize his values, he at least developed a sense of respect for them as a consequence of their apparent universality. If the father was too extreme in his role, furthermore, there were often substitute males with whom the child could form a more complete and adequate relationship.

In the isolated mobile nuclear family, however, the father does not represent a known community of adults, and there are no permanent substitutes. A specialized disciplinarian role loses any semblance of a universalistic response and takes on the appearance of malicious caprice. The father who attempts it becomes an alien intruder to his children, a state of affairs which, while tolerable in the "connected" family is severely disruptive in the isolated mobile family.

Perhaps the most dramatic expression of the difference between the two systems is the fact that while in the de-differentiated family[46] a great deal of effort is devoted to bringing the father closer to the children (often through his adoption of a tolerant, easy-going, occasional-playmate role), one of the principal mechanisms used to handle hostility in the differentiated family was distancing. This was effected not only by the general aloofness assumed by the father in the performance of his disciplinary function, but also by the mediator role played by the mother — a role which generally purports to be self-dissolving, but which in practice usually proves to be self-perpetuating.

In the most extreme case the father may play a kind of scapegoat role. If an individual is specialized in a non-rewarding direction, it is convenient to have him become the recipient of the hostile feelings occasionally aroused by more rewarding individuals. This is particularly likely to occur in a highly patriarchal family system, in which the mother may compensate for her inferior status and power in the society at large by using her strategic position as mediator to control family relationships. By a combination of public indorsement and private subversion of the father's authority she indicates to the child that the father is the source of all discomfort and she the source of all good. It should be clear that internalization of parental values under such circumstances is rather unlikely. The German *Hausfrau* who supports the father's disciplinary measures in his presence with verbal exhortations to the child to obey him, and then hustles the child off to the kitchen for candy and sympathy, is making a rather sharp distinction between what is necessary in the way of public behavior in the presence of authorities and what one may do and feel privately in their absence.

This point is sometimes misunderstood. It is assumed that because a mediator attempts to prevent conflict by establishing distance, he will ultimately be able to establish solidarity, and thus eliminate the need for his existence. But just as insulation keeps out heat as well as cold, so distance forestalls affection as well as hostility. As Simmel once pointed out, "although a bridge connects two banks, it also makes the distance between them measurable."[47] When the mother teaches her son how to please and placate the father, how to "deal with" and occasionally "get around" him, she is creating a gap between father and son which will operate effectively even in her absence, since the two will always feel a little strange with each other. This perhaps accounts for the brittleness of paternal identification in the German family — a brittleness brilliantly manipulated by Hitler. For the mother's teaching, while it establishes the superior power and status of the father and sets him up as a person worthy of imitation, does not really permit the son enough closeness to the father, or the father enough affectionate behavior toward the son, for a full internalization of paternal values to take place. Instead, she teaches the son her own role of submission, placation, and deception, thus inculcating an identification with herself. To an extent the yearning for a powerful authority which gave rise to the Nazi era may be seen as an attempt to complete the semi-identification with the father while at the same time maintaining identification with the submissive mother.

The mechanism of the maternal mediator, reasonably adequate to the task of moderating strains in a family system which had liberal access to paternal substitutes, is out of the question in a system desperately bent on intensifying the intimacy of the child-father relationship as a way of lessening the otherwise unwieldy burden on the mother produced by the relative absence in the mobile family of alternative socializing agents.

A Problem in the Comparison of Mechanisms

In an analysis of marital interaction, James March has argued that "specialization, by reducing the area of joint activity, would appear to reduce at the same time the possibility of conflict within the group."[48] It seems surprising that an otherwise perceptive author could ignore the fact that "reducing the area of joint activity" will reduce solidarity as well as conflict. It reveals the bias, common to sociologists, in favor of distancing mechanisms and raises a serious problem in the comparative analysis of social institutions.

Ambivalence is a profoundly difficult emotional state for human beings to handle. Often they are able to cope with contradictory feelings only through rigid and awkward intrapsychic and interpersonal mechanisms. When this is the case the raw material is provided for a social institution which "builds in" those components which are neglected or distorted by the individual. In other words, if the individual cannot find direct ways of expressing, in his most significant interpersonal relationships, the ambivalence of his feelings, this ambivalence is likely to reappear in social structural form.

Parental role differentiation, while it may serve many different functions in many different societies, is at one level this kind of externalizing mechanism. It tends to focus one kind of feeling toward one parent and a contrasting feeling toward the other. It facilitates displacement and dilutes the emotional intensity of the family situation by "reducing the area of joint activity" and thus increasing the psychological distance between members. In this way it displays a certain formal elegance which is lacking in the de-differentiated system; but we should bear in mind that the apparent structural simplicity of a family pattern in which both parents are equally loving and constraining serves to mask the complexity and subtlety of the interpersonal responses of the participants.

As sociologists, it is natural for us to see more clearly the function of institutions which neutralize human emotions with distancing mechanisms, as opposed to those which permit more idiosyncratic solutions to ambivalent feelings. But there is a danger in this preference — the danger that we will underestimate both the importance and the complexity of structural patterns such as we find in the de-differentiated family. In using the phrase "apparent structural simplicity" with reference to this institution, I have the uneasy feeling that this apparent simplicity may be simply a function of the inadequacy of our traditional modes of analysis. Is it not possible that we are fascinated with institutional forms such as parental role differentiation, joking relationships, and puberty rites precisely because they are simple and crude enough for us to understand? Are we not continually exposed to the risk of overrating the functional efficacy of the institutions of primitive societies because they are more transparent than our own?[49]

It may be that the more highly differentiated family, despite its prevalence, is simply too unsophisticated a structure for a technologically advanced industrial society such as ours. Its apparent dependence on a stable social context imparts to it a rigidity analogous, in its effects on the family system, to the greater rigidity of inherited as opposed to learned responses in the individual organism. It is in part this very rigidity which aids us in studying its structure and function, while the mechanics of the more undifferentiated family remain somewhat obscure.

That greater attention has been devoted to the older pattern[50] is therefore natural and appropriate, but one cannot help hoping that an analysis such as Parsons' might now be extended to the de-differentiated family. The rapidity of social change, both subtle and violent, in our own era raises the fascinating possibility that a clear understanding of the functions of emergent as well as decadent institutions might enable us to anticipate the institutional arrangements of tomorrow.

FOOTNOTES

[1] Revision of a paper read at the 1960 annual meeting of the American Sociological Association.

[2] See Talcott Parsons and Robert F. Bales, *Family: Socialization and Interaction Process* (Glencoe, Ill.: Free Press, 1955), chap. ii.

[3] *Ibid.*, pp. 91-94.

[4] *Ibid.*, p. 355.

[5] *Ibid.*, pp. 45, 80.

[6] Ernest and Pearl Beaglehole, "Personality Development in Pukapukan Children," in W. E. Martin and Celia B. Stendler (eds.), *Readings in Child Development* (New York: Harcourt, Brace & Co., 1954), p. 161.

[7] Morris Zelditch, Jr., "Role Differentiation in the Nuclear Family," in Parsons and Bales, *op. cit.*, chap. vi.

[8]Parsons and Bales, *op. cit.*, p. 286.

[9]Zelditch, *op. cit.*, p. 312.

[10]Robert Briffault, *The Mothers* (New York: Macmillan Co., 1931), *passim.*

[11]Zelditch, *op. cit.*, p. 311.

[12]Philip E. Slater, "Psychological Factors in Role Specialization" (unpublished Ph.D. dissertation, Harvard University, 1955), pp. 205-13. Particularly interesting in Zelditch's argument is the implicit assumption that whereas it is possible for persons in subordinate positions to make this transition, it is not possible for those in positions of leadership (Zelditch, *op. cit.*, pp. 311-12).

[13]Parsons and Bales, *op. cit.*, pp. 290-96; Philip E. Slater, "Role Differentiation in Small Groups," *American Sociological Review*, XX (June, 1955), pp. 308-10.

[14]Ezra F. Vogel and Norman W. Bell, "The Emotionally Disturbed Child as the Family Scapegoat," in Norman W. Bell and Ezra F. Vogel (eds.), *A Modern Introduction to the Family* (Glencoe, Ill.: Free Press, 1960), pp. 389-90 (cf. also Ezra F. Vogel, "The Marital Relationship of Parents and the Emotionally Disturbed Child" [unpublished Ph.D. dissertation, Harvard University, 1958]).

[15]Parsons and Bales, *op. cit.*, p. 80. This statement also seems to imply that Parsons' model of differentiation is unidimensional, although the underlying theory would suggest a bidimensional model.

[16]Cf. A. R. Radcliffe-Brown, *Structure and Function in Primitive Society* (Glencoe, Ill.: Free Press, 1952), p. 20.

[17]Vogel and Bell, *op. cit.*, pp. 390-91.

[18]*Ibid.*, pp. 394-97.

[19]"Identification" is here defined as any tendency for an individual to seek to maximize his similarity to another person in one or more respects. The studies I have cited in support of my position would not all serve as adequate evidence, were other definitions of identification to be used. I have elsewhere distinguished between "personal" and "positional" identification, the former based on a desire to assimilate the valued personal qualities of a

loved object, the latter based on a desire to assume the position or role of an envied and hated object. See my "Toward a Dualistic Theory of Identification," *Merrill-Palmer Quarterly,* VII (April, 1961). It is to "personal" identification that this section is devoted.

[20]Parsons and Bales, *op. cit.,* p. 80.

[21]D. E. Payne and P. H. Mussen, "Parent-Child Relations and Father Identification among Adolescent Boys," *Journal of Abnormal and Social Psychology,* LII (1956), pp. 358-62.

[22]Otto Fenichel, *The Psychoanalytic Theory of the Neuroses* (New York: W. W. Norton & Co., 1945).

[23]Cf. I. L. Child, "Socialization," in Gardner Lindzey (ed.), *Handbook of Social Psychology* (Cambridge, Mass.: Addison-Wesley, 1954), Vol. II; Susan W. Gray and R. Klaus, "The Assessment of Parental Identification," *Genetic Psychology Monographs,* LIV (1956), pp. 87-114; Payne and Mussen, *op. cit.;* Pauline Sears, "Child-rearing Factors Related to Playing of Sex-typed Roles," *American Psychologist,* VIII (1953), p. 431 (abstract); J. W. M. Whiting and I. L. Child, *Child Training and Personality: A Cross-cultural Study* (New Haven, Conn.: Yale University Press, 1953).

[24]E. G. Beier and F. Ratzeburg, "The Parental Identifications of Male and Female College Students," *Journal of Abnormal and Social Psychology,* XLVIII (1953), pp. 569-72; Slater, "Psychological Factors in Role Specialization," p. 120.

[25]Parsons and Bales, *op. cit.,* pp. 91-94; cf. also J. Kagan, "The Concept of Identification," *Psychological Review,* LXV (1958), p. 302; O. H. Mower, *Learning Theory and Personality Dynamics* (New York: Ronald Press Co., 1950), p. 608; R. R. Sears, Eleanor E. Maccoby, and H. Levin, *Patterns of Child Rearing* (Evanston, Ill.: Row, Peterson & Co., 1957).

[26]Parsons and Bales, *op. cit.,* p. 81. (Italics mostly mine.)

[27]Parsons and Bales, *op. cit.,* p. 54.

[28]*Ibid.,* p. 27.

[29]L. M. Lazowick, "On the Nature of Identification," *Journal of Abnormal and Social Psychology,* LI (1955), pp. 175-83.

[30]M. Manis, "Personal Adjustment, Assumed Similarity to Parents, and

Inferred Parental Evaluations of the Self," *Journal of Consulting Psychology,* XXII (1958), pp. 481-85.

[31] Slater, "Psychological Factors in Role Specialization," pp. 133-35.

[32] H. Wechsler, "Conflicts in Self-perceptions" (unpublished Ph.D. dissertation, Harvard University, 1957).

[33] "Husbands who had the most segregated role-relationships with their wives had manual occupations, and the husbands who had the most joint role-relationships with their wives were professional or semi-professional people" (Elisabeth Bott, "Conjugal Roles and Social Networks," in Bell and Vogel [eds.], *op. cit.,* p. 251). While Bott is primarily concerned with conjugal roles here, the type of differentiation, with its de-emphasis of shared activities, is one we would expect to be highly correlated with differentiation of socialization roles.

It is the middle-class parents, moreover, who are the principal consumers of the child-training manuals, which often specifically oppose such practices as deferring punishments for the father to administer, and which argue, in general, for an undifferentiated pattern of parental behavior (cf., e.g., Benjamin Spock, *The Pocket Book of Baby and Child Care* [New York: Pocket Books, 1956], pp. 14-15, 242-43).

[34] Slater, "Psychological Factors in Role Specialization," pp. 207-9.

[35] See Bott, *op. cit.,* p. 252.

[36] *Ibid.,* p. 439.

[37] It would seem that the sharper the differentiation of conjugal roles in a society, the greater the reliance which will be placed upon sex segregation in the training of children for these roles. For while segregation of the sexes in the youth peer group may be universal, as Parsons suggests ("The Incest Taboo in Relation to Social Structure and the Socialization of the Child," *British Journal of Sociology,* Vol. V [June, 1954]), the degree and duration of such segregation may have important consequences. In some societies (and in some segments of the American lower class) it becomes something of a Frankenstein monster, inasmuch as the individual who has spent most of his youth in one-sex groups only feels truly at ease in such groups as an adult. The stress that this creates for marital relationships, even in the mildly segregated American middle class, is the bread-and-butter of cartoonists and comedians across the nation (note the ubiquity of poker, golf, and bridge-club jokes). The consequences of the more severe forms of sex segregation are discussed by Bettelheim in his *Symbolic Wounds* (Glencoe, Ill.: Free Press, 1955).

In wartime sex segregation is sharply increased, and the resulting stresses overload the usual mechanisms. This perhaps accounts for the temporary rash, during World War II, of psychiatric papers dealing with penis envy and other forms of sex antagonism (cf., e.g., *Psychiatry*, 1940-46). While each sex experiences severe deprivation and suffering during wartime, neither is in a position fully to understand or appreciate the different nature of the sufferings of the other. The resulting resentment finds its ultimate expression in fantasies of single-sex societies (cf., e.g., Bernice S. Engle, "Lemnos, Island of Women," *Psychoanalytic Review*, XXXII [1945], pp. 353-58).

[38] Bott, *op. cit.*, p. 256.

[39] Although animal sociology is not sufficiently advanced to enable us to generalize with much confidence, J. P. Scott implies that this relationship extends to the other primates, when he contrasts the relative lack of sex role differentiation among the gibbons, who live in isolated nuclear families, with the strong differentiation among baboons, who show more extended social groupings (*Animal Behavior* [Chicago: University of Chicago Press, 1958], p. 187).

[40] Observation made to author by Theodore Mills.

[41] Riesman and Roseborough, e.g., refer to the "young married proto-executives" who "become very adept at pulling up stakes, and at being at home everywhere and nowhere" (David Riesman and Howard Roseborough, "Careers and Consumer Behavior," in Bell and Vogel [eds.], *op. cit.*, pp. 143-62, esp. pp. 152, 155, 158). The academic world is so characterized to an almost equal extent. One reason that the de-differentiation of parental roles is a useful preparation for this kind of transient adult life is that it teaches the child at an early age that his human sources of gratification are more or less interchangeable.

[42] Although loose-knit networks are, as noted before, less frequent among lower-class families, we might expect to find them in mobile or newly acculturated families. Vogel and Bell's "scapegoated" children were largely from families undergoing one or both types of transition, and there may have been a particularly strong need in such cases for the parents to place emotional demands upon the child which had previously been directed outside the nuclear family (see Vogel and Bell, *op. cit.*, pp. 384-85).

[43] R. A. LeVine, "Social Control and Socialization among the Gusii" (unpublished Ph.D. dissertation, Harvard University, 1958), p. 358. The shallowness of internalization in the differentiated family is also shown in a study by Hazel Hitson ("Family Patterns and Paranoidal Personality Structure in

Boston and Burma" [unpublished Ph.D. dissertation, Harvard University, 1959]). See also Stanley H. King and Andrew F. Henry, "Aggression and Cardiovascular Reactions Related to Parental Control over Behavior," *Journal of Abnormal and Social Psychology*, L (March, 1955), pp. 206-10. Henry reported that "reluctance to blame the other person as well as willingness to blame the self both increase the likelihood that the mother will be viewed as principal disciplinarian" ("Family Role Structure and Self-blame," in Bell and Vogel [eds.], *op. cit.*, p. 542).

[44]Eleanor E. Maccoby, "Effects upon Children of Their Mother's Outside Employment," in Bell and Vogel, *op. cit.*, pp. 528-29 (cf. also Urie Bronfenbrenner, "Socialization and Social Class through Time and Space," in Eleanor E. Maccoby, T. M. Newcomb, and E. L. Hartley [eds.], *Readings in Social Psychology* [New York: Henry Holt & Co., 1958], p. 419).
Maccoby is here assuming, of course, the desirability of internalization in American society, an assumption roundly rejected, along with the undifferentiated middle-class marital relationship, by Arnold Green ("The Middle-Class Male Child and Neurosis" and "The 'Cult of Personality' and Sexual Relations," both reprinted in Bell and Vogel [eds.], *op. cit.*, pp. 563-72, pp. 608-15, see esp. pp. 564 ff. and 614-15).

[45]Urie Bronfenbrenner, "The Changing American Child – a Speculative Analysis," *Merrill-Palmer Quarterly*, VII (April, 1961), pp. 73-84.

[46]The terms "differentiated family" and "de-differentiated family" are not intended to imply a pair of discrete types, or even a bimodal distribution of families along the differentiation continuum. In talking of such modal changes, furthermore, it should not be forgotten that they are always exaggerated in popular belief, since individual variation is overwhelming in any era. That such a de-differentiation has taken place in comparatively recent times, however, and that it has been associated with an increase in internalization, is demonstrated by a number of recent studies (cf. Bronfenbrenner, "The Changing American Child," *op. cit.*, pp. 75, 79; and Wanda C. Bronson, Edith S. Katten, and N. Livson, "Patterns of Authority and Affection in Two Generations," *Journal of Abnormal and Social Psychology*, LVIII (1959), pp. 143-52.

[47]Kurt H. Wolff, *The Sociology of Georg Simmel* (Glencoe, Ill.: Free Press, 1950), p. 129.

[48]"Political Issues and Husband-Wife Interaction," in Bell and Vogel (eds.), *op. cit.*, p. 202.

[49]A good example of this tendency to disregard more complex and subtle methods of articulating personality and social system may be found in the

remarks often made by xenocentric anthropologists regarding the lack, in our society, of institutions designed to bridge the gap between childhood and adulthood. The role of the school system in this regard is generally ignored, yet one may ask if this institution — with its increasing separation of child from mother, its finely turned system of age grading, its increasing acquaintance of the child with the adult world and adult roles, its provision of a long series of tasks and tests of gradually increasing difficulty and complexity, its careful training of internal controls through a gradual shift from minute-by-minute supervision of work to a system in which work-planning and work habits are left almost entirely in the hands of students, and its machinery for the actual training of students in adult roles — does not go a little way toward filling the appalling void posited by Benedictine observers of the contemporary scene, who seem at times to imply that a primitive adolescent, having been, in a single pubertal ceremony, tortured, isolated, and generally frightened to death, is in some magical fashion better prepared for adult life in his society than is an American graduate of high school or college.

[50]This is not meant to imply, of course, that de-differentiation is "new" but only that at the present time there seems to be a trend toward the particular form discussed here.

Comment

Bernard Bergen

Rejoinder

Philip Slater

COMMENT

Bernard J. Bergen

There are, generally speaking, two principal vantage points from which a problem of the analysis of roles can be approached. That predominant in sociology takes as its initial point of departure the designation of a specific type or category of social role. The analysis itself is usually concerned with the problem of some aspect of the relations of that class of persons who "fit" into the designated role category with one or more alters in a given social system. A number of concrete problems in such analysis have been derived from this orientation: for example, the effect of conflict on the performance of those in specified categories of role; the relation between psychological variables and performance and so on.

While this constitutes a mode of analysis which can achieve what Weber has earlier referred to as "the sociological understanding of the actions of typically differentiated human . . . individuals"[1] there is also a necessity, as he insisted, "to know what a 'king' and 'official' and 'entrepreneur,' a 'procurer' or a 'magician' does; that is, what kind of typical action, which justifies classifying an individual in one of these categories, is important and relevant for an analysis before it is possible to undertake the analysis itself."[2]

The second vantage point takes this as its point of departure and is concerned with the basis of the classification or typology of roles. Relatively little sociological effort has been expended on moving beyond the *ad hoc* labels affixed to people which designate their role, toward the formulating of a systematic classification and exploring its significance in elucidating other sociological problems.

This is, however, the vantage point from which Parsons has taken up the problem of parental differentiation of role. Slater, on the contrary, has approached the issues which Parsons' analysis has raised from the more familiar point of view. Their divergence becomes more distinct when we consider the differences in their use of the term "role."

It is abundantly clear from the content of his arguments and evidence that Slater uses the term "role" to refer to the relationships which characterize dyadic units in the family: father-child, mother-child, mother-father. The general principle underlying his use of the term is that of a referent for what Linton has called the "reciprocal behavior between individuals."[3] The problem with which Slater is concerned is thus that of accounting for role differentiation conceived as a dimension along which to measure the variable relationships between incumbents of different types of familial roles. He offers a theory centering on the psychological competence of those in parental role categories.

On the other hand, Parsons, by stating that the role of the father is concerned with instrumental functions and that of the mother with expressive functions, is not describing the relationship of mother and father to each other or to any other member of the family. He has formulated his definitions in these terms:

> The instrumental-expressive distinction we interpret as essentially the differentiation of function, and hence of relative influence, in terms of "external" vs. "internal" functions of the system. The area of instrumental function concerns relations of the system to its situation outside the system, to meeting the adaptive conditions of its maintenance of equilibrium and "instrumentally" establishing the desired relations to *external* goal-objects. The expressive area concerns the "internal" affairs of the system, the maintenance of integrative relations between the members, and regulation of the patterns and tension levels of its component units.[4]

The term "role" then, at least as Parsons uses it in this case, does not stand for a concept based on the uniformities of behavior between two specified actors in a social system but rather for a concept relating an actor to the solution of those problems which he has described in an earlier work as "inherent in or arising from social interaction of a plurality of actors."[5] It is this conceptualization which serves as the basic set of criteria for a classification of role types or categories. The problem with which Parsons is initially concerned is that of defining parental role types; more accurately, of defining the sociological character of biologically differentiated parents. His procedure is to apply to the family his functionally based classification scheme and to present evidence concerning the universal differentiation of these role types by sex. This is presented as having important implications for the process of socialization.

It is thus apparent that the issues which Slater raises in opposition to Parsons are created by his confusion over the vantage points from which the two analyses of parental roles are undertaken. The two authors, in a strict sense, do not talk about the same thing at all.

The source of confusion would seem to lie in two conditions. The first is the apparently implicit assumption by Slater that problems of importance in sociology must be conceived in strictly interpersonal terms. He has failed to realize that social relationships, to which the term "role" refers, can be conceived of at different levels of abstraction. No concept can exhaust all the information empirically obtainable on the kind of experience it organizes. The information that one uses or disregards depends upon the particular problem for which the concept has been formulated. Parsons' concept of role is formulated by abstracting from the specific dyadic relationships of an actor the kind of emergent system functions or problems for which they have relevance. This is not the level of abstraction at which Slater uses the term or, apparently, understands Parsons' use of it.

The second source of confusion is the lack of discriminating terms to refer to the two levels of conceptualization. Although it is impossible to say that there is in sociology today universal consensus over the use of "role," it seems to us that the trend is to restrict its meaning as Slater uses it. The term which seems to us to be most consistently used to refer to social relationships on the level at which Parsons conceptualizes them, is that of "status" in its non-hierarchical sense, or its more recent synonym, "position." It is possible to attribute Parsons' failure to use this term to the relative obscurity and lack of specificity still surrounding it.[6]

To indicate the lines along which the major issue of contention between the two can be clarified and resolved: Parsons states that "the mother figure is always the more permissive and supportive, the father, the more denying and demanding."[7] Considering only the father-son relationship, Slater has reformulated this using such terms as "strict," "non-rewarding," to characterize the father's role. However, Parsons also goes on to say that "the basic problem concerns the roles of the two parents in the family as a system. If the boy is to 'identify' with his father in the sense of sex role categorization there must be a discrimination in role terms between the two parents. *This is essentially a different question from that of agency in administering specific disciplines.*"[8] This latter sentence, admittedly confusing in Parsons' context, becomes clearer when we keep in mind both his theoretical approach to socialization and the particular kind of conceptualization the term "role" stands for.

Parsons' concern with the socialization process, dealing at present only with the male child, is with the progressive formation of a personality stable enough to assume his appropriate sex-linked role. Being that of an adult male, his role will be primarily focused on the occupational sphere at large. This, Parsons suggests, is accomplished by the progressive internalization of familial roles at successive psycho-sexual phases of development. Substituting, as we have suggested, the term "position" where Parsons uses "role," we can say that the father, by occupying an instrumental position, will be perceived by the male child, as a function of his identification with him, as denying and demanding: "denying," in the sense that identifying himself with the position of the father suppresses whatever regressive tendencies the male child may have to avoid orienting himself to the universalistic standards of the extra-familial world and to remain oriented to the particularistic standards of the family; "demanding," in the sense that identification with the position of father demands that the male child reject identification with his mother, in part of course, and reject his previously exclusive orientation to particularistic family standards.

The terms "denying" and "demanding" do not, then, refer to particular qualities of the relationship between father and son as a dyadic system. Parsons' use of the term is indeed "a different question from that of agency in administering specific disciplines." The specific relations between fathers and sons are not, of course, unrelated to the problem of role identification as Parsons deals with it. The evidence that Slater cites quite convincingly suggests that unless a father is warm and loving his function as denying and demanding by virtue of his particular position in the family will not be effective.

Slater's paper is thus not in contention with Parsons' formulations about differentiation in roles. He has, rather, made a different kind of contribution. His paper has sharply underscored the need for clarifying and establishing rules of terminology in the analysis of role suitable to the complexities of conceptualization.

REJOINDER

Philip E. Slater

Bergen's thoughtful comment provides considerable clarification of some of the issues I have raised. I can only argue in defense of the objections I have made to Parsons' theory of differentiation in parental role that I am not convinced that Parsons has entirely succeeded in avoiding lapses into a usage of "role" identical with mine. Certainly, other authors often quote him in contexts which make it clear that they are not thinking in terms of position.

Such lapses are not surprising in view of the temptations. For if a role is defined independent of behavior toward specified alters, one can hardly make predictions concerning its impact on them. Yet most persons interested in socialization and identification are rather anxious to make just such predictions, and I confess to a like weakness. If we adhere to a strict "position" interpretation of role, we must realize that parental differentiation can tell us nothing whatever about *why* the child identifies himself with the father or the mother, but merely explains how he can tell the difference between them.

FOOTNOTES

[1] Max Weber, *The Theory of Social and Economic Organization,* trans. Henderson and Parsons (New York: Oxford University Press, 1947), p. 107.

[2] *Ibid.*

[3] Ralph Linton, *The Study of Man* (New York: Appleton-Century-Crofts, 1936), p. 113.

[4] Talcott Parsons and Robert F. Bales, *Family: Socialization and Interaction Process* (Glencoe, Ill.: Free Press, 1955), p. 47.

[5] Talcott Parsons and Edward Shils (eds.), *Toward a General Theory of Action* (Cambridge, Mass.: Harvard University Press, 1951), p. 7.

[6] "Position," as distinct from "role," is usually conceived of as referring to a general or abstract concept (as opposed to a "specific concrete or real" one) and having "static" qualities (as opposed to "dynamic" qualities).

The attempt to discriminate two distinct concepts "covered" by the terms "position" and "role" has apparently inhibited the use of the former as a term to stand for relationships in a social system at any level of abstraction. This has, however, never really been accepted without serious reservations, even by those who made the most prodigious efforts in rationalizing the distinction. Linton himself has said that "role and status are quite inseparable, and the distinction between them is of only academic interest" (Linton, *op. cit.,* p. 114).

Gross more recently has all but directly stated that the two concepts are tautologous. "The meaning of location in a system of social relationships is not, however, entirely self evident. It is difficult to separate the idea of location from the *relationships which define it*" (Neal Gross *et al., Explorations in Role Analysis* [New York: John Wiley & Sons, 1958], p. 48). Usually no attempt is made toward resolving the implicit conflict over its continued use.

Describing "position" as a "collection of rights and duties" or a "location" in social space contributes, of course, very little with respect to its meaning. Further attempts to go beyond these definitions have usually resulted in metaphor, resembling Linton's well-known analogy of a driver in an automobile.

[7] Parsons and Bales, *op. cit.,* p. 80 n.

[8] *Ibid.* (Italics mine.)

Personal and Positional Influence in Formal Groups

Propositions and Theory for Research on Family Vulnerability to Stress

Donald A. Hansen

This article by Donald A. Hansen illustrates the utility of precision in the description and use of concepts and serves to illustrate some methods of framework construction. Hansen produces a speculative model for measuring family stress vulnerability which involves the clarification of relationships between family members and suggested solution to the problems produced by the bi-dimensional axis proposed by Slater. The model awaits empirical test.

Formal groups of apparently similar structure often respond differently to similar stresses; hardships which are the nemesis of some are easily weathered by others, and occasionally stimulate a group to develop new strengths and capacities. It is likely that an understanding of differential vulnerability to stress would offer important insights into more general interpersonal and social processes. Efforts to derive descriptive or predictive theories of differential vulnerability, however, have met with only limited success.

Reprinted, with permission of the author and publisher, from *Social Forces*, 44 (December 1965), pp. 202-210.

Most consistent and long lived of such efforts is the sociological concern with families under stress.[1] Already at the turn of the century the search had begun for qualities which distinguish families vulnerable to stress from those invulnerable; it dominated family sociology through the great Depression of the thirties, was systematically developed in study of war separation and reunion, and continues today in study of the effects of mental retardation, illness, and other stresses on the family.

An implicit definition appears to have been accepted in these studies: *The vulnerable family (or group) is that which lacks ability to influence the action of its members (i.e., lacks "behavioral influence") in such a way that even under stress they remain together and continue to share and satisfy role expectations.* This definition is but circular, however, unless it leads to predictions or hypotheses about the response of groups to future stress. Such hypotheses might be possible, given answers to two questions: How can the strength of behavioral influence be identified? What are the likely effects of stress on this behavioral influence?

These questions have never been explicitly asked in research on families under stress, but they have been implicitly approached. In his pioneering study of the Depression, Angell, for example, approached the first (unasked) question with the concept of "family integration," and the second question with the concept "family adaptability."[2] Unfortunately, these concepts, specified in later investigations by Koos,[3] and Cavan and Ranck,[4] have attracted little attention since the systematic work of Hill in 1949,[5] and in spite of their early promise, today still offer only a low-level description.

This investigation seeks to enter the main stream of theories of families under stress, through application of a distinction generally ignored in family research, and little appreciated in small group research; a distinction between the *personal influence and the positional influence* of group members on one another. The distinction arises from the insight that in interaction individuals tend to develop both *a personal relationship,* or *the relation of ego to alter as individuals,* and *a positional relationship,* or *the relation of ego to alter as status or position holders in a group.* That is, there are two kinds of cohesiveness in a group: the first involves the influence members have on one another because of their personal relationships; the second involves the influence they have on one another because of their positions in the group structure.

In the following sections the paper will: (1) Examine the concepts, personal and positional relationships; (2) Speculatively identify qualities of "ideal" types of families characterized by various combinations of high or low personal and positional influence; (3) Postulate the likelihood of family vulnerability of each of the types to general categories of stress.

Personal and Positional Relationships

Major theorists from Comte and Spencer, through Toennies to Becker have suggested that communities may be identified on a continuum: On one pole are those which hold and attract individuals because of the rewards or punishments offered through the primary (or personal) relationships; at the other are those which hold and attract with structural (or positional) relationships.[6] As one type of relationship or attraction increases in a community, the other decreases. This traditional emphasis is reflected in Parsons' and Bales' concept of an "instrumental-expressive" axis, with which they are able to incisively describe the functional importance of parental positions in meeting the "system" requirements of the family.[7] In functional analysis, it may be legitimate to present the instrumental-expressive concept as a single variable, such that if a member is characterized by an instrumental function, he cannot also be characterized by the expressive, and, further, that in a family in which roles are sharply differentiated, if one position is essentially instrumental the other is expressive. In functional consequences, instrumental and expressive may be, indeed, negatively related.

In behavioral terms, however, one parent may perform the majority of *both* instrumental and expressive roles in the family, while the other performs almost none at all; indeed, instrumental and expressive *behavior,* far from demonstrating the perfect negative correlation required by a single axis, show a positive (though far from perfect) correlation.[8]

Parsons' and Bales' focus is legitimate and promising for certain research questions, however:[9] in stress study it can well be turned to questions of who is holding what functional positions, and of how these positions rearrange under stress. But the focus allows only comparison of family members with one another on their contributions to solution of family "problems"; it is of little use in examining the strength of the group's particular role arrangement or patterns of on-going relations; in predicting its ability to weather stress or to respond to it in such a way that the relationship is strengthened, in accounting for observations of euphoric closeness and effectiveness following stresses such as temporary illness or community-wide disaster.[10]

The following theory of personal and positional relations, by contrast, posits two *interdependent* continua, and it seeks specification of major concepts primarily in behavioral (rather than functional) terms.

Toward Definitions of Positional and Personal Relationships

The vague definitions, offered in the first section of this paper, personal and positional relationships (relationships of ego and alter as persons and as position holders) convey little information, and withstand but minor criticism. Preliminary specification is attempted in the following speculations.[11]

Specifying Assumption 1: Positional and personal relationships are arrays of expectations for behavior in which ego holds it probable that alter will act in certain ways in a given situation;

Specifying Assumption 2: Positional expectations develop and are maintained in solution of group members' shared problems of meeting, concurrently, the needs, desires and demands of the individual members, of the group and of the social community;

Specifying Assumption 3: Personal expectations develop and are maintained in response to ego's and alter's perception of their own and the other's needs and desires.

That is, personal relationships develop as individuals seek solution to their own felt needs and desires and to those perceived in their alter. Because the most pressing of these needs are often not shared or even complementary, the relationship depends on concern of at least one person with the other's individual needs and desires. Positional expectations, by contrast, develop less in response to individual needs and desires than to the problems family members *share* because of conflicts in demands and requirements of members, group and community. Solutions to such problems are seen in group structures such as the authority hierarchy (to meet group and social problems of maintaining control), the division of labor (to meet group and social problems of mastering nature), and patterns of guidance or educative responsibility (to meet group and social problems of socialization).[12]

The above statements are termed "assumptions" not only to indicate that they offer a base from which the present argument might begin, but also to emphasize that they are legitimate subjects for investigation. Taking them as given, however, specification is furthered by the following propositions (also subject to research question).

Specifying propositions about the positional relationship:

1a. The array of expectations shared by ego and alter is generally shared by all or most other members of the group;

2a. The expected behavior is primarily contractual, and is seen by ego and alter as such;

3a. Given some social stability, the array prescribes actions which serve to control tension between external agents and the group;

4a. The array may be supported by community sanction as well as by sanction of group members;

5a. The array allows behavioral influence based on coercion or manipulation;

6a. Positional relations *tend* to be stable and rigid.

Specifying propositions about the personal relationship:

1b. The array of shared expectations is unique to each dyad;

2b. The expected behavior may be, in some important parts, voluntary, and may be recognized as such by the recipients;

3b. The array prescribes actions (or types of action) which contribute to the individual needs of ego and alter, and only indirectly to the solution of group members' shared problems, or to control of tension between external agents and the group;

4b. The array receives little or no positive sanction external to the dyad.

5b. The array allows behavioral influence based only on cohesion;

6b. Personal relationships tend to be unstable and flexible.

Brief discussion of the six parallel elements may be useful.

1. Unlike personal expectations for behavior, to be effective positional expectations must be generally understood and accepted by all adult members of the family, and increasingly by children as they progress from toddlerhood through puberty. As in a bureaucracy, positional influences encourage rational behavior (i.e., consciously chosen as appropriate to the perceived situation and as compatible with established routine and principles). Personal expectations within a dyad, however, need not be perceived by any other than those involved; indeed, the family (seen, for illus-

tration, as a network of such personal dyad relationships) is often stronger if kept partly secret, for unnecessary jealousies and rivalries with other group members are avoided. The focus of personal expectations on individual needs, and of positional expectations on group and social needs, though not incompatible, indicate strong possibility of conflict between the two. Possibly, heavy emphasis on either personal or positional expectations will lead to a deterioration of the other to a minimal level, leaving the dyad vulnerable to stress.

2. Behavior rarely exceeds positional expectations, for they are seen as contractual; failure to honor the contract meets with censure and, possibly, retribution; each member is aware that what he does in excess of the contract must be identified as "special" (once again emphasizing that the excess is not truly voluntary); if it is not, the contract may be quickly altered to his disadvantage. By contrast, behavior which exceeds personal expectations is not unlikely, and, because evidences of love and acceptance are sought by all but the most coddled, the recipient of such behavior is likely to recognize it as voluntary.[13] Even when responding to those personal expectations which are explicit, the actor often is unable to identify any objective for his behavior: he acts only because he acts, as a lover loves because he loves. The actor's responses to positional expectations, by contrast, are easily and quickly rationalized and goals are often quite explicit; an individual meets positional expectations because he believes that to do so will result in more profit and less loss than would an alternate act.

3. Personal expectations prescribe behavior intended to support or enhance (or, depending on the relationship, to thwart or atrophy) the personality systems of the individual involved; intended effects on the group are indeterminate (hence, expectations may stimulate behavior which, though functional to personalities, is unintentionally dysfunctional to group and social systems). Positional expectations, by contrast, prescribe behavior intended as directly functional (or dysfunctional) to the family and social systems; intended effects on personalities are indeterminate.

4. Positional expectations may gain influence over an individual (1) through the individual's desire to share the family's material and power benefits, (2) through his desire to share the community status position of the family, and (3) from community sanctions. Personal expectations, however, have little influence over an individual unless he has an intrinsic desire to participate in a particular

relationship. Positional expectations, then, are easily manipulated or enforced compared to interpersonal expectations.

5. Personal expectations can consistently influence behavior only through mutual assent or attraction, while positional influence may also rest on the threat or imposition of force: If force were imposed through a personal relationship with any regularity, the relationship would likely transform into a more contractual, positional relationship. In short, personal influence may be characterized as "cohesive"; positional influence as either "cohesive" or "coercive."[14]

6. The foregoing distinction is crucial to an understanding of the influence of stress on a group. The general effect of stress on the highly cohesive group often is to reveal or emphasize to members that desired actions of other members are indeed voluntary. This recognition may lead to reciprocation and a strengthening of the relationship, as Gouldner argues with his concept, "reciprocity multiplier."[15]   Hence, strong cohesive influence implies regenerative powers under stress. Because of potential coercion, explicitness of shared expectations and the sanction received from community and family members, positional relationships tend to be stable and rigid, compared to personal relationships, which enjoy little external support. Under stress, the strong positional relationship exhibits efficiency and stability. Minor stresses have little effect on such a relationship, but when stress grows, the relationship becomes increasingly coercive, as members recognize fewer and fewer returns from their contract, and become less and less anxious to fulfill their part of the bargain. Then imposition of force may be necessary to assure continuation of the relationship.[16]

If these assumptions and propositions are valid, then *positional influence implies efficiency and stability, but lack of regenerative powers; personal influence implies regenerative powers but lack of stability.*

Family Types, by Behavioral Influence

In theory, a family might exist without either positional or personal influence, but in real life families, such pure relationships are highly improbable: Personal and positional expectations converge on the individual and his action is influenced by a blend of the two. The question is, just how much influence each has on family members.[17]

When personal and positional expectations are treated as independent variables, four ideal types of relationships may be identified: (a) strong in both personal and positional influence; (b) strong in personal but weak in positional influence; (c) strong in positional but weak in personal influence; (d) weak in both personal and positional influence. In each ideal type, qualitative differences in groups, dyads or families can be speculatively identified.

Type (A), The J.B.'s[18] *(Strong Personal and Positional Influence):* In this type, intimate contact is as important to most members as are the authority and status relationships among themselves and with the community. A group of this type tends to stability of organization, probable durability, efficiency of operation, a high degree of satisfaction felt by participants, marked conformity of members to group mores, sensitivity of individuals to the expectations of others, and marked ability of members to predict the behavior of others. Both personal and positional relationships, in times of non-stress, exert influence cohesively but, under stress, members may be effectively coerced to conformity. Families found in this quadrant are expected to be able to take heavy stresses without great injury.

Type (B), The Tyrones[19] *(Strong Personal, Weak Positional Influence):* This type is most easily seen in the relationship of man to mistress, in the relationship of some close siblings, in some dyads low in the ranks of highly structured organizations (such as buddies in the army), and in informal cliques and casual clubs. Families of this type – a subcategory of which might be the "pseudomutual" family[20] – tend to be unstable. Though they may be mutually satisfying, they possess little power to withstand stress of many sorts, for such relationships are based directly on the mutual satisfaction of the members. Under minor stress or gradually increasing major stress, the family may be strengthened, as voluntary actions stimulate reciprocation; unless hit by sudden severe stress, and/or unless coercion is frequent under stress, this type of family may be surprisingly regenerative. If marked coercion is applied, the relationship may alter markedly under stress; either the family will splinter, or it will change to a type C or D.

Type (C), The Albas[21] *(Strong Positional, Weak Personal Influence):* This type is perhaps the most dramatic, for it contains those families which seem to completely resist a certain amount of stress and then suddenly splinter. A family of this sort – a subcategory of which might be the "empty shell" family[22] – is typified by contractual behavior, in which services are exchanged on a profit-motive basis; by a tendency toward efficient operation of the family; by stability, as long as there is no choice of escape by members; by inflexibility. Relationships tend to be coercive; one or more individuals (e.g., the patriarchal father) dominate other members, and force them, perhaps subtly, to behave as the dominators desire. Internal or covert conflict may build intensely, as members fester in submissive roles. Such relationships are brittle, although the behavioral influence may be so strong that only a dramatic, massive blow can shatter them. When a blow of sufficient strength comes, however, there is little ability to bend with the stress. Then the family breaks.

Type (D), The Boyles[23] (Weak Personal and Positional Influence): Illustrated by many couples considering divorce, the club about to die, or the ineffectual "service organization," this type of relationship is also seen in the myriad casual acquaintances of an urban person's life. Families of this type can be hampered by instability, questionable durability and little satisfaction for members. A member who offers voluntary aid is likely to be frustrated, and a member who needs help may even refuse it. Such families are highly vulnerable to stress; they evidence neither cohesion nor effective coercion. Indeed, all that holds them together may be ennui, or community sanctions against disorganization.

Hypothetical Relation of Family Types to Stress Vulnerability

The preceding discussion identifies these general propositions:
General proposition 1: The J.B. family (Type A) tends to be vulnerable to almost all stress, and under stress may increase slightly in both personal and positional influence on members.
General proposition 2: The Tyrone family (Type B) tends to develop a crisis under light stresses, but (due to the reciprocity multiplier) will regenerate personal influence. Under heavier, but slowly increasing stresses, the family will tend to increase in positional influence (as expectations are better defined), thereby becoming more like the J.B. type; under other heavy stresses it will lose its personal influence, and become more like the Boyle type.
General proposition 3: The Alba family (Type C) tends to remain unchanged in response to all but extreme stresses; when the impact becomes great enough, however, the family tends to dramatically and perhaps violently change or splinter.

General proposition 4: The Boyle family (Type D) tends to become even less strong under almost any stress, if positional influence is particularly low. Under minor stresses, if positional influence is somewhat higher, some increase in both positional and personal influence may occur, due to reciprocation.

These propositions refer to families in which dyad relationships fall within one quadrant. Many families, however, contain an isolated member: influence over one person is markedly greater or lesser than over others. Though many combinations are possible, even in a three-person group or family, two are most probable.

(Ideal Type E) The Caulfields[24]: Parents are close, and share both personal and positional influence, but little influence impinges on the child because (E1) the child rejects or ignores the parents and/or (E2) the parents reject or neglect the child.[25]

General proposition 5: The Caulfield family (Type E) will react to stress as those of the Boyle (D) type, except that the parental dyad will be less vulnerable and better able to recover from crisis if it develops. Isolation or expulsion of the offending person will be less likely in condition E1, more likely in E2 and most likely when both conditions hold.

(Ideal Type F) The Morels[26]: The anxious parent, who works alone to keep the family intact.

General proposition 6: The Morel (Type F) family will react to stress as the Boyle (D) type, except that the family will be slightly less vulnerable to stress and somewhat better able to recover from crisis if it develops. Isolation or expulsion of the offender, if any, will be less likely than in type D.

Propositions Related to Types of Stress

These general propositions can only suggest the more specific hypotheses necessary for a particular research problem. They are especially inadequate in neglecting variations in severity and types of stress. The concept of stress is itself complex, but for demonstration it will suffice to identify three general types of stress: *demoralizing* (due to a sudden change of status upwards or downwards, loss of self or family conception, reputational damage); *depriving* (material loss, such as in disaster destruction); *organizational change* (loss or addition of members). (Combination of demoralizing and depriving will, in the following analysis, follow the same pattern of hypothetical relationship as does the single category, demoralizing.)

Not all stresses in any one category influence the family in the same way. An essential variable is the *placement of blame on a family member, or on an external source.* If blame for the demoralizing or depriving stress can be placed on a family member, the likelihood of crisis developing is increased, as internal dissension and dissatisfaction build; placement of blame on an individual member denies the family the stress-resisting mechanism of externalization. Demoralizing and depriving stresses can also be differentiated on the *severity of the stress,* which here will be simply identified as *moderate* or *extreme.*

Member loss or disability is also qualitatively different in effects on the family from member addition. Once again, the stress of either type may be considered either *moderate* (that is, the member lost or added held or demands a moderately important functional position in the family); or *extreme* (that is, the member lost or added held or demands a highly important functional position).

Table 1 presents the hypothesized vulnerability of each of the four family types to each of the 12 types of stress identified by these variables. (Vulnerability is indicated with three simple categories – Invulnerable; Vulnerable; Neither markedly Vulnerable nor Invulnerable.)

Even this simple categorization of family and stress types reveals marked hypothetical differences in vulnerability. It must be recognized, however, that the table is severely limited, neglecting many critical variables, including the *response of the community* to the family under stress. Four general types of response have been suggested (Therapeutic, Social Welfare, Repressive and Persecutive),[27] each of which would yield a table of hypotheses similar to the one presented. Community response might also introduce other stress; for example, if community disapproval focuses on *inherent qualities* (which can't be escaped, such as racial characteristics) strains on the family will likely differ from those experienced when disapproval focuses on *behavior* (which the family can escape, either by changing behavior, or rejecting the disapproved members).

Such limitations, however, should not obscure the intent of the foregoing effort: to explore a possible redirection of theories of family and group resources and stress vulnerability.[28]

Conclusion

If identification of vulnerability is one objective of family stress study, an essential requirement is adequate description of family

Table 1. Table of Hypotheses: Relation of Stress Type and Severity and of Family Type to Vulnerability

Stress Type & Severity	Family Type[1]			
	A	B	C	D
Demoralizing (or Dem. and Depriving)				
A. Member Blame				
(e.g., Delinquency, Illegitimate Pregnancy)				
1. Moderate Stress	I[2]	N	I	V
2. Extreme Stress	N	V	V	V
B. External Blame				
(e.g., Religious or Racial Persecution)				
1. Moderate Stress	I	N	I	N
2. Extreme Stress	I	N/V	V	V
Depriving				
A. Member Blame				
(e.g., Loss of Job)				
1. Moderate Stress	I	I	I	V
2. Extreme Stress	I/N	N	V	V
B. External Blame				
(e.g., Disaster Loss)				
1. Moderate Stress	I	I	I	N
2. Extreme Stress	I	I/N	N/V	V
Organizational Change				
A. Member Loss or Disability				
(e.g., Illness or Death of Member; War Separation)				
1. Moderately Important[3]	I	N	I	V
2. Extremely Inportant[4]	N	V	N/V	V
B. Member Addition				
(e.g., Grandparent moves in)				
1. Moderately Important	I	N.	I	N
2. Extremely Important	I	N	N/V	N/V

[1] Family types E and F are, hypothetically, similar to type D in vulnerability.
[2] I = Marked Invulnerability Hypothesized; N = Neither, or Slight Invulnerability or Vulnerability Hypothesized; V = Marked Vulnerability Hypothesized.
[3] Member lost or added took or demanded secondary role, or moderately important functional position.
[4] Member lost or added took or demanded a conflicting or central role, or an extremely important functional position.

behavior and relationships. This essay suggests that a key to a structural description lies in the concepts of *personal and positional influence*. The relationship of each of these variables to stress vulnerability is pursued, yielding this general, summary proposition: A family will better resist stress the more:

> Positional expectations are understood and accepted by all members; Positional expectations are explicit and supported by community sanction and by the sanction of family members; Personal expectations are exceeded, in voluntary actions intended to meet the perceived needs and desires of other members; These voluntary actions are recognized as such by the recipients.

Though the present report considers the usefulness of only one aspect of personal and positional relationships (their behavioral influence), and though it focuses on the limited substantive area of family vulnerability, it offers concepts and typologies which may prove useful as sensitizers for diverse problems, as in small group research, in investigations of the community, urbanization and mobility, and in analyses of organizations and bureaucracies.

FOOTNOTES

This investigation was supported in part by a grant from the National Institute of Mental Health. The author is indebted to R. S. Adams (Queenland University, Australia), Bruce Biddle (University of Missouri), Edward Z. Dager (Purdue University) and F. W. Mitchell (Otago University, New Zealand) for criticisms, and to Reuben Hill and Roy G. Francis (University of Minnesota) for stimulating discussions.

[1] The quest has won attention not only from family sociologists, but also from researchers and theorists in the field of social work, and, more recently, from medical researchers. For discussion and bibliography, see Donald A. Hansen and Reuben Hill, "Families Under Stress," *Handbook of Marriage and the Family,* Harold Christensen, ed. (Chicago: Rand McNally & Co., 1964).

[2] Robert C. Angell, *The Family Encounters the Depression* (New York: Charles Scribner's Sons, 1936). Family integration referred to bonds of coherence and unity in family life, such as common interests, affection and a sense of economic interdependence. Adaptability referred to the family's ability to meet obstacles and shift courses.

[3] Earl L. Koos, *Families in Trouble* (New York: King's Crown Press, 1946).

[4] Ruth Shonle Cavan and K. H. Ranck, *The Family and the Depression* (Chicago: University of Chicago Press, 1938).

[5] Hill demonstrated that Angell's concepts, however vague, had descriptive power, and he suggested that the two concepts be combined into one scale for "dynamic stability." Reuben Hill, *Families Under Stress* (New York: Harper & Bros., 1949).

[6] Simplistically, the single continuum suggests that in primary communities, the personal and positional relationships are so closely interrelated that they can hardly be differentiated, while in the contractual communities, the two are quite distinct. Such a representation only makes more imperative in complex societies the general argument of this article: That to move toward causal analysis, prediction, or penetrating description of human groupings, both positional and personal relationships must be examined.

[7] Talcott Parsons and Robert F. Bales, *Family Socialization and Interaction Process* (Glencoe, Illinois: The Free Press, 1955).

[8]For an illuminating discussion of this point see both Philip Slater, "Parental Role Differentiation," *American Journal of Sociology*, 62 (November 1961), pp. 296-308, and Bernard Bergen's "Comment" on Slater's article in the same issue, pp. 308-311.

[9]For example, Blood and Wolfe, as other family researchers, suggest that at least within certain Western communities the wife-dominated family is often less satisfying to its members, and perhaps more vulnerable to stress, than is either the husband-dominated or the synergetic. Robert Blood and Donald Wolfe, *Husbands and Wives: The Dynamics of Married Living* (Glencoe, Illinois: The Free Press, 1960).

[10]Parsons and Bales do not suggest that their instrumental-expressive axis should answer such behavioral questions, yet it is often so interpreted by others. Geismar, *et al.*, for example, have employed the concepts in characterizing multi-problem families. These researchers, however, do not really follow Parsons' emphasis on the functional characteristics of family positions, but rather look at role as activity. Hence they use Parsons to sensitize, but are, in fact, closer to the theory offered in the next section than to Parsons' germinal ideas. Ludwig L. Geismar, M. A. LaSorte and Beverly Ayres, "Measuring Family Disorganization," *Marriage and Family Living* (February 1962), pp. 51-56.

[11]Although relationships may also be characterized either by regularities of behavior or by functional characteristics, neither emphasizes the futurity of the relationship. A most essential element of "relationship" is the member's agreement that it will probably exist largely unchanged in the near future; expectation thus appears the essential element of definition. Research, on the other hand, may be more fruitful if focus is on regularities of behavior. The definitions presented would then require only minor, and obvious, modifications.

[12]The above assumptions imply that "expectation" involves not only prediction of another's actions (e.g., in situation X my husband will do Y); it might involve recognition of generally held prescriptions for persons in a specifiable position (e.g., in situation X, the rest of the family expects daddy to do P); it might also involve *individual* egoistic desire that one action or another is performed (e.g., in situation X, I'd like my wife to do A no matter what people say). That is, in considering expectations, we must attend to the prediction, the norm and the egoistic desire. *Generally, though both personal and positional relations require some predictability, personal also involves especially egoistic desires, while positional relationships involve especially*

normative prescriptions. This conception of expectation might lead to a number of promising hypotheses, such as: The greater the similarity of predicted, prescribed and desired behavior between family members the stronger the family (or, the greater the behavioral force); the more similar prediction and prescription, the stronger the positional relationship; the more similar prediction and desire the stronger the personal relationship. This line of theory, however, is not followed here.

[13]Of course, not all voluntary behavior is recognized as in excess of expectations; indeed this importance of recognition of voluntary behavior underlines the utility of occasional lapses in voluntary behavior. If the individual constantly hides his own disappointments and irritations behind a mask of smiling acceptance and uninterrupted voluntary offerings — as many parents do, to protect their children from the early recognition of the harshness of life — he may miss opportunities to strengthen personal relationships, and perhaps even positional. Yet even small children may be capable of weathering occasional lapses of parental nurture, which demonstrate that parental offerings are voluntary and hence to be valued. As moderate stresses may elicit such lapses, they may actually tend to strengthen relationships in some cases.

[14]Both personal and positional relationships, however, are vulnerable to manipulative force, or the ability to influence behavior without the actor's awareness of the influence. Nonetheless, it is usually the cohesion or coercion that make the individual vulnerable to the manipulation.

[15]Alvin Gouldner, "Organizational Analysis," in Robert K. Merton *et al.*, (eds.), *Sociology Today* (New York: Basic Books, 1959), esp. pp. 423-425.

[16]In general, the less the personal influence, the more likely are members to be attached to the family by coercion. If this coercion rests on strong positional influence (with little personal influence), family relationships will be brittle, for coercion tempers a relationship as heat tempers steel, both hardening it and robbing it of its capacity to bend — under great pressure it will likely break. Though coercion often engenders inflexibility, however, it does not necessarily render the family vulnerable to all stress; if accompanied with cohesion, it can offer stability and definiteness to a relationship. (Indeed, without some coercion, a positional relationship might be almost as fickle as the personal.)

[17]Francis makes a similar distinction on the community level, in discussion of influences on migration. Francis suggests that migration might be

affected by both personal and positional appeals or repulsions of the community migrated to or from. Roy G. Francis, "The Relation of Data to Theory," *Rural Sociology,* 22 (September 1957), pp. 258-266.

[18]Archibald MacLeish, *J. B.* Names, which refer to families under stress depicted in popular literature, are offered only to aid in description of the types.

[19]Eugene O'Neill, *Long Day's Journey into Night.*

[20]Lyman Wynne, Irving Ryckoff, Juliana Day and Stanley Hirch, "Pseudo-Mutuality in the Family Relations of Schizophrenics," *Psychiatry,* 21 (May 1958), pp. 205-220. Reprinted in Norman Bell and Ezra Vogel, (eds.), *A Modern Introduction to the Family* (New York: The Free Press of Glencoe, 1961).

[21]Garcia Lorca, *The House of Bernarda Alba.*

[22]William Goode, "Family Disorganization," Robert K. Merton and Robert A. Nisbet, (eds.), *Contemporary Social Problems* (New York: Harcourt, Brace & World, 1961), pp. 440-442.

[23]Sean O'Casey, *Juno and the Paycock.*

[24]J. D. Salinger, *Catcher in the Rye.*

[25]These possibilities are combined, for it is all but impossible to distinguish one from another in most cases; indeed, a good argument could be made that the two almost always go together.

[26]D. H. Lawrence, *Sons and Lovers.*

[27]Hansen and Hill, *op. cit.*

[28]Operational specification of the variables, personal and positional influence, is neither easy nor impossible. Obviously, the relationships cannot be measured directly, with current instruments in behavioral research. Nor can respondents be asked for their evaluation of the influence. Projective techniques offer one potential means by which specification might be sought. Other indirect evidence of the relationships may be found in the reported

behavior, for example, of communications and conflicts among family members. Positional communications (dealing with subjects directed toward efficiency or effectiveness of meeting family problems, and hence usually directed toward, or elicited by, action) may be compared with personal communications (subjects directed towards integration of the involved individuals or the enhancement of either, and usually not directed toward, nor elicited by, action). Similarly, conflict may be identified as either positional (rational, and involving structural rearrangement of activities of family members, probably leading to resentment which endures beyond resolution of argument; ego wounds, if any, likely to be short-lived), or personal (topics seemingly trivial or irrational leading to resentment that probably will not endure beyond resolution of argument; ego wounds may be long-lived). Other indications may be sought in techniques of meeting problems, in the autonomy of family members (physical autonomy compared with emotional autonomy) or in the interpersonal sensitivity of members to one another: intellectual insight (positional) or emotional empathy (personal).

Symbolic Interaction as an Approach to Family Research

Sheldon Stryker

An adequate account of any theory demands firstly that under-lying assumptions be identified and concepts clearly defined and secondly that organized collections of discrete propositions be formulated. In this review of Symbolic Interaction theory Sheldon Stryker addresses these demands in attending to questions that the theory suggests and answers that the theory is competent to offer. At the same time, Stryker acknowledges the contribution of an approach which combines Symbolic Interaction and other theoretical orientations to form a more inclusive theory.

Various commentators have stated that the ideas covered by the label symbolic interaction are part of the intellectual baggage of almost all who concern themselves with human behavior. On the other hand, persons identifying themselves as symbolic interactionists commonly hold that this theory suffers from general, albeit certainly undeserved, neglect. There is a good deal of validity in both views. Many social psychologists have made at least some of the ideas of symbolic interaction part of their theoretical equipment, whether or not they are aware of their debt. Yet the

Reprinted, with permission of the author and publisher, from *Marriage and Family Living*, 21 (May, 1959), pp. 111-119.

implications of this theoretical scheme are not always perceived and appreciated even by men calling themselves symbolic interactionists. The problem seems to be that at least some of the once-novel ideas of the theory have become for many simple commonplaces or platitudes, and like most platitudes, more likely to defeat thought than to stimulate it.

This paper is above all an attempt at a straightforward review of symbolic interaction theory. Its aim is to stimulate renewed interest in a simple, but relatively powerful, set of ideas which remain largely unexploited. It is perhaps particularly in the family field that these are open to exploitation.

The theory being dealt with has a venerable tradition, beginning at least as far back as Hegel. Modern formulations have their roots in American pragmatism, in the writings of Peirce and James. Suggestions contained here were elaborated and systematized by James Mark Baldwin, John Dewey, Charles Horton Cooley and, most important of all, George Herbert Mead. Specifically in the family field, Waller, Burgess, Hill, and Foote represent persons whose work, to important degree, stems from this framework.

There is no single orthodoxy which is symbolic interaction theory. There is certainly a hard core of agreement, and there are certainly important differences, among representatives of the position. Some see it as no more than a set of concepts serving to sensitize one to aspects of social life, some as a general theory of human behavior. The present discussion proceeds on another view, which sees the theory as addressing itself to a relatively modest series of questions.

Theory can be taken to mean a set of assumptions or postulates with which one approaches some part of the empirical world, a set of concepts in terms of which this part of the world is described, and a set of propositions, emerging from the assumptions and relating the concepts, about the way this part of the world "works" which are checked against observations of that world.

This presentation begins by noting briefly the general questions to which symbolic interaction theory is addressed, and turns successively to the assumptions underlying the theory, the concepts provided by the theory, and illustrative instances of the propositions which are the answers to its questions. It concludes by considering some of the implications of the theory for family research.

The Problems to Which the Theory is Addressed

As a social psychological theory, symbolic interaction addresses a set of interrelated questions, most of which take their place in the context of two major problems. The first is that of socialization: how the human organism acquires the ways of behaving, the values, norms and attitudes of the social units of which he is a part. The focus here is on development — that which happens over time to the human neophyte: the infant, the recruit entering the army, the student entering the university, the bride entering a new set of family relationships.

The twin of the problem of socialization is that of personality: the organization of persistent behavior patterns. Such organization cannot be assumed but must be demonstrated and accounted for. The task of a social psychology is to account for such organization insofar as it depends upon social relationships. It should be added that symbolic interaction addresses itself largely to the normal person — in the sense of the person without gross physical, physiological, or psychological defect.

To say that this position is oriented to the normal person is not to say that it is concerned only with personal organization for the theory seeks to explore personal disorganization as well. As a matter of fact, one of the strengths of this position is that it treats personal organization and personal disorganization as facets of the same problem, rather than different problems, and that it can provide answers to both without invoking principles lying outside its theoretical scheme.

These are the major problems which symbolic interaction theory seeks to resolve. They have been stated in general form, for more specific formulation depends on the assumptions and concepts with which the theory approaches the parts of the world in which it has interest.

Assumptions

The initial assumption is that, insofar as interests are social psychological, man must be studied on his own level. The position of symbolic interactionism is anti-reductionist; it argues that valid principles of human social psychological behavior cannot be derived from, or inferred from, the study of non-human forms. This assertion rests on the principle of emergence. Emergence suggests the existence of qualitative differences as well as quantita-

tive continuities among the precipitates of the evolutionary process. If man is qualitatively different in some respects from other
animal forms, it follows that principles derived from other forms
cannot completely account for his behavior. The task of at least
some social psychologists is to focus on that which is different in
man.

A second assumption is that the most fruitful approach to man's
social behavior is through an analysis of society. This assumption
involves no assertion of some metaphysical priority of society over
the individual. Social psychologists of one stripe have argued that
society is *the* ultimate reality; social psychologists of another
variety give ontological precedence to the individual, denying the
reality of society. Either position leads to confusion and contradiction. Symbolic interaction has not resolved the argument:
but it has bypassed it. It has done so by beginning its analyses
with the social act. Its basic unit of observation is interaction, and
from interaction both society and individual derive. It is worth
noting that this formulation permits an articulation between sociology and social psychology which alternative frameworks can
forge, if at all, only with great difficulty. Both begin with the same
"building bricks": social actions. Sociology builds in one direction
to the behavior of collectivities. Social psychology builds in another direction to the behavior of individuals. Those whose
problems bridge the two fields, as is true of many students of the
family, are provided with a framework facilitating movement
from one level to the other, allowing systematic transactions between the two levels.

A third assumption concerns the equipment with which the
newborn enters life. The human infant is, from this point of view,
neither social nor anti-social, but rather asocial. It has the potentialities for social development. It is an active organism, it has
"impulses," but these impulses are not channelized or directed
toward any specific ends. Original nature is amorphous and plastic; it lacks organization.

A last assumption is that the human being is actor as well as
reactor. The human being does not simply respond to stimuli
occurring outside himself. In fact, what is a stimulus depends on
the activity in which the organism is engaged: objects become
stimuli when they serve to link impulses with satisfactions. The
environment of the organism is a selected segment of the "real"
world, the selection occurring in the interests of behavior which

the human being himself has initiated. It is this assumption which leads to the fundamental methodological principle of symbolic interaction: the demand that the investigator see the world from the point of view of the subject of his investigation.

These seem to be the assumptions underlying symbolic interaction theory. Not an assumption, but closely related to those discussed, is a predilection on the part of adherents of this theory to stay close to the world of everyday experience. The viewpoint develops out of such experience, and it is with such experience that it seeks to deal.

Major Concepts

An assumption of this theory, again, is emergence. The principle emergent on the human level is language behavior. The initial concern in this review of concepts thus must be with language and its correlatives.

The starting point is with the *act*: behavior by an organism stemming from an impulse requiring some adjustment to appropriate objects in the external world. A *social act* is one in which the appropriate object is another individual. But another individual does not "stand still"; he, too, acts with reference to the first actor. Thus every social act implicates at least two individuals, each of whom takes the other into account in the processes of satisfying impulses. Since such acts occur over time, they have a history. This makes possible the appearance of *gestures,* defined as any part of the act which stands for, or comes to be a sign of, those parts of the act yet to occur. Thus, in responding to one another, individuals may be involved in what Mead called a "conversation of gestures": they may come to use early stages of one anothers' acts as indicators of later stages. Such gestures have meaning. Vocal sounds can serve as gestures, and they too may have meaning. The meaning of a gesture (an early stage of an act) is the behavior which follows it (the later stages of the act): meaning is, by definition, behavior. Some gestures have an additional property. They may mean the same thing, imply the same set of subsequent behaviors, to the organism which produces the gesture and that which perceives it. When this occurs, the gesture becomes a *significant symbol.* To illustrate: the cry of the infant may serve as a sign of hunger to the mother, and she responds by feeding the infant. The cry is a gesture whose meaning lies in the parental response. At a later stage, the child may call out "milk!" and, unless the appropriate parental response is made, protest vigorously. The work "milk" is here a significant symbol. Language, basically, is a system of significant symbols. This is equivalent to asserting that language is a system of shared meanings, and this in turn implies that language is a system of shared behavior. Communication between human beings presupposes these characteristics of language symbols.

Retreat is necessary before going forward. Symbols arise in the context of social acts, and they function in completing acts: they reflect the interests from which the acts stem. We respond to symbols as predicters of further behavior, our own as well as that of others. Since these symbols predict later behavior, they provide a basis for adjusting our activity before that later behavior has occurred. Thus symbols may be said to function in the context of the act in place of that which they symbolize, and may further be said to organize behavior with reference to that which is symbolized. Symbols intail a plan of action. To illustrate and summarize:

> Thus if one hunter shouts to another, "A duck!" the second hunter immediately looks into the air and makes appropriate preparations for shooting at a bird on the wing. If the first hunter shouts, "Rabbit!" his partner responds in a different manner. Language symbols do not merely stand for something else. They also indicate the significance of things for human behavior, and they organize behavior toward the thing symbolized.[1]

Some symbols represent generalizations of behavior toward objects; these are *categories*. To categorize is to apply a class term to a number of objects, to signify that a number of different things are, for certain purposes, to be treated as the same kind of thing. Classification or categorization is essential to activity, for life would be impossible if one were forced to respond to every object in the world as unique. Class terms, or categories, are of course symbols, and as such they share the characteristics of symbols. They have meaning, they are cues to behavior, and they organize behavior.

Humans respond to a classified world, one whose salient features are named and placed into categories indicating their significance for behavior. In short, humans do not respond to the environment as physically given, but to an environment as it is mediated through symbols — to a *symbolic environment*. Persons frequently enter situations in which their behavior is problematic. Before they can act, they must define the situation, that is, represent it to themselves in symbolic terms. The products of this defining behavior are termed "definitions of the situations."

A particularly important kind of category is that called "position."[2] Positions are socially recognized categories of actors, any general category serving to classify persons: father, sergeant, teacher are positions by this usage, as are playboy, intellectual, blacksheep.

The significance of such categories is that they serve to organize behavior toward persons so categorized. An equivalent assertion is that in attaching one of these position designations to a person we are led to expect certain behaviors from him and we behave toward him on the basis of these expectancies. To the expectations with regard to behavior attached to a position the term "role" is given. These expectations are social in the same sense symbolic behavior is always social: the ultimate meaning of the positions to which these expectations apply is shared behavior. They are social in another and most important sense, namely, that it is impossible to talk about *a* position without reference to some context of *other* positions: one cannot talk about the behavior of father except with reference to the positions of mother, child, and so on. Thus every position assumes some counter-position, and every role presumes some counter-role. To use the term "role" is necessarily to refer to an interpersonal relation.

The discussion of categories has been couched in terms of an actor responding to objects in the external world, including people, by classifying them in functionally relevant ways. Under certain circumstances, an actor may apply such categories to himself: he may respond to himself as he responds to other people, by naming, defining, classifying himself. To engage in this kind of behavior is to have a *self*. Self can be defined in various ways, each calling attention to slightly different aspects of the same activity. Mead defined the self as that which is an object to itself. Others have discussed the self as a set of responses of an organism serving to organize other responses of the same organism. It is useful in the present context to define the self in terms of categories one applies to himself, as a set of self-identifications.

However defined, self refers to activity, to reflexive activity, and not to an object, thing, or essence. It is a necessary concept, from the standpoint of the symbolic interactionist, but it is one fraught with the dangers of reification. As Robert W. White notes:[3]

> The necessity of using the concept of self does not confer the privilege of misusing it. As we use concepts in our thinking, they tend to get firmer and harder. Thought about fluid events tends to curdle and form solid clots. Before long we begin to think of the self as if it were a lump in the personality. It becomes a region, an institution, an entity. ... In the end the self is standing like a solid boulder of granite in the midst of personality, and one's thinking about it is as flexible as granite.

The self is defined in terms of socially recognized categories and their corresponding roles. Since these roles necessarily imply relationships to others, the self necessarily implies such relations. One's self is the way one describes to himself his relationships to others in a social process.

The discussion thus far has presumed but not made explicit the concept of "role-taking," or alternatively, "taking the role of the other." Role-taking refers to anticipating the responses of others implicated with one in some social act. The meaning of the concept can best be elucidated through illustration. Consider the classroom instructor who presents to his students an especially difficult conception. He perhaps finds that the words ordinarily used to cover the topic do not allow the discussion to proceed beyond the immediate issue. He then casts about for words which will allow him to clarify the conception, and so allow him to move beyond it to further materials. How shall he select such words? Presumably he will do so in terms of what he knows or guesses about the backgrounds or experiences of the students before him. He will, in other words, attempt to put himself in the place of the students; he will attempt to anticipate their responses to the words he will use. He takes the role of the other.

Role-taking may involve the anticipation of responses of some particular other. More frequently, it involves the anticipation of responses of what Mead called the "generalized other." To revert to the class-room illustration, the instructor must deal with the class not as discrete individuals but as an organized unit, the members of which can be expected to behave in differentiated yet related ways. To take the role of the generalized other is to see one's behavior as taking place in the context of a defined system of related roles. The concept of reference group, as it is currently used, represents partially a restatement and partially an extension of the generalized other concept.

In comparatively recent work, the concept of "significant other" has come into use. This concept represents the recognition that, in a fragmentated and differentiated world, not all the persons with whom one interacts have identical or even compatible perspectives; and that, therefore, in order for action to proceed, the individual must give greater weight or priority to the perspectives of certain others. To speak, then, of significant others is to say that given others occupy high rank on an "importance" continuum for a given individual.

One last set of concepts must be mentioned. Symbolic interaction makes unashamed use of "mental" concepts such as thinking, volition, and self-consciousness. The case can be put in stronger fashion; its judgment is that any scheme which rules out such concepts distorts the facts of human experience. However, its usage of these terms is not traditional. Where frequently these concepts are defined in such way as to place them outside the bounds of scientific discourse, symbolic interaction defines these terms behavioristically and, in so doing, permits their treatment within the conventions of scientific procedure. Thus, thinking is defined as the internalized manipulation of language symbols. Volition becomes the process of selecting among alternatives symbolically present in the experience of the individual. And self-consciousness is the activity of viewing oneself from the standpoint of others.

The Answers Provided by the Theory: Illustrative Cases

It will be impossible, given limitations of space, to do full justice to the complexities of the problems raised or the explanations provided by symbolic interaction theory; all that can be done is to review these in barest outline.

The problem of socialization has a number of interrelated facets, among them questions of how meanings are obtained by the human infant, how the self develops and is structured, and how thinking and objectivity arises in the course of experience.

The human infant, active but unorganized, is born into an ongoing set of social relationships. Such relationships are premised upon a set of shared meanings. The infant acts, but randomly: he thrashes his arms, he exercises his vocal cords. The adult responds to these actions, say the crying of the infant, by doing something to the infant – he feeds it, or changes it, or turns it over on its stomach. He will eventually find that response which will complete the act in a desired way, that is, stop the crying. There is in this situation an "impulsive" act which is, incipiently, a gesture, and there is incipient meaning as well. The incipient meaning is that part of the act supplied by the adult. In time, both the cry of the infant and the response of the adult become specialized; when this occurs, the cry is a gesture in the previously-defined sense. The significant point is that, since it is the adult who completes the act, it is he who supplies the meaning of the gesture. What kinds of completions will he supply? He is, of course, limited by the repertory of meanings available in the social unit of which he is a part. Further, the adult will have defined the situation, including his positional relationship to the infant, for example, that of father to son, and this definition will invoke the set of expected behaviors we call the role of the father. If the father is a middle class American, and if he takes the cry of the infant to mean that the infant is thirsty, his response will be to supply milk or water – but not wine or whiskey. The meanings attached to the gestures of the infant are social meanings, and they are supplied through his relationships with already socialized participants in an ongoing society.

The early activity of the child will include random vocalization. Eventually, too, he will imitate sounds others make. Others respond to the initially random vocalization by selecting out particular sounds and responding to these. They respond to the imitated sounds as well by acts which contain the adult meanings of these sounds. For the child, the correspondence between sound and meaning will be initially vague, but in the process of interaction over time the correspondence will become more pronounced. So, for example, the child may use the sound "ba" to refer to any approximately round object and, having played this game with daddy, may be led to roll any such object – ball, orange, egg – around the floor. The response of parent to the rolling of an egg – especially an uncooked one – will soon make clear that an egg is not a "ba" and thus is not to be rolled on the floor. In the course of time, child and parent will come to agree on what is and is not a ball, and thus a significant symbol will have come into existence. A sound, initially meaningless to the child, comes to mean for the child what is already means for the adult.

The "self" comes into existence in the same way. Just as the sound "ba" took on meaning through the responses of others, so too the human organism as an object takes on meaning through the behavior of those who respond to that organism. We come to know what we are through others' responses to us. Others supply us with a name, and they provide the meaning attached to that symbol. They categorize us in particular ways — as an infant, as a boy, et cetera. On the basis of such categorization, they expect particular behaviors from us; on the basis of these expectations, they act toward us. The manner in which they act towards us defines our "self," we come to categorize ourselves as they categorize us. and we act in ways appropriate to their expectations.

The evolution of the self is, of course, gradual; moreover, it is continual. This development is one of increasing complexity, in a sense, for as the child moves into the social world he comes into contact with a variety of persons in a variety of self-relevant situations. He comes, or may come, into contact with differing expectations concerning his behavior, and differing identities on which these expectations are based. Thus he has, through the role-taking process, a variety of perspectives from which to view and evaluate his own behavior, and he can act with reference to self as well as with reference to others. In short, the socialization process as described makes possible the appearance of objectivity. Furthermore, since these processes may be internalized through the use of language symbols, it also makes possible the appearance of self-control.

The individual, at the same time and through time as well, occupies a variety of positions in sets of social relationships. If he responded in each of these in terms of unique sets of role-expectations and self-definitions, his behavior would be discontinuous. Usually, however, there is continuity and organization among the behaviors of a given individual. The question is how such personal organization can be accounted for. The basic answer provided by symbolic interaction theory uses the concepts of self, role, and definition of the situation. On entering an ongoing social situation, one responds to that situation by defining it. This definition includes the assignment of positions to others, and thus the setting up of expectations concerning their behavior. It, further, includes an assessment of self, that is, the assignment of positional identities to oneself. Others in the situation are, of course, engaged in the same kind of activity. The behavior that ensues is a function of such definitions. A crucial question thus becomes one of the congruence of definitions, situation, role and self, of the interacting persons. Congruence permits efficient, organized behavior. Expanding this, again noting that the individual moves through a variety of interpersonal situations, the congruence of definitions, and so the behavioral expectations these imply, is fundamental to continuity of behavior. Personal organization is thus seen as a function, not simply of that which the individual carries around with him, but of the relationship between that which he carries with him – in the form of self-concepts – and the situations in which he interacts with others as these are mediated symbolically.

When one asks what kinds of social conditions foster or permit such congruence, the generalized answer is that when meanings are widely shared in a society, or among those persons within a society with whom one actually interacts, congruence is likely.

What happens when meanings are diverse among the others with whom one interacts? Reversing the above process, but maintaining the same explanatory principle, it may be said that incongruities in definition and so incongruities in expectations will result, and that personal disorganization is the outcome. A number of possible types of incongruity may be suggested: conflicts or lack of coordination between self concepts and the expectations of others; conflicts among aspects of self called into play in the same situation; the temporal succession of expectations which do not articulate, and so on.

It may be worthwhile to take one type of incongruity, say lack of coordination between self concepts and expectations of others, and note more closely its relevance to personal disorganization. At the same time, the question can be raised: under what circumstances do identities change? Suppose one enters a situation with a set of self identifications which include the name "professor," and suppose he defines the situation – for example, as a classroom – in such a way that this identity is appropriate. He will then presumably conduct himself in ways indicated by that identity. He speaks in judicious, measured tones, he adopts a knowledgeable air, and so on. He can behave this way only so long as his audience accepts this definition of himself and so responds in such ways as validate his behavior, by taking notes, by concentrating attention upon him, by directing questions at him. Suppose, however, the audience fails to accept this definition; they think him a fool rather than a professor (although perhaps the two are not completely incompatible). They disregard what he is saying, they challenge his competency, they pay more attention to friends in class than they do to him. In short, they fail to validate his self identification. How will he behave? It is highly probable that behaviors ordinarily inappropriate to the classroom will ensue. He will likely lose his judicious tones and become emotional. He is likely to act confused, uncertain, embarrassed, ambivalent. At the same time, since persons typically have considerable investment in identities, he very probably will attempt to defend himself. He may do so by redoubling his efforts to act the complete professor, by dismissing the incident as a joke, by regarding the audience as consisting of morons. But if, persistently, his identity as professor fails to be validated by others, he cannot retain that identity. Others validate identities by behaving in appropriate ways, ways which provide cues on the basis of which further performance in terms of the identity is possible. If these cues are not provided, then such performance is no longer possible, and the identity will fade.

Implications for Family Research

Rather than attempt to detail implications of symbolic interaction for family research, a few brief indications of researchable questions stimulated by this theory will be presented.

One question, or set of questions, has to do with differential commitment to family identities. It is obvious, for example, that not all persons who are objectively fathers are equally committed to such identity. What accounts for such differentials, for the fact that for one man identity as father supersedes all other ways in which he sees himself, while for another the father identity is relatively low on the self totem pole? The theory suggests that this will be a function of the extent to which one is defined by significant others as a father. It also suggests that the degree of congruence of definitions by significant others will be of import. Borrowing a phrase from studies of political behavior, could the presence or absence of "cross-pressures" deriving from others with whom one interacts account for this differential commitment, at least in some degree?

Perhaps of greater significance to students of the family is the question of the consequences of differential commitment to familial identities. Foote[4] has contended that differences in motivation of role performances may fruitfully be seen in these terms. Political apathy seems to be in good part a consequence of lack of commitment to a clear-cut political identity; it seems reasonable to suspect that apathetic familial behavior has a similar source. It is also quite possible that, for example, the prediction of divorce would be on sounder ground when questions dealing with commitment to family identities are included in batteries of predictive items.

Closely related to these questions is another set. Are there extra-familial identities which are in varying degree compatible with familial identities? What are the effects of identities deriving from diverse spheres of activity on one another, and on behavior in these diverse spheres? Someone has suggested that the deviant behavior of a man in a work situation which appears to be idiosyncratic when viewed in this limited context, may rather be a consequence of his position and role within his family. That is, for example, the rate-buster on the job may not be acting "selfishly," but may simply be acting in accord with his conception of self as family breadwinner. It is certain that one's extra-familial identities operate within the family situation. Which identities so operate, their specific mode of articulation with family identities, and their consequences for family relationships are questions of obvious importance.

Another set of questions can be phrased around the relationship of crises to identity. Crises will always threaten identifications, for the latter depend on stable activities of others with reference to oneself; and crises are likely to be important in the process by which identities change. It may be that adaptation in crisis situations is a function of the ease with which identities alter; adaptation to the death of a spouse, for example, might profitably be approached in these terms. Yet that ease with which identities are altered is not always functional is suggested by Hill's[5] research on war separation and return; in such multi-phased crises it may be that, at least for some, easy alteration of identity at one point creates problems at still another point. Such questions, too, are worth the research energies of students of the family.

A different kind of question suggested by the theory may be prefaced by relating an overheard conversation. A young lady was speaking of her relationships with her boy friend. The two were, apparently sufficiently involved to talk about marriage and their future. But, it seems, they argued when they engaged in such talk. The basis for the argument was this: she labelled such talks "plans," he called them "dreams," and each bridled at the other's conception of their conversations. Nonsense? Arguing over mere words? Not when one has in mind the significance of defining behavior and the consequences of classification. Plan implies a greater stake in a projected course of action than does dream. Dreams suggest freedom of action, plans a commitment. Suggested here is the potential fertility of studying the courtship process, marital role relationships, parent-child relationships, and so on, in terms of role-linked symbolic behavior: for example, the investigation of possible sex-linked differences in defining family situations, and the consequences of such differential definitions as may exist.

Finally, the theory suggests that studies focusing on the role-taking process may be rewarding. Role-taking is a variable; anticipation of the responses of others is not always correct. Foote[6] and his associates have conducted an impressive series of studies designed to uncover means by which role-taking ability can be improved, on the assumption that role-taking ability, or empathy in their language, is one aspect of interpersonal competence. While this may well be justified, some research[7] indicates that if one expects that interpersonal adjustment will always result from accurate role-taking, he is likely to be disappointed. But this still leaves open questions of the specific consequences, under varying conditions, of role-taking accuracy. Are the consequences the same, for example, when husband and wife share the same value framework and when they do not? Might it not be that accurate role-taking differs in its consequences as role relationships change, when a couple moves through the sequential stages of courtship, early marital experience, and later family experience? These, too, are questions worth raising and answering.

One final remark: symbolic interaction is not a general theory of human behavior. That is, it does not incorporate all the variables presumably important in accounting for human behavior, but rather selects from these a few for concentrated attention. Thus it would not do to deny the contributions of alternative theoretical views from which human behavior can be approached. It is contended, however, that alternative views can be enriched by taking into account the set of ideas which have been developed.

FOOTNOTES

A slightly amended version of a paper presented to the 21st Groves Conference on Marriage and the Family, Washington, D. C., April 15, 1958.

[1] Alfred R. Lindesmith and Anselm L. Strauss, *Social Psychology*, New York: Dryden Press, 1956, p. 63.

[2] Others have used the term "status" here. I prefer "position" in order to avoid the hierarchical implications of status. Positions may certainly be hierarchized, but hierarchy and position are conceptually distinct and it is important to distinguish between them.

[3] Robert W. White, *The Abnormal Personality*, New York: Ronald Press, 1948, p. 140.

[4] Nelson N. Foote, "Identification as the Basis for a Theory of Motivation," *American Sociological Review*, 16 (February, 1951), pp. 14-21.

[5] Reuben Hill, *Families Under Stress*, New York: Harpers, 1949.

[6] Nelson N. Foote, Editor, *Developing Interpersonal Competence: A Manual of Procedures for Family Life Educators*, unpublished manuscript.

[7] See, for example, Sheldon Stryker, "Role-Taking Accuracy and Adjustment," *Sociometry*, 20 (December, 1957), pp. 286-296.

Toward a Theory
of Family Development

Roy Rodgers

A necessary step towards meeting the challenge of developing wide-ranging family theory is the construction of a conceptual framework capable of combining compatible concepts abstracted from a variety of conceptual traditions. Roy Rodgers' proposals establish the potential of the developmental framework for the formulation of propositions about an extensive range of family situations and conditions. Rodgers outlines some of the advantages of an eclectic approach while urging caution over methodological and theoretical problems yet to be solved.

The term "theory" has been used in a variety of ways in the field of sociology, as have the terms "conceptual approach" and "conceptual framework." Merton[1] identifies six types of sociological work which are often labeled "theory" in a somewhat undifferentiated manner. Zetterberg[2] also sees the term used with several different meanings. The consensus of these writers appears to be that "theory" is most legitimately used to mean a set of interrelated propositions which are empirically verifiable, universally valid, and parsimonious in their explanation of phenomena.[3]

Reprinted, with permission of the author and publisher from *Journal of Marriage and the Family*, 26 (August 1964), pp. 262-270.

On the other hand, a "conceptual framework" consists, according to Hill and Hansen, of "clusters of interrelated but not necessarily interdefined concepts generally applicable" to a particular area of sociological interest. They view a theory as "a set of interrelated concepts, a set of underlying and unifying assumptions, and a set of postulates."[4] Hill and Hansen's conceptual framework is similar to Zetterberg's "taxonomy," which he states is "an orderly schema for the classification and description of anything social."[5]

Finally, while none of the writers cited deals explicitly with the term, a "conceptual approach" might be viewed as a set of concepts which are rather loosely tied together and which are not in any definite sense interrelated and interdefined.[6] While in a conceptual approach there is some attempt to consider a problem at a level of abstraction above the purely descriptive, the approach does not achieve the tight interrelatedness of a framework nor the universal validity and parsimony of a theory.

The objective of this paper is to consider an area in the sociology of the family which might best be called an approach in its present state and to propose a conceptual framework for analysis of this area. While the ultimate goal is the development of a theory, the working out of a conceptual framework appears to be the most fruitful next step toward this goal.

Family Development as an Approach

The history of the developmental approach in family sociology has been traced in considerable detail elsewhere.[7] The basic characteristics of the approach are described by Hill and Hansen as follows:

> The developmental approach is not at this moment a precisely unique framework but is really an attempt to transcend the boundaries of several approaches through incorporation of their compatible sections into one unified scheme. From rural sociologists it borrowed the concept of stages of the family life cycle. From child psychologists and human development specialists came the concepts of developmental needs and tasks. From the sociologists engaged in work in the professions it incorporated the concept of the family as a convergence of intercontingent careers. From the structure-function and interactional approaches were borrowed the concepts of age and sex roles, plurality patterns, functional prerequisites, and the many concepts associated with the family as a system of interacting actors.[8]

The unique contribution of the family development approach to family theory has been its attempt to deal with the dimension of time in the analysis of the family as a small group association. That is, much of the previous work which deals with change in the family over time has tended to be macroanalytic in character. The result has been a focus on broad institutional patterns with a consequent loss of almost all analysis of the change in the dynamics of family interaction. Microanalytic studies of family dynamics, on the other hand, have tended to be restricted to a static view of the family at one point in time or, at the most, to a comparison of two points in time which are not too far removed from one another. The major interest of family development has been the attempt at the analysis of the dynamic changes in the nuclear family from its establishment at marriage to its dissolution in death, separation, or divorce. By utilizing the basic ideas cited in the quotation above, family development attempts to account for changes in the societal-institutional, associational-interactional, and individual-personality variables over the entire career of the family system. In this attempt, the approach has encountered a number of theoretical and methodological problems which remain to be solved.

At the heart of the family development approach has been the idea of "stages" of the family life cycle. Over the years, a variety of life cycle stage schema have been suggested, each with its strengths and weaknesses.[9] The rationale behind most of these systems has been that changes in family internal dynamics are primarily related to the changing membership composition of the family over time. The basic method of determining the individual stages, therefore, has involved selecting various patterns of numbers, age, or sex (or combinations of these) which reflected differing qualities of internal interaction. Since the potential number of such combinations is almost infinite, some criterion for the identification of the most significant patterns is demanded. The choices made by the several developers of stage schema appear at times to be somewhat arbitrary. The contention of this paper is that the primary reason for this apparent arbitrariness lies in the lack of an explicit conceptual framework to serve as a guide in the construction of stages. It must be recognized that any such set of stages is essentially a system of categories for the analysis of the continually changing patterns of interaction in the family system. The stages are in no sense real entities, though some of the literature in the area would appear to approach the point of reification. It is for this reason that the term family life cycle "category" is preferred to the term "stage" and will be used in the subsequent discussion.[10] In summary, then, a conceptual framework for family development investigations should lead to a better understanding of the phenomena being described in the various life cycle category schemes and, ultimately, should lead to some theory of family development.

Again, Zetterberg can be of help in this task. He has laid out several steps which he states lead to "axiomatic" theory.[11] These can be summarized into four general processes.

1. List a series of primitive terms or basic concepts.
2. Define the derived concepts obtained from the combinations of the basic concepts. The basic and derived concepts form the nominal definitions of the theory.
3. Formulate hypotheses of the theory using no other concepts than the nominal definitions derived above.
4. Select and empirically test a number of propositions based upon the derived hypotheses. Verification of these propositions leads to verification of the hypotheses and, ultimately, of the theory.

First, then, is the list of the basic concepts.

Basic Concepts[12]

Family. In family development literature, the definition of the family is clearly related to the work of Ernest W. Burgess and Reuben Hill. Hill revised Burgess's original discussion of the family as a "unity of interacting personalities"[13] by adding the idea of the family as a "closed system."[14] This conceptualization has been further revised in Hill's thinking and in the literature of family development until at this point the family is viewed as a *semi-closed system of interacting personalities.* This definition captures the following aspects of family dynamics: (1) the family is not entirely independent of other social systems, neither is it wholly dependent, thus it is a *semi*-closed system; (2) the family as a small group system is interrelated in such a manner that change does not occur in one part without a series of resultant changes in other parts; (3) the family is composed of dynamic persons who are both group members and individuals, and, therefore, changes in both group relationships and individual personality factors must be taken into account. This conceptualization, then, takes cognizance of both the internal and external structure of the system and the dynamic behavioral aspects of members. Thus, it joins the social system approach with the closely allied ideas of structure-function theory and of social-psychological analysis of group life.

At the same time, it must be recognized that this definition does not express the unique character of the family in the societal context as opposed to other groups. Attempts at defining the family in terms of its unique structure and functions are numerous, but in terms of universal applicability (which is necessary if a general theory of the family is to be derived), these attempts have generally fallen short of the mark. Such a definition must be sufficiently broad to avoid the omission of certain kinds of family forms and sufficiently specific to state what is the precise character of the group being analyzed. The presentation of the following suggested addition to the above definition is not to be taken as an implication that this problem has been solved. It is presented, rather, with the hope that it will lead to such a solution.

The definition of the family proposed is, "The family is a semi-closed system of interacting personalities which is composed of interrelated positions and roles defined by the society of which it is a part as unique to that system." This definition adds to the above-listed characteristics the notion that every society has at least one group in which it specifies certain positions and roles as related in a way which no other group in the society possesses. In some societies, it may be that this includes reproduction and socialization of new members. In others, this may not be the case. The definition does not specify the content of the positions and roles, but only the existence of such a structure of unique positions and roles. In the set of concepts presented below, it will be seen that the framework remains content free, specifying only the structure of the system.

Position. Gross and others have defined a position as a "location of an actor or class of actors in a system of social relationships."[15] Position thus deals with the structure of a system, defining the system in terms of interrelated positions.

Norm. A norm is "a patterned or commonly held behavior expectation. A learned response, held in common by members of a group" as defined by Bates.[16] Norms, thus, are part of the structure of a group.

Role. Again following Bates, roles are "a part of a social position consisting of a more or less integrated or related sub-set of social norms which is distinguishable from other sets of norms forming the same position."[17] Bates emphasizes that this definition places the concept in the area of analysis of group structure rather than in group dynamics or interaction. In discussing the relationships between the three structural concepts of position, role, and norm, he points up certain significant characteristics which are relevant to the present discussion. These include: (1) in any given culture there are a limited number of roles making up a limited number of positions; (2) each position contains dominant and recessive roles; (3) roles are always paired with a reciprocal role of another position; (4) in a pair of related positions, there is always at least one pair of reciprocal roles composed of reciprocal norms requiring certain kinds of expected behavior.[18] Applying these characteristics to the family, a limited number of positions appears within the family system of any culture. Assuming an American nuclear family, these could be listed as husband-father, wife-mother, son-brother, and daughter-sister. Each of these positions contains a number of dominant and recessive roles which are broadly defined by the culture in terms of norms. Furthermore, each of the roles of these positions is related reciprocally to at least one role in each of the other positions of the system.

Role Behavior. Role is a structural concept encompassing the expected behavior of an actor. Since individual behavior rarely follows precisely the expectations of the group, a concept is necessary to express the manner in which an individual meets group expectations. Gross *et al.* use the concept role behavior to mean "An actual performance of an incumbent of a position which can be referred to an expectation for an incumbent of that position."[19] This concept, then, is the behavioral counterpart of the structural concept of role.

Sanction. Groups will tolerate, within limits, deviate role behavior. Beyond these limits, group members respond with role behavior designed to achieve closer conformity to the group-defined role. By the same token, groups will respond positively to role behavior which meets the group expectations. According to Gross *et al.,* "A sanction is a role behavior the primary significance of which is gratificational-deprivational."[20]   As a matter of fact, there are clearly defined norms which demand certain types of gratificational or deprivational role behavior in response to approved or disapproved role behavior on the part of the incumbent of a reciprocal role in the system.

The concepts presented thus far may be utilized to analyze the family at one point in time. They are the basic concepts. It will be recalled, however, that the family development approach attempts to take account of family change through time. The concepts that follow attempt to cope with this problem. These are all derived from the basic concepts.

Derived Concepts

Role Sequence. Irwin Deutscher has pointed out that

> As an individual moves through the life cycle he is called upon to play a series of roles *sequentially,* in distinction from the many roles he may play *concurrently* at any one period of his life. In the family cycle, the young childless couple is not required to play the same roles as they will be when they have children, and the postparental couple, childless again and older, presumably is faced with role expectations which are different from those of preceding stages of the cycle.[21]

Thus, it may be concluded that within any social position, the norms associated with a particular role change over time. For analytical purposes, each time a change takes place in the normative content of a role, a new role exists. These roles, when linked together longitudinally, may be termed a role sequence. To illustrate, the norms defining the roles of "father" are not the same vis-à-vis the reciprocal roles of "infant" as they are vis-à-vis the "pre-school child" or the "teen-age child." While the occupant is still "father," the expectations of the group for the occupant of the role change, so that an analysis of these changes would reveal a sequence of roles of slightly, sometimes radically, different normative content over time.

Role Cluster. As has been stated, a position is the sum total of roles occupied by an actor in a group. To distinguish between the general concept of position which exists in a group over time and the specific role content of a position at a specific point in time, the concept *role cluster* is used. Thus, a set of concurrent roles which are the content of a position at any one point in time is a role cluster.[22] This content will vary, with some roles being added and others removed from the position.

Role Complex. The family is a *system* of positions. At any point in time, this system is composed of several role clusters possessed by the actors in the system. Therefore, two or more sets of role clusters held concurrently by two or more actors or occupants of positions in an interlocking system at one point in time may be called a role complex.[23]

Positional Career. Bernard Farber uses the term "career" to refer to the "course of a person's life."[24] Relating this to what has been presented above, it can be seen that a position, when viewed over time, consists of a set of role clusters in sequence. This sequential set of role clusters of a specific position in a system may be called a positional career.[25]

Family Career. The family system at a single point in time, it has been stated, may be seen as a set of role clusters called a role complex. The sequential linking of role complexes over the life history of the family system may be conceptualized as a family career.[26] The family career concept is at a high level of generality and abstraction, including as it does all of the concepts presented above. This fact leads to the contention that the conceptual framework level, as opposed to the conceptual approach level, has been reached. If this is the case, a detailed analysis of the proposed framework should yield some theoretical and methodological insights into the problem of family life cycle analysis.

The Framework

Figures 1, 2, and 3 are provided as aids to the discussion to follow.[27] Figure 1 shows the position composed of roles which are further composed of a set of norms. The behavioral expression of role, role behavior, and the special form of role behavior of a gratificational-deprivational nature, sanction, are not shown since they relate to the functioning of the group rather than to its structure. Figure 2 presents the longitudinal character of the single position in its depiction of the longitudinal aspect of a single role, the role sequence, and the longitudinal aspect of a role cluster, the positional career. Finally, Figure 3 brings two positions together in a role complex at a single point in time, and additional positions appear as time progresses, so that ultimately the longitudinal expression of the role complex is seen in the

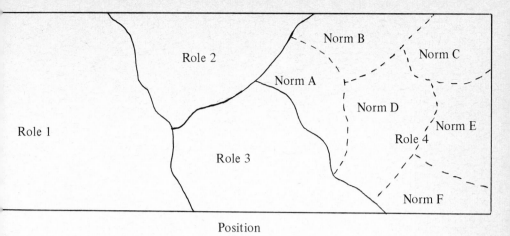

Position

Fig. 1. Relationship of Position, Role, and Norm
(After Bates, "Position, Role, and Status: A Reformulation of Concepts,"
Social Forces, 34 (May 1956), 313-321.)

family career. For clarity, the reciprocal relationships between the roles of the positions which make up the role complexes are not shown.

Functional Prerequisites and the Family System. Social system theory has paid attention to the question of the basic conditions under which a social system exists. Bennett and Tumin present six functional prerequisites necessary for the continuance of any social group: (1) maintenance of biological functioning of group members, (2) reproduction of new group members, (3) socialization of new members, (4) production and distribution of goods and services, (5) maintenance of internal and external order, and (6) maintenance of meaning and motivation for group activity.[28] In the framework developed here, the family system is seen as organized in such a way as to insure that these basic conditions are met, though this is not the only meaning of family organization. Thus, the family system contains within it specific roles defined in such a manner that the system will continue to exist. It must be emphasized that these functions refer to the continuance of the family system *as a system* and not necessarily to the functions which a given society may allocate to the family system for the continuance of the society as a whole. That is, while a given society may allocate the function of socialization primarily to the educational system in order to maintain the societal existence, the family system must still carry out a basic socialization process in order to continue as a system as well. Similarly, while most societies look to the family system for the reproduction function, the family would still be required to carry out reproduction in some form for its continuance even if the society at large assigned the basic reproductive function to some other system. The concern, therefore, is with the functional prerequisites as carried out within the family system, rather than with the particular functions which the family may carry out for the larger society.

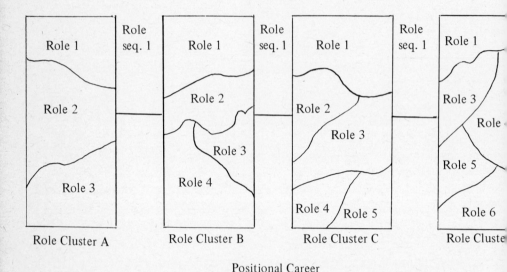

Positional Career

Figure 2. Role Sequence, Role Cluster, and Positional Career

Origin of Normative Pressures. The norms of the family system may be seen as arising from three chief sources: (1) the society of which the system is a part, (2) the family group, and (3) the individual within the group. Societal norms impinge on the family *as a group* and on individual members within the family group. Since all societies have expectations concerning what the family group ought to do, in a basic sense these norms are designed to carry out the functional prerequisites mentioned above. Thus specific roles, which must be carried on by the occupants of specific positions in the family system, are clearly defined and applicable to all families in a society. At the same time, it has been noted that some roles are dominant or obligatory in a position, while others are recessive or discretionary. It is generally obligatory in the United States society, for example, that the male adult head of the family

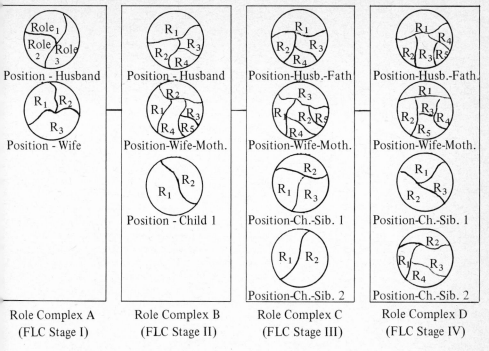

Role Complex A	Role Complex B	Role Complex C	Role Complex D
(FLC Stage I)	(FLC Stage II)	(FLC Stage III)	(FLC Stage IV)

Figure 3. The Family Career

occupy the role of bread-winner, but this same role may be discretionary or obligatory for the adult female under specified circumstances.

A second set of societal norms which apply to positions is related to the age and sex of the occupants of these positions. That is, certain age- and sex-specific roles apply broadly in every society. Again, in American society, an old woman would not be expected to perform the latest dance craze or dress as a teen-ager. As above, there are both obligatory and discretionary age and sex roles.

Family norms are directed internally toward individual family members and externally toward occupants of positions in other social systems. The family norms which define the expected behavior of members of the family will follow the general societal norms to a great extent but will also have unique qualities present only within that family system. The normative pressures which the family system places upon other systems of the society are many and complex. This transactional behavior of families has

Toward a Theory of Family Development   151

yet to be adequately analyzed at the role complex level in either cross-sectional or longitudinal form.

Finally, the individual family member is a source of normative pressures. While individual expectations may not be properly called norms, they may gain group acceptance and thus become norms. To the extent that an individual's role behavior is able to influence other members to place similar expectations upon the occupant of a particular position with respect to a particular role, he may be the source of definition and redefinition of roles in the family system. In like manner, the individual, either as an individual *per se* or as a representative of the family system, also occupies positions in other social systems of the society which have implications for the definitions of norms in those systems.

Origin of Change in the Family System. The groundwork for identifying the sources of change in the family system has been laid in the discussion immediately above. Throughout the career of a family, the changes which occur in the system arise from three principal sources: (1) the physical maturation of the individual; (2) the behavioral expectations of the other family members and of the larger society; and (3) the desires, aspirations, and values of the emerging personality.[29]

As the individual grows older, the societal and family age and sex norms relevant to his roles change. At the same time, the abilities of the individual — motor, intellectual, and social — also change. Therefore, out of the basic fact of maturation of the individual, some changes in roles take place.

Secondly, as time moves on, situations within the family and in the society at large change. These situations may be historical, as a result of cultural inventions, cultural diffusion, or any number of other influences. In addition, the number and sex of members in the system fluctuate and, therefore, more or fewer positions are occupied. These changes bring about redefinitions of situations within and outside the family and, concomitantly, changing role patterns.

Finally, from within the individual (and aside from his physical growth) there develops a kind of personal "life view" which will bring pressure for change in systemic organization. The extent to which these individual aspects are the result of the social-cultural situation in which the individual is placed or the result of basic biological heritage has been the basis of many "nature-nurture" debates. Suffice it to say here that the family development approach, and this conceptual framework, makes explicit recognition that this source of change in the family system is one of more than passing interest for analytical investigation.

The set of concepts developed above, when placed in the setting of the functional prerequisites, the specification of the origins of normative pressures, and the accounting for changes which occur in the family system, provide a framework which should allow for the development of a theory of family development. This paper, then, has attempted to carry out only the first two steps of Zetterberg's outline for the development of "axiomatic theory," i.e., the listing of the basic concepts and the definition of the derived concepts. Further specification and elaboration of these will doubtless be found necessary as the formulation of hypotheses, postulates, and theorems from the framework and the selection and testing of propositions are undertaken in order to validate the theory. While this is not the goal of the present paper, some of the theoretical and methodological implications of the framework may be mentioned.

Implications of the Framework

The major implication of the development of such a conceptual framework is, of course, the opening up of the possibility of moving from mere description to analysis, verification, and, ultimately, explanation. A number of areas in which "miniature theories" may be developed in the building of a more general theory come to mind. For example, the problem of crisis proneness of families may be further illuminated through the development and testing of a set of hypotheses derived from the framework. In a similar way, a set of verified generalizations may be accumulated concerning the relationship of the developmental state of a family to its ability to make decisions which will achieve the goals viewed as desirable by the members. There are, in fact, few areas which have been of concern to family sociologists in the past which may not be subjected to test within this framework.

A somewhat subtle bias which has been implicit in much of the previous work in family development is removed by the use of the framework. The tendency has been to treat families in various kinds of categories as essentially different from one another and noncomparable. Thus, subcultural and cross-cultural analyses have been virtually ignored in family development research. A definite white urban middle-class Protestant American bias has been present. Much work has been carried out on the "normal" family of husband, wife, and not more than three or four children who move from establishment through dissolution without interruption. Little attempt has been made to analyze the family as it exists with unexpected death, disability, abnormality of either a physical or mental kind, adoption of children, remarriage, or the occurence of separation and divorce. These events have been sorted out of the sample of subjects studied because they disrupted the smooth pattern of development postulated. By the same token, varying combinations of age, sex, and plurality patterns have been troublesome and not adequately accounted for in most previous work. Finally, attempts at cross-cultural and subcultural comparisons of developmental patterns are almost nonexistent.

Much of this is due to methodological limitations in data gathering and analysis, but it is also due to the absence of a specific theoretical focus. What has most often happened is that a set of life cycle categories has been developed and imposed upon the data. Since the categories were based on the initial bias, all cases which did not "fit" were rejected. Consequently, little is known of the developmental characteristics of such families. The conceptual framework, however, demands no specific set of life cycle categories, nor is it culture bound, but allows for development of a set of categories which will fit the kind of family under study. Its limitations are only those of the researcher's ability to devise methods of data gathering and analysis which will provide him with generalizations concerning these various types of families. The framework states that *all* family groups have roles, role complexes, positions, careers, and the like, which change over time. The problem is to discover what the characteristics of these patterns are and how they are related to the specific variables under study.

Finally, the opening up of the area of transactional behavior of family systems with other societal systems on a longitudinal basis provides a broad area of untapped data. Almost nothing is known concerning the relationship between the developmental status of families and the economic, educational, governmental, or religious systems of the society. Most of the work done in the transactional area has been on the relationship of family to consumer behavior. What of the relationship between family careers and occupational careers, educational careers, residential mobility careers, political participation careers, or religious activity careers?

There are still many unsolved theoretical and methodological problems associated with the family development approach. A paper discussing these in detail is in preparation. Through the publication of this suggested conceptual framework, it is hoped that scholars with interests in this field will be prompted to criticize, revise, refine, and extend it so that progress may continue toward a theory of family development.

FOOTNOTES

Revised version of a paper presented at the annual meeting of the Pacific Northwest Council on Family Relations, Pullman, Washington, April 3-4, 1964.

[1] Robert K. Merton, *Social Theory and Social Structure*, Glencoe, Ill.: Free Press, 1957, rev. ed., pp. 85-99.

[2] Hans L. Zetterberg, *On Theory and Verification in Sociology*, Totowa, N. J.: Bedminster Press, 1963, rev. ed., pp. 1-10.

[3] Merton, *op.cit.*, pp. 96-99; and Zetterberg, *Ibid.*, pp. 9-10.

[4] Reuben Hill and Donald A. Hansen, "The Identification of Conceptual Frameworks Utilized in Family Study," *Marriage and Family Living*, 22 (November 1960), pp. 300-301.

[5] Zetterberg, *op. cit.*, p. 7.

[6] Roy H. Rodgers, *Improvements in the Construction and Analysis of Family Life Cycle Categories*, Kalamazoo, Michigan: Western Michigan University, Department of Sociology, 1962, p. 6.

[7] *Ibid.*, pp. 12-21. See also Roy H. Rodgers and Reuben Hill, "The Developmental Approach," in *Handbook of Marriage and the Family*, ed. by Harold Christensen, Chicago: Rand McNally, 1964, Chap. 5.

[8] Hill and Hansen, *op. cit.*, p. 307.

[9]Cf. Evelyn M. Duvall, *Family Development,* New York: J. B. Lippincott, 1962, 2nd ed., p. 9; Paul C. Glick, *American Families,* New York: John Wiley, 1957; John B. Lansing and Leslie Kish, "Family Life Cycle as an Independent Variable," *American Sociological Review,* 22 (October 1957), pp. 512-519; Lowry Nelson, *Rural Sociology,* New York: American Book Company, 1955, 2nd ed., pp. 307-312; and Andrew Collver, "The Family Cycle in India and the United States," *American Sociological Review,* 28 (February 1963), pp. 86-96.

[10]For further development of this point, cf. Rodgers, *op. cit.,* pp. 23-25.

[11]Hans L. Zetterberg, *On Theory and Verification in Sociology,* Stockholm: Almquist and Wiksell, 1954, pp. 16-17.

[12]In the discussion to follow, the author is keenly aware of the contributions to his thinking of a number of people. Where possible, specific credit is acknowledged. Beyond this, however, the contributions through publication and conversation of Reuben Hill, Evelyn M. Duvall, Nelson Foote, Paul C. Glick, Roy G. Francis, and Theodore B. Johannis, Jr. must be cited specifically.

[13]Ernest W. Burgess, "The Family as a Unity of Interacting Personalities," *The Family,* 7 (March 1926), pp. 3-9.

[14]Willard Waller and Reuben Hill, *The Family: A Dynamic Interpretation,* New York: Dryden Press, 1951, rev. ed., 25-36.

[15]Neal Gross, Ward S. Mason, and A. W. McEachern, *Explorations in Role Analysis,* New York: John Wiley, 1958, p. 48.

[16]Frederick L. Bates, "Position, Role and Status: A Reformulation of Concepts," *Social Forces,* 34 (May 1956), p. 314.

[17]*Ibid.*

[18]*Ibid.,* pp. 315-317.

[19]Gross *et al., op. cit.,* p. 64.

[20]*Ibid.,* p. 65.

[21]Irwin Deutscher, *Married Life in the Middle Years*, Kansas City, Mo.: Community Studies, Inc., 1959, p. 18.

[22]*Ibid.*, p. 24.

[23]Rodgers, *op. cit.*, p. 42.

[24]Bernard Farber, "The Family as a Set of Mutually Contingent Careers," in *Household Decision-Making*, ed. by Nelson Foote, New York: New York University Press, 1961, pp. 276-297.

[25]Rodgers, *op. cit.*, p. 43.

[26]Farber, *op. cit.;* and Rodgers, *op. cit.*

[27]These diagrams follow closely those presented by Bates, *op. cit.*, and are reproduced from Rodgers, *op. cit.*, pp. 45-47.

[28]John W. Bennett and Melvin W. Tumin, *Social Life*, New York: A. A. Knopf, 1948, p. 49.

[29]Duvall, *op. cit.*, p. 35. This discussion is similar to that of Duvall's with respect to the origin of "developmental tasks," except that these three factors are generalized here to account for change in the total family system, rather than change only in the individual actors.

Models of Marital Adjustment

Jessie Bernard

Jessie Bernard illustrates an approach which is sensitive to both morphostatic and morphogenic processes. In employing concepts from game theory to describe aspects of the interaction between married partners, Bernard identifies a systems theory approach to family sociology. Zero-sum and nonzero-sum models are tested against the criterion of appropriateness for describing processes and consequences of interaction between married mates. Bernard is led to the conclusion that the mixed-motive model offers the best resource for the conceptualization of marital interaction.

The Dimensions of Marital Adjustments

The major dimensions of any human adjustment problem are: (a) the degree or extent or nature of the differences between or among the parties involved; (b) the degree or extent or nature of the communication between or among the parties; and (c) the quality of the relationship between or among them, that is, its positive or negative affectivity, friendliness, or hostility. If the differences are so extensive or so deep that no rapprochement is possible, that is one thing; if they are relatively minor, that is another. If they are matters of principle, that is one thing; if

Reprinted, with permission of the author and publisher, from *Handbook of Marriage and the Family,* edited by Harold T. Christensen, Chicago: Rand McNally, 1964, pp. 690-711, 733-737.

they are matters of degree, that is another. If communication is open and free, that is one thing; if it is blocked or if it is meant to deceive or mislead, that is another. If the quality of the relationship is one of love and affection, that is one thing; if it is one of hatred and hostility or enmity, that is another. And so on. Each of these dimensions is therefore important for understanding the processes of adjustment.

Degree or Extent of Difference

Any of the kinds of differences referred to above may be categorical or matters of degree. Matters of principle are usually categorical: such-and-such is wrong, period. No exceptions. No mitigating circumstance. No leeway. If this is the nature of the differences between people, adjustments are difficult, if possible at all. They are particularly likely to occur with respect to sexual behavior, tending to complicate adjustments in this area, as noted below.

Differences which are matters of degree on the other hand, may be amenable to "bargaining," as discussed below. But they may also be subject to so-called salami tactics, by which rights and privileges are nibbled away. The phenomena of limits come into play (Schelling, 1960). No one case seems significant enough to make an issue of, but slices add up. Just how far can the partner be pushed? There comes a time when he (she) can stand it no longer. There is a breaking point. There is a last straw. The spouse may be completely surprised at the result. All of a sudden, it seems, the wife (husband) packs up and leaves. "I'm fed up. I just can't stand it any longer. I can't take it any more." The difference was too great to be bridged by one partner alone; "bargaining" might have worked.

Communication

The responsibility for failure in such cases may rest on the partner who did not protest, who did not warn, who did not put up the storm signals as the limits of patience or endurance approached. For communication is essential in arriving at satisfactory relationships.

Interaction implies — indeed, consists of — communication. Communication may be explicit or tacit. Explicit communication is usually verbal, although it may also use other conventional symbols. It may be used to convey correct or incorrect information, to clarify or to mislead, to enlighten or to deceive. The importance of information is fundamental in all human adjustments, but especially in those which conform to the specifications of strategic models. Explicit communication is basic to any form of adjustment which seeks to persuade or cajole or bargain.

Tacit communication – by way of body movements or "strategic moves" – is peculiarly important in sexual adjustments because, for so many people, verbal communication in this area is impossible (Rainwater & Weinstein, 1960). A vast amount of communication in the field of sex consists of gestures. But tacit communication is not at all precise: the message is hard to read. Misreading is common. The rejected swain hotly accuses the indignant miss of "leading him on." She rejects the accusation; she did not lead him on! The husband and the wife, each hungry for the loving caress of the other, lie side by side immobilized by their inability to communicate or fearful that an advance by one may be rejected by the other.

In some situations, tacit communication takes on the aspect of a cat-and-mouse game of move and countermove. There is often an intent to confuse, to create uncertainty. What does he mean by that? Why did she do that? What is he up to? What's her idea? Often the tacit move is designed deliberately to arouse such fears and suspicions in order to humiliate the partner when the true nature of the "move" is later made clear. What was the meaning of the lipstick on his handkerchief, which he was at great pains to leave where she would find it? After suffering as long as she can, she breaks down and asks him, accusingly. With obvious pleasure and enjoyment, he offers an innocent and perfectly plausible explanation, backed by incontrovertible proof. Strange as it may seem, some couples seem to enjoy this cat-and-mouse game of tacit move and countermove: it is intense; it is interesting; it adds excitement to their essentially dull lives (Lantz & Snyder, 1962).

The importance of communication in marital relationships highlights the seriousness of breakdowns or failures in communication. These may take many forms. At one extreme they may result from general inarticulateness: one or both partners do not have the verbal skills to express themselves. The result is tacit or behavioral communication, by acts rather than by words, and the chances of misinterpretation are great.

At the other extreme, however, is an aberration resulting from

too great articulateness. This difficulty is more commonly reported or commented upon in women than in men; it may be pan-
cultural, not necessarily because of biological differences in the
sexes — although they may be involved, since the vocal cords of
women have greater innervation than those of men — but perhaps
because of inevitable relational conditions. The stock figure here
is the nag, the scold, the woman who talks incessantly at, rather
than to, her husband. This phenomenon has not been subjected
to scientific inquiry, but it appears constantly in folk culture, and
it is observable in the social circle of many people. This is the
woman to whom others are primarily objects to talk at or against;
she is little interested in what the other person has to say or even
in how he (or she) reacts to what she herself is saying. She is, in
effect, talking to herself in the presence of another person. The
contents of her talk may be pleasant or hostile; it is nearly always
boring after a few minutes, if not actually antagonizing. It is to
escape this barrage of noncommunicatory articulateness, allegedly,
that men sometimes seek refuge in the club or tavern, if not in
desertion.

Communication between spouses is often honestly blunted because of sex differences. "I just can't understand women (men),"
says the baffled spouse who has failed to communicate or to
receive communication. "I just don't know what he (she) expects
of me," is a common complaint of spouses, even those with the
best of intentions.

Refusal to be communicated with, that is, "to get the message,"
is another form, this time deliberate, which communication failure
may take. It is a powerful defense. The spouse becomes deaf, or
inaccessible. Or pretends not to understand or shakes his (her)
head incredulously. The strategic use of such blocking of communication will be discussed below in connection with mixed-
motive models.

Women appear to be especially dependent on sympathetic communication with their spouses. "Striking differences in marital
satisfaction," for example, are reported "between marriages in
which the wife's problems are understood by the husband and
those in which she is unable to communicate her troubles to him
or is rejected for doing so" (Blood & Wolfe, 1960, p. 261).

Quality of the Relationship

Adjustments may not be any easier when the parties involved

are friendly or loving. They may, indeed, be more difficult than when the parties are unfriendly or hostile. But they are more likely to be motivated in the direction of a suitable accommodation. The rewards for success are likely to be greater. If the partners in a marital relationship love one another, the costs or sacrifices demanded of them in adjusting their differences seem slight. It may not be true that love conquers all, but it goes a long way in making changes palatable.

Hostle people held within the vise which marriage imposes may also adjust their differences, but the resulting relationship is more likely to be a standoff than a victory for both.

The kinds of models suitable for interpreting or understanding marital adjustments will differ according to the quality of the relationship. Assimilative models and mixed-motive models fit relationships in which there is affection; zero-sum and schismatic models, those in which there is not.

Models of Marital Adjustment

The incompatible differences which demand adjustments in marriage, as in other relationships with similar interlocking of parties, may be handled on several levels: (a) the differences may be eliminated and similarities substituted; (b) each partner may attempt to optimize his or her position vis-à-vis the other; (c) the degree of interaction may be reduced to a minimum so that there is relatively little influence of one on the other, each arranging his (her) life in such a way that no matter what the other does, the effect is slight; or, finally, (d) the relationship may be destroyed, each going his or her separate way; conflict is avoided, if not resolved, by getting rid of the relationship. Processes at the first level are assimilative in nature, those at the second and third, strategic, and those at the fourth, schismatic.

Level I: Assimilative Models

Several techniques have been distinguished for achieving change in one or both partners so that they are no longer different: (a) brainwashing, based on the theory of conditioned response; (b) explaining away an opponent's image of the situation, based on Freudian theory; and (c) removing the felt threat associated with alternative images, based on Carl Rogers' theory of understanding and permissiveness (Rapoport, 1960).

Brainwashing. Brainwashing is a subtle use of the carrot-and-stick method of manipulating responses. For maximum effectiveness, it requires isolation of the subject, removing him or her from competing stimuli. It requires alternate punishment and reward in a way that creates willingness to accept control as an alternative to the anxiety of uncertainty. It seems to work best when carried out in a spirit of ostensible friendliness. The best-known applications of brainwashing techniques were those used by communists in prisoner-of-war camps; but in less sophisticated ways they are commonly used in everyday life, even in marriage. The husband manages to cut his wife off from contacts with her family or friends so that his definition of any situation cannot be counteracted by theirs. To the outsider, the spouse seems to be in thrall. "He has her hypnotized." "She doesn't dare to call her soul her own." The taming of the shrew, Kate, by Petruchio, as described by Shakespeare, is an illustration of change by brainwashing using the conditioned response. A wife might, similarly, make certain behavior on the part of her husband so painful that he would cease to indulge in it in order to avoid the punishment she inflicted; we say he is "henpecked." Either spouse may be so conditioned in the direction of compatibility with the other. The punishments may take many forms: weeping, sex refusal, beating, coldness, withdrawal, money deprivation, brawling, or what have you. Whatever it is, the spouse comes in time to prefer to concede whatever is under issue rather than endure the punishment, and finally the very anticipation of the punishment is enough to make him avoid the situation. A change has been effected; the difference has been removed. The entire cost has been borne by one of the partners. The resulting relationship may or may not be stable.

Explaining away. The "explain away" technique is often used by therapists, but it can be used by anyone. It is especially likely to be used by articulate people with a smattering of Freudian theory. The wife tries to change her husband by telling him he has an Oedipus complex; or the husband tries to change his wife by telling her she is a compulsive housekeeper. The general ideal is that if the underlying origin of the offending behavior can be explained, the behavior itself will stop. In a sense, the adverse labeling of unwanted behavior is a subtle form of punishment; it defies the opponent to change in order to escape the onus of the explanatory factor. The husband has to prove he does not have an Oedipus complex by not going to visit his mother; the wife has to prove she is not a compulsive housekeeper by never mentioning the husband's slovenliness about the house. Otherwise, the "I-told-you-so" tactic can be used: "See, what I said about you is true; your behavior proves it."

Threat removal. The threat-removing technique is an application of the theory of permissiveness in human relationships. It has three components: (a) it conveys to the opponent a feeling that he is understood but not judged; (b) it delineates clearly the area of validity of the opponent's position; and (c) it induces an assumption of similarity (Rapoport, 1960).

(a) One of the commonest characteristics of verbal conflict is the failure of one or both parties to listen to or even to hear the other. Each is so busy stating his or her own case in the most forceful manner that the time during which the other is talking is used merely to regroup forces for further assault. The opponents are unwilling or unable to listen to one another. There is no communication. A basic condition for changing people, however, is that they be assured that the opponent understands what their position is. Thus, the spouse who is eager to change a partner by persuasion must learn first of all to be able to state the partner's position to the partner's own satisfaction. By so doing he, or she, demonstrates that at least he understands the other's position. He not only can take the other's role, put himself in the other's position; he can also convince the other that he has done so. This is the first step in removing a sense of threat.

> There is no guarantee that the opponent will continue to listen after you have presented his case and gone on to present your own. But there is at least hope, indeed on two counts. First, having had the experience of listening and agreeing (when his own case was being presented), the opponent may carry some of his responses over at least for a while to listening to another point of view. Second, he too has a job of presenting your case to your satisfaction. He will want to do it well, because getting an admission from you that he has succeeded is a minor victory in the debate. Listening to your case will make the job easier for him. He therefore has some motivation for listening (Rapoport, 1960, p. 291).[1]

This is a form of role-taking; it teaches each one how the situation looks to the other. It gives each one the experience of viewing himself as he looks to the other. By proving that each understands the other, each mollifies the other. Change becomes easier.

(b) A second step in the threat-removal technique is to grant that the opponent's position may be justified under certain conditions. "It is hard to find a statement in ordinary language without *any* region of validity. There are, roughly speaking, no absolutely false assertions. If one tries hard enough, one can usually think of circumstances under which any given assertion might be true" (Rapoport, 1960, p. 292). Sometimes differences that are incompatible result from differences in definition of the situation, or in perception, or in interpretation. Establishing the extent of validity of both points of view is itself cooperative, and hence itself tends to reduce felt threat; but, in addition, it also clarifies the boundaries of the differences and thus offers a transition to a recognition of the area of disagreement, related to the now recognized differing frames of reference. "You hate me!" "Why, yes, I can see how you think so if you think my absorption in my work is a sign of hatred. But couldn't it also be a sign that I love you because I want to get ahead to do more for you?" "The idea . . . is to steer the debate away from polarities and toward the examination of contexts. If both parties do this (if one starts, the other may follow — imitation is a surprisingly widespread principle of human conduct), progress may be made toward the resolution of the issue" (Rapoport, 1960, p. 302). The idea is to avoid charge and countercharge or accusation and defense, both of which are threatening. The idea is, rather, to accept the charge or the accusation but to show its limitations or to reinterpret it in a different context.

(c) The third phase of the threat-removal technique is to induce an assumption of similarity rather than to emphasize the differences. Usually, we attribute bad qualities to our opponents; the threat-removal technique suggests that we look for these bad qualities in ourselves. Usually, similarly, we attribute good qualities to ourselves; the threat-removal technique suggests that we look for these good qualities in our opponents.

> Our ultimate purpose in raising questions about ourselves is to induce the opponent to raise similar questions about himself. We see ourselves as intelligent, honest, and considerate. It will often serve us well to imagine that the opponent possesses these qualities to some degree. Maybe he does not, but maybe this "delusion" of ours will induce a similar delusion in him about us (Rapoport, 1960, p. 306).

Again, this is an exercise in role-taking. By seeing ourselves as we look to the other, we begin to understand his, or her, fear or resentment. We know better how to behave in order to dissipate it. We come to see that both of us share good as well as bad qualities.

The net effect of brainwashing, explaining away, and threat removal is, presumably, to change the spouse in such a way as to get rid of differences and foster similarities. They may be used in either the parallel or the interactional form of marital relationship, but inasmuch as they depend on explicit communication, they are probably more likely to occur in the interactional form: If they are used manipulatively only, that is, if the change is only in the way differences are interpreted, the change or adjustment may last only a short time. If the quality of the relationship is one of basic hostility and resentment, it may not be amenable to any of these techniques.

It should be pointed out that even if and when such techniques succeed in changing a spouse, the result may not be what was anticipated. It has been noted in the literature, for example, that the wives of alcoholics who have learned to control their illness by abstention are sometimes greatly disappointed in the result. Some found that they preferred the man who, however difficult he might have been when intoxicated, was more lovable when sober than the man who is sober always. The serious husband who finally succeeds in muting his wife's exuberance sometimes finds that he has lost something he much loved in his wife; the difference he has erased was not divisive in the first place.

Levels 2 and 3: Optimizing or Strategic Models

*   *   *

The assimilative models just described are straightforward; they embody fairly simple principles of conditioning, analysis, and persuasion. There is control, in varying degrees, by one person in the situation; he is acting on or "adjusting" the other. It is a transitive kind of adjustment.

But in many marital situations, as in other kinds, it is not a matter of independent action. In most organizational or systemic situations, and most especially in marriage (as we noted in discussing the specifications for marital relationships) decisions are interdependent. The success or failure of Ego's policies depend on Alter's policies. Decisions must therefore always be made with the probable behavior of someone else in mind. What if Alter decides to do this? or that? Ego has to know how to select his own alternatives of behavior in terms of what Alter may do. Such situations, sometimes known as interdependent decision situations, are usually explored by means of strategic game models. Marriage fits the specifications very well, especially with modifications introduced by T. C. Schelling (1960).

The components of strategic models. The components of strategic game models are the following: (a) there are players – in our case, husbands and wives – who have conflicting goals; (b) each has alternative courses of action available to him from which he can choose; (c) each combination of alternatives of the players has an anticipated outcome; and (d) each outcome has a certain value or payoff to the players. It is specified that each player has some control over the situation, to the extent, at least, that he can decide his own behavior; but he does not have complete control, because he is tied into this relationship with the other players whose decisions also affect the situation. Decisions with respect to what course of action to follow have to be made bearing in mind that the success or failure of any course of action depends on what the other player also is going to do.

The components are usually presented for analysis in the form of a matrix, although, of course, the people involved in the situation are not always aware of the existence of such a matrix.

Ego's Alternatives	Alter's Alternatives			
	A	B	C	D
1	A-1	B-1	C-1	D-1
2	A-2	B-2	C-2	D-2
3	A-3	B-3	C-3	D-3
4	A-4	B-4	C-4	D-4

Figure 1.

Each outcome (A-1, B-2, etc.), or result of combination of strategies, has a value for each player. When these values are specified, the result is called a payoff matrix. By convention, the sign used in the matrix refers to Ego's payoff. In some situations, to be noted below, the payoff for Alter is the same, but with reversed signs. If the payoffs are different for Ego and Alter, the payoff for Ego is given at the lower left corner and that for Alter in the upper right.

In real life, of course, people rarely evaluate alternatives in any such neat and formal way; nor are evaluations as precise as implied by the use of specific numbers. But in a nonverbal way, a "calculus" is posited, and a value is arrived at. There *are* ranked preferences among outcomes. Some *are* considered more desirable than others; some *are* feared more than others. "I'd rather die than. . . ." "It's better to . . . than to. . . ." We are always expressing such sets of preferences. It is in this sense that the use of specific numbers is justified; their use does not imply that a true metric has necessarily been imposed on the outcomes, although such a metric is feasible under laboratory conditions (Siegel, 1956).

Adjustment situations under strategic models. Games of strategy may be classified in a great many ways; for our purposes here, two salient criteria are (a) the presence or absence, or the degree, of communication between the partners, or, in other words, the amount and accuracy of information available to them, and (b) the degree of conflict or the extent of the differences or divergences between the partners. On the basis of these two criteria, the adjustment situations may be viewed as in Table I.

For our purposes here, Situations A and B may be disregarded; they do not involve divisive interspousal differences.

Situations E and F fall at Level 3. They are zero-sum models and, while not suitable for many ongoing marriages, may fit a marriage in which each partner fences himself (herself) off from the other and, in effect, reduces the other to a thing, behaving in such a way that no matter what the other does, he (she) is safe. There is only as much interaction as the expectation that each will behave in a way to maximize gains or minimize losses. Beyond this, the other becomes a natural phenomenon, like the weather, which one cannot influence but which one must take into account in one's own behavior. The situation reflects a stalemate or standoff. Neither can improve the situation by his (her) own efforts. Strictly speaking, there is no process of adjustment here. It is a static situation in which any change must be for the worse. It may be a very stable relationship, even though unfair to one party. Alienated or estranged partners may find themselves in such a relationship; so also may hostile partners in a

TABLE I
Categorical Classification of Strategic Adjustment Situations

Nature or Degree of Differences	Nature or Degree of Communication	
	Communication Is Absent or Tacit in Nature	Communication is Present or Possible
There are no differences, or the differences are integrative; common interests predominate.	Situation A: Coordination game involved. For some reason or other there has been a breakdown in communication. Each must behave according to the expectations of the other to achieve the common goal without communicating with the other.	Situation B: No interspousal adjustments are necessary. The pair may have to adjust as a unit to other systems—in-laws, friends, church, school, job, etc.—but no marital adjustments, as here defined, are necessary.
Both conflicting and common interests are present. (Level 2)	Situation C: Coordination game involved, as above. See Matrix 1, Appendix, for illustration.	Situation D: Bargaining game involved; strategic moves to manipulate partner are important. See Matrixes 2, 3, and 4, Appendix, for illustrations.
"Pure conflict" is present; that is, there are no common interests. (Level 3)	Situation E: Secrecy, bluff, deception are important; the classic zero-sum game of strategy without saddle point.	Situation F: Communication is not important one way or another here; knowing what an opponent is going to do does not help. The outcome which maximizes the gains of one also minimizes the losses of the other. (A "saddle point" is said to be present when this occurs.) The classic zero-sum game with saddle point; a "standoff" or "stalemate."

parallel relationship. The distinction between E and F lies in the fact that communication makes no difference in F; in E secrecy is so important that, mathematically speaking, the player himself does not know which strategy he is to use until he is ready to use it. There are techniques to tell him how often to use one and how often another (Williams, 1954).

At Level 2, Situations C and D — called cooperative or mixed-motive games — do fit the specifications of marriage and are useful models for explaining or interpreting marital adjustments.

The mixed-motive model uses the same conceptual equipment as does the zero-sum model, but it changes the specifications. In the zero-sum model, neither player attempts to change the payoff or values of the several outcomes; both accept the matrix as given. In the mixed-motive model, however, one player, or both, may attempt by his own behavior to change the payoff or value of the several outcomes for his opponent. He behaves in such a way (to be elaborated presently) as to make it more to less rewarding for his opponent to select certain alternatives rather than others. In the zero-sum model, the gains and losses of the two players cancel out; what Ego wins, Alter loses, so only one set of figures in the payoff matrix is called for. In the mixed-motive model, the pay-offs may be different, not only in terms of gains and losses, but also in terms of amount. It is characteristic for mixed-motive models that it is possible for both players to win or for both to lose.

Because the mixed-motive model fits so many marital adjust-ment situations and is so illuminating when it does fit, it is elaborated in some detail below. It is merely introduced here. In order to complete our description of the models at the several levels of adjustment, however, escalation and schismatic models are presented before continuing with the discussion of the mixed-motive model.

Level 4: Escalation and Schismatic Models

Useful as they are, strategic concepts do not explain the pro-cesses by which situations change. They are dynamic only in the sense that they explain how in any given situation one player manipulates the other to make him select one alternative rather than another. But each situation requires a new "frame." Game concepts are useful dynamically, that is, in a given situation, but not for changes in the situation over time. For changes over time, "moving pictures" rather than separate "frames" are needed. Escalation and schismatic models, with parameters moving the partners either farther and farther apart, or closer and closer together, provide such a "moving picture."

The escalation model. The mathematical model for this process — designed originally to explain arms races, psychological epidemics, and the like — is useful also for understanding marital adjustments. In general, this model refers to a situation in which the rate of increase or decrease in a certain kind of behavior of one party is related to (a) the rate of increase or decrease in certain kinds of behavior on the part of the other party, (b) costs or inhibitions which brake the increase or decrease, and (c) permanent grievances between them which keep the process going. In the equations for this model, the interdependence variable and the braking variable are assumed to be positive; but the permanent grievance variable may be either positive or negative. If negative, it refers to the opposite of a grievance, to something, that is, which holds the parties together, like love or friendliness.

Applied to marital relationships, this model states that the rate of increase of hostile acts by Ego is positively dependent on the amount of hostile behavior on the part of Alter, negatively on the cost involved in engaging in such hostile behavior, and positively on some stable issue, such as the "permanent grievances" which are present (Rapoport, 1960). The equations for these statements are:

$$dx/dt = ay - mx + g,$$
$$dy/dt = bx - ny + h.$$

Here dx/dt refers to rate of change; x and y refer to the amount of hostility present in the two partners; m and n stand for the effort or cost involved in pursuing the hostile behavior; and g and h stand for the "permanent grievances." The parameters a and b stand for the degree of mutual dependence of one party's behavior on the other party's behavior. For understanding the relationships to which such a model applies, it is not necessary to solve the equations which represent it. The chief purpose the model serves, in fact, is simply to help see how marital relationships function. Since the parameters a, b, m, and n may sometimes have the value of zero, and g and h may be negative as well as positive (the opposite of a grievance as well as a grievance), this model explains how partners may move toward, as well as away from, one another; it also explains stability. Rapoport summarizes four situations which may result from his model, according to the relationship among the parameters.

1. If the product of the braking forces or costs in the two parties (mn) is greater than the product of the degree of mutual dependence (ab), and if there is an underlying grievance (g and h are positive), there will be stability in the relationship; there will be no escalation, one way or another.

2. If, as above, the braking force (mn) is greater than the mutual dependence (ab), and there is the opposite of a grievance present (g and h are negative), hostile behavior will cease.

3. If the braking force (mn) is less than the mutual dependence (ab) and there is an underlying grievance (g and h are positive), there will be runaway escalation; the partners will move farther and father away from one another.

4. If the braking force (mn) is less than the mutual dependence (ab) and there is the opposite of a grievance present (g and h are negative), the situation will be equivocal, depending on the initial level of hostility. If the initial level is above a certain point, there will be upwardly escalating hostility; if it is below that point, there will be declining hostility.

We shall have more to say about escalation in our discussion of divorce below.

Rapoport summarizes the interpretation of the escalation model as follows, but here the application to marital adjustments is substituted for his application to an arms race:

> What can we learn from this analysis? Let us review what we have done. We have contrived an extremely artificial situation, a model, which bears *some* resemblance to what we can abstract from the dynamics of [marital interaction]; that is, we have put into the simplest type of mathematical equations the usual arguments given about the causes of [hostile behavior in marriage], namely, underlying grievances and mutual resentment, and the limiting factors, such as the constraints of [difficulties in the way of hostile behavior]. So long as these factors were discussed in conventional language, not much could be concluded as to what would happen, for example, whether the [hostile behavior] could be stabilized, whether a runaway race would result, or whether total [ending] was thinkable. Once a translation was made into quanti-

tative relations, at least theoretical conclusions about the "fate of the system" could be made. The truth of these conclusions depends, of course, entirely on the accuracy of the model. It goes without saying that the model here depicted is grossly inaccurate and oversimplified. Note, however, that the "would-be" conclusions are in accordance with common sense, to a degree. The presence of grievances would prevent total [ending of hostile behavior]. Balance of power is possible if the degree of mutual [hostility] is sufficiently tempered by constraints on the [extent of hostile behavior]. Underlying good will can insure [cessation of hostile behavior], provided mutual [hostility] is not too great or provided the level of [hostile behavior] had already been brought down below a certain critical level or had not risen above it, etc.

What the model gives us that common sense conclusions do not is a neat quantitative way of expressing these results. So far, these results are little more than shorthand notation for the common sense conclusions although it can be argued that being rigorously deduced they deserve more confidence as conclusions (Rapoport, 1960, pp. 29-30).

As in the case of other models, the major contribution of this one is not necessarily in determining measures for the parameters but rather in showing that there are processes at work which, under certain circumstances, can lead inevitably and even irreversibly to stepped-up hostility and widened breaches. Adjustment involves somehow or other changing these parameters at the most feasible point. If x and y cannot be changed, perhaps m and n can; perhaps the "permanent grievance" can be reduced or eliminated; if nothing else, perhaps a and b can be reduced to zero by temporarily separating the spouses.

Perhaps other variables must be inserted into the model to make it fit marital adjustments. But in any event, the concept of escalation and the formulation of a model to describe it is a useful one in thinking about marital adjustments.

Other schismatic models. Schismatic models refer to situations where the differences between or among parties are so great that no accommodation is possible. The relationship must be destroyed. Conflict is not resolved in this way but it is avoided. The parties go their separate ways. One partner leaves or divorces the other. Schismatic models attempt to explain how such social systems fall apart.

One such model, not further elaborated here, is in terms of the relative costs and/or rewards involved in remaining within the system as opposed to destroying it. ". . . the increased attainment of a given end entails increased utility [rewards] to the system up to a certain point, though with decreasing increments of utility [rewards] as that point is approached. Beyond that point, at first with small decrements but with progressively increasing decrements as the given end is further pursued, utility decreases" (Firey, 1948, pp. 21-22).

The statement of this model is purely theoretical and general; the application varies, of course, according to the specific situation. That is, the costs and the rewards have to be determined specifically in each case. What constitutes a cost or a reward would be different in different marriages, according to personality variables as well as institutional variables. Where, for example, beatings are defined as a form of attention, they might be evaluated as rewards; where they are defined as cruelty, contrariwise, they would certainly be evaluated as costs.

Another model not elaborated here which may be classed as schismatic refers to groups characterized by four variables, all of which apply to marriages: (a) intensity of interaction; (b) level of friendliness; (c) amount of activity carried on by partners; and (d) amount of activity imposed by the external environment. In addition, there are three postulated sets of relationships among these variables: (a) intensity of interaction is dependent upon and increases with the level of friendliness and the amount of activity within the group; (b) the level of friendliness will increase if or when the actual level of interaction is greater than the amount appropriate at the existing level of friendliness; and (c) the amount of activity is higher than the existing amount of activity (Simon, 1952). This model can derive the conditions of stability and of instability in a relationship. It finds that if a group is dissolved, as one of the parameters is reduced, it cannot necessarily be restored by once more increasing that parameter; that is, a group – in this case a marriage – may be destroyed by reducing one of the parameters so irretrievably that attempting to restore it by increasing the parameter becomes impossible. There is a point, in brief, when marriages are so severely strained that mending them becomes impossible.

All these models may be useful in interpreting or explaining marital adjustments, although with varying degrees of frequency. Models which specify explicit communication will not fit marriages in which communication tends to be tacit; models which specify verbal interaction will be more appropriate for the interactional pattern of marital relationships than one which does not. For a relationship as diverse and as complex as marriage, a variety of models is necessary.

One family of models, based on the theory of games of strategy, especially as modified by Schelling, is of such special interest that it is discussed now in greater detail.

The Mixed-Motive Models

There are few if any marital adjustment situations which conform to *all* of the following specifications of classic zero-sum game theory: (a) one which states that what one wins the other loses; (b) one which states that the payoffs for all outcomes are identical, signs opposite, for both players; and (c) one which requires the existence of uncertainty and/or risk.

There are, to be sure, some kinds of situations which might fit the first of these specifications, such as one in which the wife wished to rear the children in one religious faith, the husband in another. Or one in which the wife wanted the husband to reject the proffered job that would require the family to move away from the home community and in which the husband wanted to accept it. Indeed, the specification of the marital relationship as a unit often imposes this zero-sum characteristic on it; there is an either-or choice. In such situations only one partner can win.

There may also be, perhaps, situations in which the second specification holds, the payoffs for all outcomes being identical, signs reversed, for both players. The loss "means" as much to one as the concomitant "gain" does for the other. If money has exactly the same value for both of the spouses, this specification of classic game theory is met in situations involving the expenditure of family income. The "loss" to the husband in not getting the power mower exactly balances the "gain" to the wife in getting the new drapes for the living room. But even so, we are, as all students of the subject recognize, on perilous ground when we come so near to comparing the utilities or values of one person to those of another.

So, also, is the third specification for the application of classic game theory — the existence of either uncertainty or risk — uncharacteristic of the marital relationship. A major idea in game theory, viewed normatively, is to guide the players when they do not really know what they are up against; it is designed to help them decide what to do when they do not have all the information they need about the probable behavior of their opponents. It is a gambler's tool. Such uncertainty is not a major characteristic of marriage. There will, of course, be some day-by-day adjustment situations of most marriages in which uncertainty and/or risk are involved. What kind of mood will John be in when he gets home from work today? Mary doesn't know exactly. If he is in a good mood, strategy A will yield her the highest payoff; but if he is in a bad mood, strategy B is her best bet. She has to decide before he gets home. She might try "espionage," that is, have one of the children telephone him to see if she can judge from his reaction what his frame of mind is; or she might depend on her past observations or knowledge of his behavior. Monday is the day he has to make a report to the committee; he was uncertain about it when he left; he will probably feel frustrated and depressed. Conclusion: don't try strategy A. He will say "no," and once having committed himself, he won't feel like changing when his mood lifts. Or, Monday is the day he gets his citation for best performance in his department this year; he will probably feel elated and on top of the world. Conclusion: strike while the iron is hot; he will be in an expansive mood tonight and ready to concede anything. And once having promised, he won't be in a position to renege. In such situations, there is an element of uncertainty and/or risk involved in a marital adjustment. But here, again, as in the other game-theory specifications, the most characteristic aspect of marital adjustment situations is not the presence of uncertainty and/or risk, but rather, in fact, the opposite. "Winning" often depends on "making known" one's behavior.

Although any one, or even two, of the specifications of the zero-sum situation may be present in marital relationships, it is not likely that all of them will be. For this reason, the model that perhaps best fits the usual marital situation is the so-called cooperative or mixed-motive game in which (a) if one wins the other does not automatically lose, that is, in which both may win — or lose; (b) the payoffs or values for all outcomes may be different for husband and for wife rather than identical with reversed signs; and (c) in which there is little or no uncertainty and/or risk. Strange as it may seem, the model which least well fits the specifications of classic game theory appears to be the most useful one in explaining or interpreting marital adjustments.

Schelling (1960), by shearing or peeling away many of the basic specifications of game theory — especially the specification of uncertainty and/or risk — has given us a valuable way of looking at marital adjustment situations. Perhaps it is no longer game theory, but it is based on concepts borrowed from game theory.

The cooperative game, as Luce and Raiffa (1957) call it, or the mixed-motive game, as Schelling (1960) calls it, is one in which (a) there are both conflicting and common interests in the relationship, a situation characteristic of marriage; (b) there is not a zero-sum situation but one in which both partners can either win or lose; (c) the values of all outcomes may differ for both spouses not only in sign but also in magnitude; and (d) the strategic use, not of secrecy and misleading information, but of precisely the opposite — information convincingly communicated — is important. It is this last-named specification which is of major importance.

> There is probably no contrast more striking, in the comparison of the mixed-motive and the pure-conflict (zero-sum) game, than the significance of having one's own strategy found out and appreciated by the opponent. Hardly anything captures the spirit of the zero-sum game quite so much as the importance of "not being found out" and of employing a mode of decision that is proof against deductive anticipation by the other player. Hardly anything epitomizes strategic behavior in the mixed-motive game so much as the advantage of being able to adopt a mode of behavior that the other party will take for granted (Schelling, 1960, p. 160).

In his analysis of the so-called coordination game, Schelling makes a great deal of expectations and in his analysis of bargaining he shows how the payoffs — since there is no longer uncertainty and/or risk present perhaps the term should be value instead of payoff — of opponents can be changed by proclaiming loudly one's own strategies and thus forcing opponents to do something they would originally have preferred not to do.

Referring back to Table I, two relevant situations will be described here. One is the so-called coordination game characterized by the presence of both common and conflicting interests and the absence of communication (Situation C); here *expectations* are the key elements. It is, of course, true that expectations are fundamental in all strategic games; but there is a difference. In the classic game, strategies do not change the incentive structure of an opponent; the payoffs are not altered by the expectations. Each player expects his opponent to select a strategy which will maximize his gains or minimize his losses; he bases his own strategy on this expectation. But in the coordination situation, the players can change the incentive structure of their opponents. In Matrix 1 (See Appendix), for example, it is Mary's expectation that John will expect her to come to the prize fight that gives this outcome so much value to her. If, however, the nature of their relationship were such that she could expect him to expect her to go to the concert and therefore to go there himself, outcome 1A would have a higher value.

The other relevant situation is the bargaining game, characterized by the presence of both common and conflicting interests and presence of communication (Situation D); here a convincingly communicated *commitment,* which nails down the expectation, is the basic element.

Coordination

No conflict present. Problems of coordination may arise even though there is no conflict present; if for some reason or other communication is impossible, how should each spouse act in order to achieve a common goal (Situation B)? A husband and wife, for example, get separated in a crowded department store; they want to locate one another in the shortest time. They have this common interest and no conflicting interests. What should they do? How do they "adjust" to one another in such a situation? Each has to "read the other's mind." Success depends on each acting in a way that will conform to what each expects the other to expect of him or her. By accurate expectations of what each will expect the other to do, and by acting in accord with these expectations, they coordinate their behavior and achieve their common goal.

Conflict present. More difficult are coordination adjustments when there are conflicting, as well as common, interests present (Situation C). How, in the absence of communication, does adjustment take place? "The problem is to develop a modus vivendi when one or both parties either cannot or will not negotiate explicitly or when neither would trust the other with respect to any agreement explicitly reached" (Schelling, 1960, p. 53). This kind of situation might arise in a marriage during a quarrel in which communication has broken down. Neither one wishes the breach to proceed to the point of divorce; this much they have in common. But neither one wishes to recognize the other to the extent of open interaction and explicit communication.

Coordination under these circumstances can be achieved on the basis of mutual knowledge of expectations. A trivial example will illustrate. John and Mary quarreled at breakfast over how to spend the evening. John wanted to go to a prize fight, Mary to a concert. This is the conflicting interest. But neither wanted to go anywhere alone, and neither wanted to stay home, together or alone. This is the common interest. In the absence of communication, how can they coordinate their activities to attain the most satisfactory result? John would rather go to a concert with Mary than to a prize fight alone; Mary would rather go to a prize fight with John than to a concert alone; both would rather go to either event than stay home.

If Matrix 1 (See Appendix) accurately reflects the values for both John and Mary of the several outcomes in this situation, the choice narrows down to outcome concert-concert or outcome prize fight-prize fight. Thus Mary, on the basis of her knowledge of her husband, might reason as follows: "John knows I know how much he enjoys a prize fight; he'll take it for granted that I'll give up the concert tonight, so he'll expect me to meet him at the prize fight. I might as well go. It's worth more being with him there than either with him at home or along at the concert." John might, on the basis of his knowledge of his wife, reason like this: "Mary knows how much I enjoy a prize fight and she wouldn't stand in the way of my seeing this one, so I'll go ahead and meet her there." On the basis of their knowledge of one another they know what to expect — "to take for granted" — hence what to do to optimize their payoffs or values. The situation might, of course, have been reversed: he might have said, "She knows I know how much she wants to go to the concert tonight so she'll expect me to go there; I'd rather go there with her than to the prize fight alone." And she might have said, "He knows how much I want to hear the concert tonight and he wouldn't stand in the way of my going, so I'll go and meet him there."

As a matter of empirical fact, however, in a satisfactory marriage, the chances are greater that Mary will coordinate her behavior to adjust to John's expectations rather than the other way round, for it has been found that congruence between a wife's perception of her husband and his perception of himself is related to satisfactory marriage whereas the reverse was not found. The author concluded that "if it is the wife who does the adjusting [as Burgess and Locke and as Goode contend], it is to the benefit of the relationship if she knows what she's adjusting to! If she sees the husband as he sees himself, she is better able to make adjustments which bring more satisfaction to the marriage" (Luckey, 1960, p. 157).

The above situation, whoever expects the other to conform to his (her) preferred outcome, assumes a good relationship between the spouses. But expectations can also be used negatively. In reverse coordination, one spouse can use expectations to reduce the satisfaction of the other. For it is always possible for one or the other to "cut off his nose to spite his face." In such a case, the values in the above matrix change so that Mary, let us say, now derives more satisfaction from going to the concert alone or staying home, either alone or with John, than she does from being with him either at the concert or the prize fight. Reducing his pleasure rather than enhancing her own is her objective (Matrix 1A, Appendix). "I'll show him" by acting contrary to his expectations, by disappointing him, reflects her attitude. It is worth being miserable herself to make him miserable. People who know one another well know best how to hurt, as well as how to please, one another. Now, both can lose.

Ordinarily, however, it the situation in Matrix 1 rather than Matrix 1A is a true reflection of the situation, each optimizes his payoff or satisfaction by acting on the expectations of the other, for an

> . . . odd characteristic of . . . [this type of situation] is that neither . . . can gain by outsmarting the other. Each loses unless he does exactly what the other expects him to do. Each party is the prisoner or the beneficiary of their mutual expectations; no one can disavow his own expectation of what the other will expect him to expect to be expected to do. The need for agreement overrules the potential disagreement, and each must concert with the other or lose altogether (Schelling, 1960, p. 60).

The precise decision will depend, of course, on the satisfaction resulting from each outcome for each player. The end result is that conforming to the expectations of the other yields the maximum satisfaction or payoff.

There is, of course, no assurance that coordination without communication will succeed, or that it will yield results as favorable as or more favorable than those achievable by explicit interaction. A set of experiments has convinced Schelling that in most such situations, "the outcome is determined by something that is fairly arbitrary. It is not a particularly 'fair' outcome, from either an observer's point of view or the points of view of the participants" (1960, p. 65). He concludes also that "when agreement must be reached with incomplete communication, the participants must be ready to allow the situation itself to exercise substantial constraint over the outcome; specifically, a solution that discriminates against one party or the other or even involves 'unnecessary' nuisance to both of them may be the only one on which their expectations can be coordinated" (p. 75). In explicit interaction a wife might be able to "bargain" for the husband's going to the concert; but in the absence of communication, this is not possible, and her best bet is to do what she expects her husband to expect her to do.

The possibility of error in coordinating behavior without communication highlights the importance of keeping the channels of communication open. "At a minimum," says Schelling, "this might mean assuring that a surrender offer could be heard and responded to by either side" (p. 78). After a quarrel it is important that channels for communication be open enough at least to send apologies and an "I'm sorry, let's kiss and make up."

Schelling, speaking of war, says that practice in the use of referees and mediators might be a useful prior arrangement to serve as a coordinating mechanism in a serious crisis. There is thus established a precedent which both parties might be expected to recognize and which would thus coordinate their behavior in a situation where communication has broken down. An analogy in marital adjustments would be prior agreement on a trusted mutual friend or even professional counselor to whom both would be expected to turn when communication broke down.

In the coordination situation, each spouse is manipulating or influencing the behavior of the other by an "unseen hand" or by "remote control," so to speak. Each is adjusting his (her) own behavior to the expected expectations of the other. The matter of expectations is related no doubt to the phenomenon of social or interpersonal perception, on which a fairly large literature of empirical research has developed in recent years.

The bulk of theory and interpretations of research findings indicate that interpersonal behavior is closely related to, if not dependent upon, the way in which individuals perceive themselves, others, and the situation of the moment. Both the role theorist and the phenomenologist would agree that where individuals perceive similarly, and frames of reference are thus shared, communication is easier, and the relationship existing between the individuals concerned is more satisfactory (Luckey, 1960, p. 153).

In general, marriages in which the wife perceives her husband as he perceives himself tend to show higher marital satisfaction scores than those in which she does not (Luckey, 1960). The implication is that she knows what he expects of her and can therefore coordinate her behavior with his on her expectations of his expectations.

In a bargaining type of situation, these expectations become explicit. Ego knows exactly what to expect from Alter, not on the basis of social perception, but because Alter has committed himself to a certain course of action and has communicated it convincingly to Ego.

Bargaining

Popular wisdom has long recognized that marital adjustments are a matter of give and take. The conception of the relations between the sexes as a bargaining situation is very old. Quite aside from the patent form of bride purchase or the dowry, the psychological give and take between men and women has long been viewed as essentially a duel of wits for advantage. The courts of love in the twelfth century dealt with the nature of such bargains; who owed what to whom and why. A knight must perform certain feats in order to obligate his lady to become his love. ". . . in the service of love, pain and sorrow were necessities; . . . there was never a joy which was not purchased at the expense of a hundred griefs" (Rowbotham, 1895, p. 240). The courtly give and take or bargain was highly conventionalized; its rules were enforced in the so-called courts of love.

It was Willard Waller who formulated most elaborately and insightfully the bargaining model of relations between the sexes. His application was primarily to the premarital period, but the fundamental processes are the same, although the specific "goods" involved in the exchange may vary greatly — love, mink coats, sex relations, approval, "freedom," etc.

The kind of bargaining which has to do with marriage has had a long history, and folk wisdom recognizes its importance. As in dating, so in marriage, one gets about what he deserves according to the accepted standards of the group. In the simple, homogenous group this is very clear. In modern society, groups are confused, and cultural imperatives are in conflict, and therefore the nature of the bargaining process is more complex and its outlines are confused. Further, the current emphasis upon marriage for love causes the bargaining element to be concealed, and yet no thoughtful person will contend that it is not present (Waller & Hill, 1951, p. 160).

These intuitive insights have been refined and incorporated in the mixed-motive model. It is specified that some bargain or exchange is considered preferable to none at all by both parties; this guarantees a common interest. If one partner does not feel this way, he is not likely to enter the relationship; or if he does, to remain long in it. The bargaining model is suitable in any situation "in which adversaries watch and interpret each other's behavior, each aware that his own actions are being interpreted and anticipated, each acting with a view to the expectations that he creates" (Schelling, 1960, p. 21).

These expectations are established now not by social or interpersonal perception, as in the coordination game, but rather by convincing and explicit commitments, clearly communicated. Commitment is thus a central core in Schelling's analysis of bargaining. One of the players makes a commitment to a specified line of action rather than to any other; he convinces his opponent that he is committed to this line of action. There must be no uncertainty about this; the commitment must be binding. It is precisely the lack of uncertainty, the complete conviction on the part of the opponent, that renders the commitment effective.

In Matrix 2 (Appendix), for example, the usual solution would be for Ego to select strategy A, knowing that Alter would expect him to do so and hence would himself select 1 rather than 2, even though 2 would yield him a higher payoff. That is, under classic game theory, each would expect the other to expect his opponent to behave in a way to minimize expected losses or to maximize expected gains. But suppose that Alter makes it unequivocally clear that no matter what Ego does he is going to select strategy 2. Ego now has no better alternative than B. Alter has changed Ego's expectations with respect to his behavior. By such a commitment, one party can manipulate the other.

Manipulation may permeate any bargaining situation, as, indeed, any interactional one. In manipulation (Situation D as shown in

Table I) there is an attempt to place the burden of change or adjustment on the other partner. The object is to change the opponent's payoff or satisfaction matrix by removing all uncertainty from the alternatives, so that his problem becomes one of simple maximization, in one's own favor. The manipulating party removes any uncertainty from his own behavior by committing himself unequivocally to a certain course of action.

But a commitment is useless unless the opponent knows what it is: a threat, for example, cannot be made if the opponent does not hear it or understand it or believe it; a promise has no effect if it is not received or if it is not believed. Serious strategic errors in choice of behavior may result from lack or defects in the system of communication. So communication becomes extremely important; it is of the essence. Not secrecy and suprise, not deception and misrepresentation but, on the other hand, convincing proof of what one is going to do is the important characteristic of this situation.

Basic, then, to the strategic moves about to be presented, is a firm commitment persuasively communicated; this commitment eliminates uncertainty. Once Ego has committed himself and convinced Alter of his commitment, Alter is in no doubt about what will happen. He is no longer making a decision in the face of uncertainty; the probability is 1.00 that Ego will behave in a certain way. His choice is now between the alternatives which net him most; and Ego's behavior has predetermined this by means of his strategic moves.

Three basic strategic moves are: "first move," strategic threat or "second move," and strategic promises. All depend on commitments:

> If the essence of a game of strategy is the dependence of each person's proper choice of action on what he expects the other to do, it may be useful to define a "strategic move" as follows: A strategic move is one that influences the other person's choice, in a manner favorable to one's self, by affecting the other person's expectations of how one's self will behave. One constrains the partner's choice by constraining one's own behavior. The object is to set up for one's self and communicate persuasively to the other player a mode of behavior (including conditional responses to the other's behavior) that leaves the other a simple maximization problem whose solution for him is the optimum for one's self, and to destroy the other's ability to do the same (Schelling, 1960, p. 160).

"First move." If one party can commit himself irrevocably to a certain position as described above, and convince the other party that his position is indeed irrevocable no matter what, he has won. The other party can only take it or leave it and, by definition, any solution is preferable to a breakdown in the relationships. In order to make first move effective, the commitment must be so convincing that there can be no question about it; preferably there is a penalty attached to nonfulfillment.

The *fait accompli* is a form of first move. "I've already bought the tickets to the concert; we'll have to go," says the spouse who did not want to go to the prize fight. Or a situation is created in which the commitment is validated by putting the onus on some third party. "I can't go to the party with you tonight, dear, much as I'd like to because I promised the boss I'd work tonight; if I don't he'll fire me." She cannot bargain against such a commitment; he has won.

Strategic threats. Strategic threats, like "first move," depend on commitments, but they are characteristic of situations where the opponent has "first move." They are, in fact, an attempt to gain the advantage of "first move."

> The threat differs from the ordinary commitment . . . in that it makes one's course of action *conditional* on what the other player does. While the commitment fixes one's course of action, the threat fixes a course of reaction, of response to the other player. The commitment is a means of gaining *first move* in a game in which first move carries an advantage; the threat is a commitment to a strategy for second move (Schelling, 1960, p. 124).

A theoretical distinction is made between a warning, which is also conditional, and a strategic threat. The essential characteristic of a warning is that it reminds the other party what will happen if he does, or does not do, something or other; it conveys information. In this sense it may be mutually beneficial; it prevents an inadvertent outcome by improving the warned person's understanding. In a warning, there is a clear incentive on the part of the warning person to do what he is warning the other that he will do. "If you continue to charge so many things, I'll refuse to pay the bills," is a warning. The husband has an incentive to do what he warns the wife he will do.

A strategic threat, however, is a more complex phenomenon.

The person who makes a strategic threat surrenders choice, renounces alternatives; more important, he changes his own incentive structure in such a way as to constrain his opponent. He commits himself to a course of action which he, as well as his opponent, wishes to avoid, a course of action, further, which has no necessarily logical relationship to the action of his opponent.

In a warning, there is a logical and understandable relationship between the action of Ego and the reaction of Alter. There is a tit-for-tat situation. It is easy to see why the husband will refuse to pay the bills if the wife continues to overspend. His incentive is clear; he will save money. In a strategic-threat situation, however, there is no necessarily logical relationship between the action of Ego and the threatened reaction of Alter, such, for example, as going through bankruptcy. Alter must therefore create an incentive. He can do this by making the threatened behavior preferable to any alternative. In both warning and strategic threat, there are dire consequences; but in the strategic threat they are made relatively less dire for the threatener than alternatives and more dire for the threatened than alternatives. Matrix 3 (Appendix) illustrates the strategic threat.

A strategic threat places on the threatened person the responsibility for the dire consequences to the threatener himself. It shifts blame. "If you continue to run home to your mother, I'll go back to drinking," says the husband as he brings home a fifth of whiskey. In order to be even more convincing, he tells her he has told his cronies what he will do. Neither he nor she wants him to go back to drinking; the strategic threat now puts her in the position of having to save him from doing something he doesn't want to do anyway in order to save his face vis-à-vis his friends and herself. He has changed the game. He has given himself an incentive (face-saving) to do something he prefers not to do (return to drinking). "If you don't stop running around with other women, I'll divorce you," says a wife, "and I have told mother so." Neither wants a divorce. She has given herself an incentive (again, face-saving vis-à-vis her mother) to do something she prefers not to do. She is putting him in the position of being to blame for the divorce, for ruining the marriage which neither wants to end. The threatened person must, in effect, protect the threatener in order to protect himself.

To be effective, of course, strategic threats must be credible. "If you don't get home for meals on time I'll kill myself" is an empty, meaningless threat for which it would be difficult to create a credible incentive. But "if you don't get home for meals on time I'll simply not eat at all" might be a credible threat; in order to keep himself from the onus of responsibility for her hunger and malnutrition, he must get to meals on time. In order to be credible, the strategic threat must make carrying out the threat the only alternative; reneging must be more painful than carrying it out. Otherwise, it may be taken as a bluff and called.

The strategic threat is especially interesting for interpreting marital relationships because its effectiveness is often based on love, pity, forbearance rather than – as in classic game theory, especially zero-sum game theory – on fear and hostility. The strategic threat is effective against people who care. One coerces an opponent by presenting him with an alternative that he just can't bring himself to select unless he is inhuman. It uses coercion by the self. It is the kind of thing that Gandhi exploited so successfully. The Hindus who chained themselves to railroad tracks knew that the engineer would not run over them; he couldn't, not because his engine was incapable of doing it, but because his self was. They won because their opponent was unable to select so horrible an alternative. Hunger strikes represent another example. The strategic threat puts both parties in a situation where, in order to save himself – literally "his self" – the threatened person must also save the threatening person.

Strategic promises. Strategic promises differ from conventional promises in that they are designed to induce or prevent behavior in an opponent. "If you promise to give up drinking, I'll promise to be more careful about keeping the house in order" is a bilateral commitment, similar to a bargaining situation. Sometimes unilateral promises may be used to get the opponent to do something good for both partners. "I promise to take you to the theater tonight" is reassuring to the wife; she doesn't have to promise to stay home. Being home and ready to go to the theater is more rewarding to both her and her husband than going out to play bridge with the girls.

To be effective as strategic moves, promises must truly commit. A person who offers no guarantee that he will fulfil his promise will find it hard to convince people; he must prove that he will fulfil it. He must also, if he wishes future promises to be effective, carry out his commitment. If he welshes on a promise, he will find it difficult to use it again; he cannot induce anyone to act in his favor, no matter what he promises. There is hardly anything more devastating than to find oneself faced with a dishonored promise after one has based his own choice of action on confidence in its fulfilment. The young man promises to marry the girl; she has sex relations with him. He reneges on his promise. "But you promised!" He replies cynically, "What are you going to do about it?" The promise to marry is usually validated by publishing banns or by getting a license or by wearing an engagement ring; there is now some penalty for reneging on the promise. "I want it in writing," or "Let's tell the family," or "a legal contract" are ways of giving promises genuine commitment value. Within the marriage relationship, such shoring up of promises is more difficult. Success in the strategic use of promises is more likely to rest on previous behavior, confidence, and trust.

Strategic release from commitments. Important as strategic commitment is — whatever form it may take — there is always a "risk of establishing an immovable position that goes beyond the ability of the other to concede, and thereby provoking the likelihood of stalemate or breakdown" (Schelling, 1960, p. 28). So some provision must be made for tactfully permitting an opponent to get out of commitments without loss of face. One must, in effect, reduce his losses and one's own gains by not "rubbing it in" or gloating over his capitulation.

Or sometimes one party may wish to make a concession and hesitate, not because of the loss of face involved, but because openly making a concession may lead an opponent to misinterpret his position. It may not only be construed as capitulation, but it may also "mark a prior commitment as a fraud, and make the adversary skeptical of any new pretense at commitment. One, therefore, needs an 'excuse' for accommodating his opponent, preferably a rationalized reinterpretation of the original commitment, one that is persuasive to the adversary himself" (Schelling, 1960, p. 34). The wife, that is, must persuade her husband that he is not really committed; or that he is not really giving in; or that his original commitment was genuine and he is acting on it; or that he has miscalculated his commitment; or that no precedent is being established; etc. She saves not only his face but also his reputation for use in future commitments. This verbal use of strategy has been called "casuistry." She also protects him from his friends or family by making it impossible for them to determine whether he has held to his commitment or not.

... when the opponent has resolved to make a moderate concession one may help him by proving that he can make a moderate concession consistent with his former position, and that if he does there are no grounds for believing it to reflect on his original principles. One must seek, in other words, a rationalization by which to deny oneself too great a reward from the opponent's concession, otherwise the concession will not be made (Schelling, 1960, p. 35).

There is no "I told you so," no gloating, no emphasis on the concession; but rather, face-saving and casual understatement.

Refusing communication. A major defense against strategic moves is simply not to permit oneself to be communicated with. It is often to Alter's advantage to be stupid, uncomprehending. This characteristic of the mixed-motive model helps to explain why it is that the weaker or the stupider partners in a marriage often seem to have the upper hand. They refuse to listen or they cannot understand, and thus cut off communication; this gives them, in effect, the advantage of first move. The partner must take it or leave it, and, often, he takes it. Or, if they listen, they fail to understand and thus cut themselves off from having to give. Marriages of this kind may last for years; they illustrate for the mate who cannot "get through" to the other the quiet desperation that Thoreau noted in the lives of many people. These marriages last as long as the rewards of remaining married exceed the costs, or as long as there is no preferable alternative. The time may come, of course, when the payoff or value of this outcome changes: it is no longer worth the costs to remain married; alternative outcomes seem preferable. Desertion or divorce may result. The spouse who has refused for years to accept communication may, in all sincerity, be surprised to find that the marriage has failed. "I just don't understand," he might say, after never having permitted himself to be enlightened.

Extortion and blackmail. A spouse who "has something" on a mate is in a position to exact blackmail. He (she) must pay to keep her (him) quiet. A spouse who is in a position to do a great deal of damage to a mate can use extortion. If a man's position in the community or his career would be greatly damaged by a divorce, his wife is in a strategic position to demand payment for being discreet. The time may come, of course, when he may feel that it is no longer worth while to protect his position at the expense of bribing his wife. The problem of limits would become involved. How far can she go before his value structure changes?

Despite the fact that the mixed-motive model is useful to explain and interpret hostile and fear-motivated behavior, however, it is most useful because it explains and interprets manipulative behavior based on love or compassion or pity or forbearance, as noted above. A spouse may win because he or she knows that the other "just can't" do what is required to win. The wife accepts an invitation in public, knowing that her husband "just can't" embarrass and humilitate her before others by rejecting the invitation she so obviously wishes to accept. Or the wife puts herself in a situation that will end in great embarrassment unless the husband does something or other, knowing that he "just can't" do this to her. Or the wife bails her husband out of a situation because she "just can't" let him down. A characteristic of the mixed-motive game, in brief, and one that makes it especially relevant for understanding marital adjustments, is that the preferred alternatives of an opponent may be changed by manipulating the matrix, by making the payoff or value of one alternative too costly in terms of pity, self-acceptance, self-image, self-conception, or what have you. One player makes a sacrifice of his gain because he "just can't" pursue his advantage. The loss of winning is greater than the loss of losing. He would hate himself if he won under these circumstances; he has to lose. The payoff for a strategy which demands giving in may be greater than for a strategy which demands winning. The wife may get a higher return for making a sacrifice than for insisting on her rights.

The Detroit study referred to above concluded that power in the sense of decision-making tended to gravitate toward those who were competent to exercise it.

> . . . the balance of power . . . is determined by the comparative resource-fulness of the two partners and by the life circumstances within which they live. . . . Husbands can no longer take for granted the *authority* held by older generations of men. No longer is the husband able to exercise power just because he is "the man of the house." Rather, he must prove his right to power, or win power by virtue of his own skills and accomplishments in competition with his wife (Blood & Wolfe, 1960, p. 29).

Yet in situations where decision-making involves conflict, it is sometimes noted that the less competent, the less able spouse wins. Strategic models help to explain this illogical situation when it occurs.

The mixed-motive model is valuable also because it highlights the fact that fairness or justice is not a necessary attribute of a marital adjustment. There are some situations in which men have an intrinsic advantage, others in which women do. Since, for example, sexual deprivation appears to be harder on men than on women, women have an advantage here. Women can use sex rejection as a strategic "chip" more successfully than men can. Contrariwise, men are usually the breadwinners; control of the pocketbook may give the husband an advantage in other areas. The double standard is not "fair" either; women are more likely than men to be condemned in extra-marital affairs. Even within the relationship itself, it is by no means "fair" that the person who values the marriage more should be at a strategic disadvantage vis-à-vis the spouse who values it less. It is not at all "fair" that the rigid, unyielding spouse should dominate in the relationship, or that the stupid one should have his (her) way. It is not "fair" that the more compassionate one, the more understanding one, the more generous one should yield to the less compassionate, understanding, or generous one. The mixed-motive model helps us understand why it is so difficult to achieve a "fair" adjustment in marital relationships.

*   *   *

Appendix: Illustrative Matrixes

The following matrixes are purely illustrative in nature. Even so, several caveats must be offered in order to prevent misunderstandings:

1. The numbers have no significance except that of describing a scale of preference of the players with respect to the several anticipated outcomes. They do not imply that a metric has been imposed on them. In Matrix I, the numbers mean only, for example, that Mary prefers to be at a prize fight with John (B2) to being at a concert with him (A1) or to being home with him (A3), and that she prefers being anywhere with him (A1, B2), except at home (C3), to being apart from him anywhere, etc.

2. The two numbers in any cell are never compared with one another. The comparisons are always among either the upper righthand numbers (Alter's values) or the lower lefthand numbers (Ego's values). If Mary's scale of preferences, as describ-

ed in Matrix 1, were set along a linear scale, they might look like Figure 2.

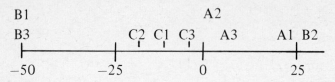

Figure 2

John's might look like Figure 3.
The units are not the same; John has greater capacity for enjoyment than Mary; he enjoys things more than she does. But their satisfactions are never compared with one another's, always with their own.

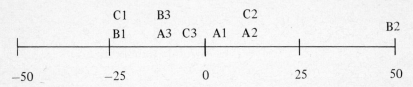

Figure 3.

3. It is not necessary to assume that people think as precisely about their preferences as the payoff matrix seems to imply. But it must be assumed that people do prefer certain outcomes to others. If all outcomes have equal value, there is no problem, chance can determine the outcome without regard to the players.

Illustrative Matrix 1.

Coordination Game: Common and Conflicting Interests Present, No Communication (Situation C)

Problem: John and Mary have quarreled at the breakfast table; they are not talking to one another when he leaves. How can they coordinate their behavior so that they can have the most enjoyable evening?

Preferences: The following matrix describes the relative value which each possible outcome has for each one.

Possible outcomes without communication:

Mary's Alternatives	John's Alternatives		
	Go to Concert (1)	Go to Prize Fight (2)	Stay at Home (3)
Go to Concert (A)	20 ^{5} (A1)	0 ^{10} (A2)	0 $^{-10}$ (A3)
Go to Prize Fight (B)	−50 $^{-20}$ (B1)	25 ^{50} (B2)	−50 $^{-10}$ (B3)
Stay at Home (C)	−10 $^{-20}$ (C1)	−20 ^{10} (C2)	−5 $^{-5}$ (C3)

Matrix 1.

A1. Both go to the concert. Mary enjoys the music but John is restless, looks bored, and thus detracts from the enjoyment. All he gets out of it is the pleasure of being with Mary. This outcome is "worth" 20 to Mary but only 5 to John, as shown in the cell for outcome A1.

A2. Mary goes to the concert and John goes to the prize fight. She doesn't get much enjoyment from the concert because John is not with her. John goes to the prize fight and enjoys it only moderately because Mary is not with him. This outcome has a value of zero for Mary and only 10 for John, again as shown in the cell for outcome A2 above.

A3. Mary goes to the concert and John stays home. She doesn't get any enjoyment because John is not with her. John is very bored and lonely without Mary.

B1. Mary goes to the prize fight and John goes to the concert. Both are miserable, not only because they are alone, but because neither enjoys the performance.

B2. Both go to the prize fight. Mary doesn't care for the performance but John enjoys it so much that she enjoys his pleasure and she enjoys being with him.

B3. Mary goes to the prize fight and John stays home. Both are miserable.

C1. Mary stays home and is lonely and miserable; John goes to the concert and is both bored and lonely.

C2. Mary stays home and John goes to the prize fight. She is lonely and miserable; he gets only moderate enjoyment from the prize fight because Mary is not with him.

C3. Both remain home and are bored and resentful because each missed a performance he (she) would have enjoyed.

Illustrative Matrix 1A.

Negative or Reverse Coordination Situation:
Mary Uses John's Expectations to Frustrate Him

Mary now gets more satisfaction out of deliberately disappointing John's expectations than by fulfilling them. She knows, as in Matrix 1, that he expects her to meet him at the prize fight (outcome B2), because he expects her to prefer being with him at the prize fight to being alone either at the concert or at home. So, knowing he will go to the prize fight, she deliberately disappoints his expectation that she will also go there by going to the concert or staying home (A2 or C2), thus reducing his satisfaction. She has reduced her own satisfaction also (as compared with Matrix 1), but this seems worth while to her in order to reduce his as well. She has "cut off her nose to spite her face."

Mary's Alternatives	John's Alternatives		
	1	(2)	(3)
(A)	0 $\quad^5$ (A1)	10 $\quad^{10}$ (A2)	20 $\quad^{-10}$ (A3)
(B)	−50 $^{-20}$ (B1)	0 $\quad^{50}$ (B2)	0 $\quad^{-10}$ (B3)
(C)	20 $^{-20}$ (C1)	10 $\quad^{10}$ (C2)	0 $\quad^{-5}$ (C3)

Matrix 1A.

Illustrative Matrix 2.

Advantage of First Move (Situation D)

If Ego had first move, he would select A, assuming that Alter would select 1 and the outcome would be A1. But if somehow or other Alter can manage to appropriate first move, he will select 2 and Ego will have to settle for B. The outcome would then be B2.

Ego's Alternatives	Alter's Alternatives	
	1	2
A	7 $\quad^8$ (A1)	4 $\quad^3$ (A2)
B	2 $\quad^1$ (B1)	5 $\quad^{10}$ (B2)

Matrix 2.

194 *Jessie Bernard*

Illustrative Matrix 3
Manipulative Use of Strategic Threat by Alter
When Ego Has First Move (Situation D)

In this situation Ego prefers alternative A. This leaves for Alter the choice between 0 and −6, according to whether he selects 1 or 2. He could select 1, and the result would be outcome A1. If, however, he can threaten Ego with selecting 2 and convince Ego that he will carry out this threat, then Ego will prefer B to A, since the payoff is greater. Outcome B2 results. If Ego is not deterred by Alter's threat, both lose with outcome A2.

Ego's Alternatives	Alter's Alternatives			
	1		2	
A	6	0 (A1)	1	−6 (A2)
B	−3	8 (B1)	2	12 (B2)

Matrix 3.

Illustrative Matrix 3A.
Warning Distinguished from Strategic
Threat (Situation D)

Ego, in the absence of information about the probabilities of Alter's choice of 1 or 2, might be tempted to select A, taking a chance that Alter will select 1, leading to outcome A1. Alter's warning supplies the information Ego needs to make a better selection. When Alter "warns" that he will select 2, Ego changes his mind and selects B, leading to outcome B2. Alter's warning is not a threat, because 2 is preferable to him. He is not coercing Ego. If Ego had had all the necessary information in the first place, he would have known that B2 was as good a solution as he could expect; Alter's warning has clarified the outcomes and helped him select the one he would have selected in the first place.

Ego's Alternatives	Alter's Alternatives	
	1	2
A	6 11 (A1)	1 11 (A2)
B	−3 11 (B1)	3 12 (B2)

Matrix 3A.

Illustrative Matrix 4.
Manipulative Use of Strategic Promise by Alter When Ego Has First Move (Situation D)

Ordinarily Ego, to avoid the possibility of losing 6, selects A. This leaves for Alter the choice between gaining 5 or 0, according to whether he selects 1 or 2. He would select 1, and the result would be outcome A1. If, however, Alter can promise Ego that he will select 2 if Ego will select B, both can double their payoffs with the outcome B2. If alter should renege on his promise and select 1 in order to raise his payoff from 10 to 12, leaving Ego with a loss of 6, the basis of trust between them would be shaken if not destroyed, and Alter would lose his ability to promise in the future.

Ego's Alternatives	Alter's Alternatives	
	1	2
A	3 5 (A1)	6 0 (A2)
B	−6 12 (B1)	6 10 (B2)

Matrix 4.

WORKS CITED

Blood, R. O., Jr. and Wolfe, D. M. *Husbands and Wives; the Dynamics of Married Living.* Glencoe, Ill.: Free Press, 1960.

Firey, W. "Informal Organization and the Theory of Schism," *American Sociological Review,* 13 (1948), pp. 15-24.

Lantz, H. R. and Snyder, Eloise C. *Marriage: An Examination of Man-Woman Relationships.* New York: Wiley, 1962.

Luce, R. D. and Raiffa, H. *Games and Decisions.* New York: Wiley, 1957.

Luckey, Eleanore B. "Marital Satisfaction and Congruent Self-Spouse Concepts," *Social Forces,* 39 (1960), pp. 153-157.

Rainwater, L. and Weinstein, Karol K. *And the Poor Get Children.* Chicago: Quadrangle Books, 1960.

Rapoport, A. *Fights, Games, and Debates.* Ann Arbor: University of Michigan Press, 1960.

Rowbotham, J. M. *Troubadours and Courts of Love.* New York: Macmillan, 1895.

Schelling, T. C. *The Strategy of Conflict.* Cambridge: Harvard University Press, 1960.

Siegel, S. "A Method for Obtaining an Ordered Metric Scale," *Psychometrika,* 21 (1956), pp. 207-216.

Waller, W. and Hill, R. *The Family, a Dynamic Interpretation.* New York: Dryden Press, 1951.

Williams, J. D. *The Compleat Strategyst.* New York: McGraw-Hill, 1954.

Interpersonal Perception

Ronald Laing, Herbert Phillipson

and A. Russell Lee

In this paper, a mixed-motive model is employed in the discussion of semantic difficulties that arise in the selection and definition of concepts in complex interpersonal interactions. Demonstrating that it is possible to theorize about complex interrelationships with a manageable number of concepts, Laing, Phillipson and Lee *provide conceptual resources which could aid family sociologists, focusing on situational interactive processes as family members relate to one another "personally" as well as "positionally."*

Human beings are constantly thinking about others and about what others are thinking about them, and what others think they are thinking about the others, and so on. One may be wondering about what is going on inside the other. One desires or fears that other people will know what is going on inside oneself.

A man may feel that his wife does not understand him. What may this mean? It could mean that he thinks she does not realize that he feels neglected. Or he may think that she does not realize that he loves her. Or it may be that he thinks that she thinks that he is mean, when he just wants to be careful; that he is cruel, when he just wants to be firm; that he is selfish when he just does not want to be used as a doormat.

Reprinted, with permission of the authors and publisher from *Interpersonal Perception*, London: Tavistock Publications, 1966, pp. 23-34.

His wife may feel that he thinks that she thinks he is selfish when all she wants is to get him to be a little less reserved. She may think that he thinks that she thinks he is cruel, because she feels he always takes everything she says as an accusation. She may think that he thinks he understands her, when she thinks he has not begun to see her as a real person, and so on.

One sees both that this area is the very heart of many relationships, and that we have in fact very little systematic and scientifically tested information about it. But let us first of all *think* about the problem a little further.

One or both persons in a twosome may spiral off into third, fourth, even fifth levels of what we have suggested may be called *meta*perspectives. Such a spiral develops, for instance, whenever two persons mistrust each other.

We do not know how people resolve mistrust that takes on this formal structure, but we know that such mistrust is common, and that it sometimes seems to go on endlessly. Logically, the possibilities are that it may end by unilateral or bilateral disarmament; by unilateral separation or mutual divorce; or by a parametric change occurring. Let us consider a simplified version of this spiral.

Jack and Jill are ostensibly in love, and each feels he or she loves the other, but Jack is not sure whether Jill loves Jack, and Jill is not sure whether Jack loves Jill. Jack feels he loves Jill, but does not know whether Jill really believes in his love. Jill feels she loves Jack, but is not sure whether Jack believes she loves him. How can each prove to the other that each loves the other?

Suppose that Jack is what is psychiatrically termed paranoid. This term is a rather inadequate descriptive generalization for certain regularities in Jack's experience and actions, one of which is a persistent tendency to mistrust certain significant others. He persistently refuses to infer from Jill's behaviour towards him, however loving, that she "really" loves him, but believes, despite evidence from Jill's manifest behaviour (he may sooner or later have to invent her "behaviour") that she loves Tom, Dick or Harry. A curious feature of Jack's tendency to attribute to Jill a lack of love for him and a love for Tom, Dick or Harry (for reasons we do not pursue at present) often seems to be that he tends to make this attribution in inverse proportion to Jill's testimony and actions to the contrary.

Jack may reason: "Look at all the things that Jill is doing to try to prove to me that she loves me. If she really loved me she would not have to be so obvious about it and try so hard. The fact that she is trying so hard proves she is pretending. She must be trying to cover up her feelings — she must be trying to cover up her true feelings. She probably loves Tom".

At this point Jill is in a double-bind. If she tries to act even more loving, she further activates Jack's assumption that she is pretending. If, on the other hand, she pretends to act less loving and more aloof then she certainly will activate his view that she does not love him. He then can say: "See, I told you so, she really doesn't love me. Look at how aloof she has become."

Jack's phantasy coefficient in his experience of Jill rises as his perception of her tends to discount his phantasy of her.

Thus, the *issue* that he is preoccupied with is love. The *direction* of this issue is Jill's love for Jack. His prototypical expectation is that Jill does not love him. For Jack this issue shapes every other issue in that he coordinates his whole field of experience and his whole field of action around this issue. Now, let us suppose that Jill feels she loves Jack, but realizes that he thinks she does not. The situation then is: Jack thinks Jill does not love him. Jill thinks she loves Jack, but Jill realizes that Jack thinks that she does not love him.

Now, Jack may decide to resolve his mistrust by various moves that one generally regards as part of the paranoid strategy. He may pretend to Jill that he does think she loves him, so that, in his view of her, she will think she has fooled him. He will then mount evidence (she has exchanged glances with a man, she smiled at a man, her walk gives her away because it is the way a prostitute walks, etc.) that seems to him to substantiate his secretly held view that she does not love him. But as his suspicion mounts, he may discover that the evidence he has accumulated suddenly looks very thin. This does not prove, however, that his attribution is incorrect; it proves that he has not taken into account how clever she is. In other words, he invents a meta-meta-perspective for her, to cap his metaperspective. Thus, he reasons: "I have not been smart enough. She realizes that I am suspicious so she is not giving anything away. I had better bluff her by pretending to some suspicions that I do not feel, so that she will think I'm on the wrong track". So he pretends to her that he thinks she is having an affair with Tom, when he "knows" that she is having an affair with Dick.

This type of reflection occurs empirically in almost the "pure" form outlined above. This aspect of the paranoid's strategy has still not been adequately explored, but even less is known about how Jack's behaviour and experience is really influenced by and influences Jill and others.

Another form of unilateral spiral is the spiral of concern. Here, the decisive direction of issue is Jill's view of Jack's view of Jill's acts towards Jack. (I want you to know I love you.) The persons in whom we see this in purest form are, in clinical terms, depressed and/or obsessional.

However, I may act not only on my own experience but on the other person's experience, by acting on the other so that he will experience me and himself as I wish him to do and act in the way that will enable me to experience him in the way I wish. Reciprocally, the other is experiencing and acting in relation to me, so that I am subject to his actions as he is to mine.

. . . Peter may attempt to control the situation by acting directly on Paul, so that Paul will act towards Peter in a way which Peter wishes, and that this may be either so that he, Peter, can continue to experience himself and Paul suitably, or so that he can be experienced by Paul as he wishes to be. In a system constantly sustained by two agents and comprising nothing other than their behaviour and experience, action either "internally" on self or outwardly through behaviour on the other is the medium for effecting change or for negating change. If it is a steady state that is desired, then, in this dyadic system, it is by *action* by each on self and on other that the steady state of the system is maintained.

Let us consider the way a husband's behaviour towards his wife functions in terms of the husband-and-wife conceived *as a system*.

Husband acts on wife so that wife will experience husband's actions in a particular way. But wife has to *act* in such a way before the husband can realize that she experiences his act conjunctively or disjunctively to his intention; thus, husband's behaviour towards wife affects her experience of him, which, mediated back to him by her behaviour towards him, in turn influences his experience of her. Through this circuit he may feel that his experience is directly related to her experience. For instance, let us say he has acted in some way that he meant to be helpful, but she feels is unhelpful and even cruel. Through the circuit of B and E he then may feel that he *has* been unkind, so that his own self-experience is now implicated. In order to keep his own self-experience and self-identity as he wants it (I am a helpful person, now I feel unhelpful and even cruel), he has to initiate another dyadic circuit by actions toward *her*, by saying, for instance, "I'm sorry", and making amends, reparation, and so on.

We see that in a dyadic system, there is no isolated individual person. The one person, in order to maintain *his own* self-identity, has to *act towards the other,* and however adroit a strategist he may be, he can never rely on controlling the other. She wishes to see herself as kind, but he feels her to be cruel. He wants to be helpful; she finds him a nuisance. Each person has to act outwardly in order to achieve and maintain his or her own inner peace. At best this intimate intermeshed coexistence can be reciprocally confirmatory; at worst it is a mish-mash in which both can lose themselves.

If the other is at one and the same time a threat and necessary to self's identity, then he or she may require to be permanently disarmed and controlled.

There are a number of ways of doing this. We have mentioned some of them. One acts towards the other to control his experience; through his experience, his behaviour; through his behaviour one's experience of his behaviour; finally, by a sort of ellipsis, through one's experience of the other's experience, one's experience of oneself. What I think you think of me reverberates back to what I think of myself, and what I think of myself in turn affects the way I act towards you. This influences in turn how you feel about yourself and the way you act towards me, and so on. One may, however, seek to eliminate this dyadic circuit, at any rate from one's own point of view. If one can act upon one's *own* experience of the other, so that one can shape to one's own desire the way one sees the other and hence the way one supposes the other sees oneself, is it worth the bother to act toward the other in order to shape *the other's* experience? Perhaps not, if it could work. Action towards the other would then be only a gesture performed before a mirror.

Let us consider one facet of an extremely simplified dyadic phantasy system, reverberating around the issue of greed and meanness.

Jack feels Jill is greedy. Jill feels Jack is mean. That is, Jack feels Jill wants too much from him whereas Jill feels Jack does not give her enough. Moreover Jack feels that Jill is mean as well as greedy. And Jill feels that Jack is greedy as well as mean. Each feels that the other has and is withholding what he or she needs. Moreover, Jack does not feel he is either greedy or mean himself, nor does Jill. Jack, however, realizes that Jill thinks he is mean, and Jill realizes that Jack thinks she is greedy. In view of the fact that Jack feels he is already overgenerous, he resents being regarded as mean. In view of the fact that Jill feels that she puts up with so little, she resents being regarded as greedy. Since Jack feels generous but realizes that Jill thinks he is mean, and since Jill feels deprived and realizes that Jack thinks she is greedy, each resents the other and retaliates. If, after all I've put up with, you feel that I'm greedy, then I'm not going to be so forbearing in the future. If, after all I've given you, you feel I'm mean, then you're not getting anything from me any more. The circle is whirling and becomes increasingly vicious. Jack becomes increasingly exhausted by Jill's greed and Jill becomes increasingly starved by Jack's meanness. Greed and meanness are now so confused in and between each and both that they appear to take on a life of their own. Like two boxers dominated by the fight that they are themselves fighting, the dyad, the system, the marriage, becomes "the problem" to each of the persons who comprise it, rather than they themselves. Jack and Jill are not divorced from each other, but they are divorced from the system that their own interaction and interexperience has generated, which now presents itself to each of them as a container, a mechanical machine in which both are being mangled. Each has now become caught and entangled in the properties of a system of a relationship that is experienced by *both* as a prison. Each may now experience the system as a third party — in phantasy terms, a container, a persecuting machine, a suffocating prison, something one is inside, in which one cannot move or breathe, in which one is entangled. Only when it is impossible to live in an impossible situation any more may the process be reversed. It is just from the experience of the *common situation,* now *shared,* that a ray of deliverance may be glimpsed.

Jack and Jill in the above example are much more in touch with each other than usually is the case. On the level of direct perspective that each has of self and other, they are in disagreement. However, each realizes how the other feels. That is, each person's metaperspective is in play, and is correct. Furthermore, each realizes that he or she is understood, in so far as one's point of view is at least recognized. That is, no disjunction is postulated between direct and meta, or between meta-meta and metalevels of experience.

Now, in the terms of the present discussion:

a) *understanding* can be defined as the conjunction between the metaperspective of one person and the direct perspective of the other;

b) *being understood* is the conjunction between the meta-metaperspective of the one person and the metaperspective of the other.

c) the *feeling* of being understood is the conjunction of one's own direct perspective with one's *own* meta-metaperspective.

There is a peculiar satisfaction in feeling that one understands another person, and in feeling that one is being understood.

Patently, however, two people may neither understand each other completely nor wish to. They may understand each other while supposing that they do not understand. Understanding may be greater over some issues than in others. The relationship may be relatively symmetrical, in that each understands the other to about the same extent over the same issues, or it may be lopsided, one person, in Jung's sense, being the container and the other the contained. The feeling of being understood entails feeling that the other person's *meta*perspective is correct; in other words, that one's own meta-metafeeling corresponds to one's own direct perspective. One is now operating between all three levels. The feeling of being understood or misunderstood may be desired or feared. Its presence may be comforting or disconcerting. Its presence may mean a sense of being together, its absence a sense of solitude.

People will vary as to whether or not they would rather be understood or understand. An important aspect of each person's *self*-concept is the extent to which he feels capable of being understood. An important aspect of one's image of the other is the extent to which one feels the other can or does understand oneself.

Whether or not it is easier to make guesses between second and first order perspectives, or between third and second order perspectives, is an interesting question, and one towards which our method can contribute an answer.

We must remember that some people feel extremely persecuted because they persist in attributing to the others a capacity to know what is going on in them far higher than the others actually do possess. This may be because they grew up with another who had such an ability (e.g., identical twin), or who in fact laid claims to such understanding. In intergroup and international as well as in interpersonal dyadic systems, the desires to be understood in some respects, the fears of being known in others, the efforts taken towards being understood, and the precautions taken against being known, together with the complementary manoeuvers to achieve knowledge of the other, legitimately and illegitimately (espionage), quite evidently play a large part.

From the point of view of the subject, the starting point is often between the second and third order level of perspective. Jill thinks that Jack thinks that she does not love him, that she neglects him, that she is destroying him, and so on, although she says she does not think that she is doing any of these things. In this position, it is open to Jill to do a number of things. She may constantly complain to Jack that Jack does not realize how much she is doing for him, and that he is always sorry for himself. He may protest that he thinks she is doing all sorts of things for him, but she does not believe him. She may express fears lest he think that she thinks that he is ungrateful to her for all she is doing, when she wants him to know that she does *not* think that he thinks she thinks he thinks that she does not do enough. Here, the *initial* situation from Jill's point of view is: Jill thinks that Jack thinks that Jill neglects him. One move that the other may make in order to break such a unilateral spiral is to break into it at one level of perspective. Thus, Jill thinks Jack does not believe that Jill loves Jack. Jack's move may be to say: "But I *do* believe you *do*." This direct contradiction, in this case intended as reassurance, is usually thought by psychiatrists, psychoanalysts, marriage counsellors, and so on to be ineffective.

A way to enter such a situation therapeutically is to get both Jack and Jill to define their criteria for generosity and to define how their parents defined generosity. One discovers that Jack's father treated his mother very differently than Jill's father treated her mother. Jack's father was too poor to have brought home enough money to make his family feel secure against the possibility of being evicted or not having enough food. Jack remembers vividly how his mother complained to his father about his inadequate income. From this Jack developed the viewpoint that if his father had simply made enough money his mother would have been eternally grateful. Since he is now successful financially, he expects Jill to be eternally grateful to him for providing her with a security that his mother never had. On the other hand, Jill has come from a wealthy family in which there was never any comparable issue of financial insecurity. In Jill's family, consideration, love and kindness were expressed through the giving of gifts, the remembering of anniversaries, etc. She had learned to take it for granted that the man will provide her with an economically secure home. What she looks for are the little niceties which she feels indicate true considerateness, kindness and love. For Jack these niceties are irrelevant; they are minor details, trivia by comparison to the other things he does for the family. However, if each can discover his or her own and the other's value system and thereby see the conjunctions and discrepancies between them, it becomes possible for each to explain himself or herself to the other. It is now, for the first time, feasible for Jack to say: "Well, if it really is that important to you that I remember your birthday, I'll do my darndest to try". It is now possible for Jill to "appreciate" Jack more as a provider in the family. If bitterness and revenge (I am going to hurt you for the hurt you have done to me) have not intensified too much, it may still be relatively simple for each to satisfy the other's expectations according to their idiosyncratic value systems. Such an incredibly simple move can sometimes produce very powerful effects, particularly, early in a relationship. Once a history has been developed of pain and misery, the matter becomes correspondingly more complex and difficult to reorient.

There are innumerable such unilateral and bilateral spirals as well as those of giving-taking, trust-mistrust, indifference and concern. There are "ascending" "manic" spirals (I'm happy that you're happy I'm happy), and "descending" "depressive" ones (I'm sad that you're sad, etc.); all are in a sense "obsessive". Such spirals can be attempts to get out of a *false or untenable position.* The danger to the persons involved is that the next *move* may be catastrophic. It may be the *last move ever;* it may be the end of the relationship, or the end of the world.

Here we are particularly concerned with how such a unilateral spiral functions in the dyad system. After the twists of the spiral have been extended to a third, even fourth, level, at some point a relatively steady state of reciprocal mistrust, precarious happiness, common misery or terror becomes established. It may be that the only hope at the precatastrophic position is to make a move to change the whole axis of orientation, to change the issue, both in content and direction, and one person has to make the change initially.

Psychoanalytic interpretations often have this form.

Thus, Jack maintains that the issue is: does Jill love Jack, or Tom, Dick or Harry? An analytic interpretation to Jack might be that the "real" or more basic issue is: does *Jack* love Jill, or Tom, Dick or Harry? That is, the analyst (Freud in the Schreber case) registers that in Jack's view the issue is whether or not Jill is unfaithful to him, but feels that Jack should come to examine both the nature of his relation to *Jill* (rather than Jill's relation to him) and of his relation to Tom (rather than Jill's relation to Tom). That is, in the twosome Jack and Jill, the analyst would wish to change Jack's axis of orientation away from his attempt to infer the quality of Jill's experience of him *from* the testimony of her behaviour towards him *to* the nature of his feelings about Jill and Tom. The analyst's thesis in this case might be expressed as: Jack attributes to Jill's feelings towards Tom what he is afraid to infer about his own feelings about Tom, if he were to examine his own behaviour.

A family therapist would feel that it was insufficient to relate to Jack alone in such an interpersonal nexus. He would wish to observe directly how Jack, Jill, Tom, Dick or Harry all relate to one another. In the course of his close examinations of how Jill, for instance, actually behaves with Jack and with Tom, Dick or Harry, he may discover that she indeed is much more demonstrative with them than she is with Jack. And this might even fit her idea of how a wife should be. Jack, however, may feel that Jill's increased demonstrativeness to them is proof that she loves these other men more than himself. One such wife in therapy stated: "But of course I make a bigger fuss over your friends than I do over you. When I am with your friends I put on my social self. When I am with you I'm my real self". The implication being that she saw it as her duty to act in a "charming" way in social situations, but with her own husband she felt able to "be herself". Said she, "Would you want me to act with you, too"? Said he, "No I just would prefer that you would stop acting with others and be your natural self all the time".

Another form of reciprocal alienation gives rise to some very strange situations. Let us suppose again that the pivotal issue between two persons is love. Then my concern may be my love for you, or your love for me. My concern, however, may not be whether I love you or you love me, but whether you need my love. Similarly, your concern may not be whether you love me, or whether I love you, but whether I need your love.

This is a common issue in modern marriage, how common one does not know. Neither party is concerned so much about direct perspectives or direct issues, but about a second or third level. In these terms, I do not want someone to love or someone to love me, but I need someone to need me, and the other is someone who needs me to need her. This reciprocal dependence on the other's dependence is a form of reciprocity tending towards a spiral effect wherein each may become reciprocally more estranged from the act of directly giving or receiving love, and each in greater and greater alienation may even suppose that this is to grow deeper and deeper "in love".

This can be elevated to a system of rights and obligations. If each person is concerned about what the other thinks, feels, does, he may come to regard it as his *right* to expect the other to be concerned about him, and to be under an obligation to feel concern toward the other in turn. I make no move without feeling it as my right that you should be happy or sad, proud or ashamed, of what I do. And I regard you as callous if you do not concern yourself about my concern for you when you do anything.

My need has then ceased to be a matter of direct loving and being loved. My need is for the *other's* need of me. His or her need is that I need him or her. It is my need to be needed by the other. My desire is no longer to love and to be loved. My solicitude is not for another, but for another to want me. My want is a want to be wanted; my longing, a longing to be longed for. And in the same way, my emptiness is that the other does not require me to fulfill him or her. Similarly the other wants to be wanted by me, longs to be longed for by me.

The most natural thing in the world is the desire to love and to be loved. Which is the greater misfortune, to love without being loved or to be loved without loving? Very few people would admit to wanting either contingency. Yet we find people driving themselves into such situations all the time. Why? We say it is "compulsive". We are fortunately not trying to explain the why of this, but to describe the what. And one of the most hellish whirligigs of our contemporary interpersonal alienation is that of two alienated loves, two self-perpetuating solitudes, each in emptiness feeding on the other's emptiness, an inextricable and timeless confusion, tragic and comic — the ever fertile soil of endless recrimination and desolation.

Selected Bibliography

Institutional

1. Definitive studies

KOENIG, Daniel J. and A. E. Bayer, "The Institutional Frame of Reference in Family Study," in *Emerging Conceptual Frameworks in Family Analysis,* ed. by Ivan F. Nye and Felix M. Berardo, New York: The Macmillan Co., 1966, pp. 78-96.

SIRJAMAKI, John, "The Institutional Approach," in *Handbook of Marriage and the Family."* ed. by Harold T. Christensen, Chicago: Rand McNally, 1964, pp. 33-50.

2. Definitive and Illustrative studies

CALHOUN, Arthur W., *A Social History of the American Family: From Colonial Times to Present,* New York: Barnes and Noble, Inc., 1945.

KENKEL, William F., *The Family in Perspective,* 2nd ed. New York: Appleton-Century-Crofts, 1961.

SIRJAMAKI, John, *The American Family in the Twentieth Century,* Cambridge: Harvard University Press, 1953, pp. 3-10.

3. Illustrative studies

KEPHART, William, "Legal and Procedural Aspects of Marriage and Divorce," in *Handbook of Marriage and the Family,* ed. by Harold T. Christensen, Chicago: Rand McNally & Co., 1964, pp. 944-968.

MACE, David and V. Mace, *Marriage East and West,* New York: Doubleday & Co., Inc., 1960.

QUEEN, Stuart A. and J. B. Adams, *The Family in Various Cultures*, Philadelphia: J. B. Lippincott Co., 1952.

THOMAS, John L., "Family Values in a Pluralistic Society," *American Catholic Sociological Review*, 23 (1962), pp. 30-40.

THOMAS, John L., *The American Catholic Family*, New Jersey: Prentice-Hall, Inc., 1956.

VINCENT, Clark E., "Unmarried Fathers and the Mores: 'Sexual Exploiter' as an Ex Post Facto Label," *American Sociological Review*, 25 (1960), pp. 40-46.

ZIMMERMAN, Carle C., *Family and Civilization*, New York: Harper & Row, 1947.

Anthropological

1. Definitive studies

EISENSTADT, S. N., "Anthropological Studies of Complex Societies," *Current Anthropology*, 2 (1961), pp. 201-222.

LEWIS, Oscar, "An Anthropological Approach to Family Studies," *American Journal of Sociology*, 55 (1950), pp. 468-475.

2. Illustrative studies

LEWIS, Oscar, *Pedro Martinez*, Toronto: Random House, 1964.

MEAD, Margaret, "The Contemporary American Family as an Anthropologist sees it," *American Journal of Sociology*, 53 (1948), pp. 453-459.

MURDOCK, George P., *Social Structure*, New York: The Macmillan Co., 1949.

MURDOCK, George P., "Family Stability in Non-European Cultures," *The Annals*, 272 (1950), pp. 195-201.

RADCLIFFE-BROWN, A. R. and D. Forde, eds., *African Systems of Kinship and Marriage*, New York: Oxford University Press, Inc., 1950.

ZELDITCH, Morris, Jr., "Cross Cultural Analysis of Family Structure," in *Handbook of Marriage and the Family*, ed. by Harold T. Christensen, Chicago: Rand McNally, 1964, pp. 462-500.

ZELDITCH, Morris, Jr., "Family, Marriage and Kinship," in *Handbook of Modern Sociology*, ed. by R. E. L. Faris, Chicago: Rand McNally, 1964, pp. 680-733.

Structure Function

1. Definitive studies

BARBER, Bernard, "Structure-Function Analysis: Some Problems and Misunderstandings," *American Sociological Review*, 21 (1956), pp. 129-133.

BELL, Norman W. and E. F. Vogel, "Toward a Framework for Functional Analysis of Family Behavior," in *A Modern Introduction to the Family*, ed. by Bell & Vogel, Glencoe, Ill.: The Free Press, 1960, pp. 1-33.

BREDEMEIER, Harry C. and R. M. Stephenson, *The Analysis of Social Systems*, New York: Holt, Rinehart & Winston, Inc., 1962.

COSER, Rose L., ed., *The Family: Its Structure and Functions*, New York: St. Martin's Press, Inc., 1964.

GOODE, William, "The Sociology of the Family," in *Sociology Today*, ed. by Robert K. Merton, Leonard Broom, and Leonard S. Cottrell, Jr., New York: Basic Books, Inc., 1959.

McINTYRE, Jennie, "The Structure-Functional Approach to Family Study," in *Emerging Conceptual Frameworks in Family Analysis*, ed. by Ivan F. Nye and Felix M. Berardo, New York: The Macmillan Co., 1966, pp. 52-77.

PARSONS, Talcott and R. F. Bales, with J. Olds, M. Zelditch, Jr., and P. Slater, *Family, Socialization and Interaction Process*, Glencoe, Ill.: The Free Press, 1955.

PITTS, Jesse R., "The Structural-Functional Approach," in *Handbook of Marriage and the Family*, ed. by Harold T. Christensen, Chicago: Rand McNally, 1964, pp. 51-124.

2. Illustrative studies

GOODE, William, *After Divorce*, Glencoe, Ill.: The Free Press, 1956.

KOMAROVSKY, Mirra, "Functional Analysis of Sex Roles," *American Sociological Review*, 15 (1950), pp. 508-516.

LEVY, Marion J., *The Family Revolution in Modern China,* Cambridge, Mass.: Harvard University Press, 1949.

PARSONS, Talcott, "The Social Structure of the Family," in *The Family: Its Function and Destiny,* ed. by Ruth Anshen, New York: Harper & Row, 1959, p. 263 ff.

SCOTT, Frances G., "Family Group Structure and Patterns of Social Interaction," *American Journal of Sociology,* 68 (1962), pp. 214-228.

SUSSMAN, Marvin B. and L. Burchinal, "Kin Family Network: Unheralded Structure in Current Conceptualizations of Family Functioning," *Marriage and Family Living,* 24 (1962), pp. 231-240.

WINCH, Robert F., *The Modern Family,* New York: Holt, Rinehart & Winston, Inc., 1963.

WINCH, Robert F., R. McGinnis and H. R. Barringer, eds., *Selected Studies in Marriage and the Family,* New York: Holt, Rinehart & Winston, rev. ed., 1962.

Situational

1. Definitive studies

BOSSARD, James H. S. and E. S. Boll, *Family Situations,* Philadelphia: University of Pennsylvania Press, 1943.

CARR, Lowell J., *Situational Analysis: An Observational Approach to Introductory Sociology,* New York: Harper & Row, 1948.

ELIOT, Thomas D., "Human Controls as Situation-Process," *American Sociological Review,* 8 (1943), pp. 380-388.

RALLINGS, Elisha M., "A Conceptual Framework for Studying the Family: the Situational Approach," in *Emerging Conceptual Frameworks in Family Analysis,* ed. by Ivan F. Nye and Felix M. Berardo, New York: The Macmillan Co., 1966, pp. 130-151.

RAUSH, Harold L., A. T. Dittman and T. J. Taylor, "Person, Setting, and Change in Social Interaction," *Human Relations,* 12 (1959), pp. 361-377.

2. Illustrative studies

BOULDING, Elise, "Family Adjustment to War Separation and Reunion," *The Annals,* 272 (1950), pp. 59-68.

BLOOD, Robert O., Jr., "A Situational Approach to the Study of Permissiveness and Child Rearing," *American Sociological Review*, 18 (1953), pp. 84-87.

CARR, Lowell J., "A Situational Approach to Conflict and War," *Social Forces*, 24 (1946), pp. 300-303.

FREIDSON, Eliot, "The Relation of the Social Situation of Contact to the Media in Mass Communication," *Public Opinion Quarterly*, 17 (1953-54), pp. 230-238.

HILL, Reuben and E. Boulding, *Families Under Stress*, New York: Harper & Row, 1949.

RALLINGS, Elisha M., "Family Situations of Married and Never-married Males," *Journal of Marriage and the Family*, 28 (1966), pp. 485-490.

STREIB, Gordon F., "Intergenerational Relations: Perspectives of the Two Generations on the Older Parent," *Journal of Marriage and the Family*, 27 (1965), pp. 469-479.

Symbolic Interactional

1. Definitive studies

BURGESS, Ernest W., "The Family as a Unity of Interacting Personalities," *The Family*, 7 (1926), pp. 3-9.

KOMAROVSKY, Mirra and W. Waller, "Studies of the Family," *American Journal of Sociology*, 50 (1945), pp. 445-451.

KUHN, Manford H., "Major Trends in Symbolic Interaction Theory in the Past 25 Years," *Sociological Quarterly*, 5 (1964), pp. 61-84.

MANIS, Jerome G. and B. M. Meltzer, eds., *Symbolic Interaction*, Boston: Allyn & Bacon, 1967.

MEAD, George H., *Mind, Self and Society*, Chicago: University of Chicago Press, 1934.

SCHVANEVELDT, Jay D., "The Interactional Framework in the Study of the Family," in *Emerging Conceptual Frameworks in Family Analysis*, ed. by Ivan F. Nye and Felix M. Berardo, New York: The Macmillan Co., 1966, pp. 97-129.

SHIBUTANI, Tamotsu, *Society and Personality: An Interactionist Approach to Social Psychology*, New Jersey: Prentice-Hall, Inc., 1961.

STRYKER, Sheldon, "The Interactional and Situational Approaches," in *Handbook of Marriage and the Family*, ed. by Harold T. Christensen, Chicago: Rand McNally & Co., 1964, pp. 125-170.

2. Illustrative studies

DYER, Everett D., "Parenthood as Crises: A Re-Study," *Marriage and Family Living*, 25 (1963), pp. 196-201.

GOMBERG, Robert, "Family Diagnosis, Trend in Theory and Practice," *Social Casework*, 39 (1953), pp. 73-83.

HILL, Reuben, J. M. Stycos, and K. W. Back, *The Family and Population Control: a Puerto Rican Experiment in Social Change*, Chapel Hill: University of North Carolina Press, 1959.

LAING, Ronald D., *et al.*, *Interpersonal Perception: a Theory and a Method of Research*, London: Tavistock, 1966.

MIYAMOTO, Frank S. and S. M. Dornbusch, "A Test of Interactionist Hypotheses of Self Conception," *American Journal of Sociology*, 61 (1956), pp. 399-403.

MOWRER, Ernest R. and H. Mowrer, "The Social Psychology of Marriage," *American Sociological Review*, 16 (1957), pp. 27-36.

MOWRER, Harriet, "Getting Along in Marriage," in *Family, Marriage, and Parenthood*, ed. by Howard Becker and Reuben Hill, Boston: D. C. Heath & Co., 1948, Chapter 11.

ROSE, Arnold M., *Human Behavior and Social Processes: An Interactional Approach*, Boston: Houghton-Mifflin Co., 1962.

STRYKER, Sheldon, "Relationships of Married Offspring and Parent: A Test of Mead's Theory," *American Journal of Sociology*, 62 (1956), pp. 308-319.

SUSSMAN, Marvin, "The Help Pattern in the Middle-Class Family," *American Sociological Review*, 18 (1953), pp. 22-28.

WALLER, Willard and R. Hill, *The Family: A Dynamic Interpretation*, rev. ed., New York: The Dryden Press, Inc., 1951.

Developmental

1. Definitive and Illustrative studies

DUVALL, Evelyn M., *Family Development*, Philadelphia: Lippincott, 2nd ed., 1962.

HARRIS, Dale B., ed., *The Concept of Development,* Minneapolis: University of Minnesota Press, 1957.

HILL, Reuben, "A Critique of Contemporary Marriage and Family Research," *Social Forces,* 33 (1955), pp. 268-277.

HILL, Reuben and R. H. Rodgers, "The Developmental Approach," in *Handbook of Marriage and the Family,* ed. by Harold T. Christensen, Chicago: Rand McNally & Co., 1964, pp. 171-211.

LEIK, Robert K. and M. Matthews, "A Scale for Developmental Processes," *American Sociological Review,* 33 (1968), pp. 62-75.

MAGRABI, Frances M. and W. H. Marshall, "Family Developmental Tasks: A Research Model," *Journal of Marriage and the Family,* 27 (1965), pp. 454-458.

RODGERS, Roy H., *Improvements in the Construction and Analysis of Family Life Cycle Categories,* Kalamazoo: Western Michigan Univsity, 1962.

ROWE, George P., "The Developmental Conceptual Framework," in *Emerging Conceptual Frameworks for Family Analysis,* ed. by Ivan F. Nye and Felix M. Berardo, New York: The Macmillan Co., 1966, pp. 198-222.

STROUP, A. L., *Marriage and Family: A Developmental Approach,* New York: Appleton-Century-Crofts, 1966.

2. Illustrative studies

BIGELOW, Howard F. and R. L. Bond, "Financial Plans in the Family Life Cycle: What are Usual Family Patterns?" *Journal of Home Economics,* 42 (1950), pp. 27-29.

BLACKWELL, Gordon W., "Correlates of the State of Family Development among Farm Families on Relief," *Rural Sociology,* 17 (1942), pp. 161-174.

BLOOD, Robert O., Jr. and D. M. Wolfe, *Husbands and Wives,* Glencoe, Ill.: The Free Press, 1960.

FOOTE, Nelson, "Matching of Husband and Wife in Phases of Development," in *Sourcebook in Marriage and the Family,* ed. by Marvin Sussman, 2nd ed., Boston: Houghton-Mifflin Co., 1963, pp. 14-20.

McARTHUR, Arthur, "Developmental Tasks and Parent-Adolescent Conflict," *Marriage and Family Living*, 24 (1962), pp. 189-191.

MORIOKA, Kiyomi, "Life Cycle Patterns in Japan, China, and the United States," *Journal of Marriage and the Family*, 29 (1967), pp. 595-606.

RODGERS, Roy H., "The Occupational Role of the Child: A Research Frontier in the Developmental Conceptual Framework," *Social Forces*, 45 (1966), pp. 217-224.

Game Theory and Systems Theory

1. Definitive studies

BERNARD, Jessie, "The Theory of Games of Strategy as a Modern Sociology of Conflict," *American Journal of Sociology*, 59 (1954), 411-422.

BUCKLEY, Walter, *Sociology and Modern Systems Theory*, New Jersey: Prentice Hall, 1967.

HOMANS, George C., "Contemporary Theory in Sociology," in *Handbook of Modern Sociology*, ed. by R. E. L. Faris, Chicago: Rand McNally & Co., 1964, pp. 951-977.

VON NEUMANN, J. and O. Morgenstern, *Theory of Games and Economic Behavior*, Princeton: Princeton University Press, 1944.

RAPOPORT, Anatol, *Two Person-Game Theory: The Essential Ideas*, Ann Arbor: University of Michigan Press, 1966.

SCHELLING, Thomas C., *The Strategy of Conflict*, Cambridge: Harvard University Press, 1960.

WILLIAMS, John D., *The Complete Strategyst*, New York: McGraw Hill, 1954.

b. Illustrative studies

BERNARD, Jessie, "Some Current Conceptualizations in the Field of Conflict," *American Journal of Sociology*, 70 (1965), pp. 442-454.

BERNARD, Jessie, "Counselling Techniques for Arriving at Optimum Compromises: Game and Decision Theory," *Marriage and Family Living*, 21 (1959), pp. 264-274.

KIMMEL, Paul R., "Game Theory Versus Mutual Identification: Two Criteria for Assessing Marital Relationships," *Journal of Marriage and the Family*, 28 (1966), pp. 460-465.

RAPOPORT, Anatol, *Fights, Games and Debates*, Ann Arbor: The University of Michigan Press, 1960.